The Complete Book Of
Home
Crafts

Colour Library Direct

A QUINTET BOOK

CLD 21627
This edition published in 2000 for
Colour Library Direct Ltd.
New Mill
New Mill Lane
Witney
Oxfordshire OX8 5TF

ISBN 1-86155-293-9

CTF

Conceived, designed and produced by
Quintet Publishing Ltd.
6 Blundell Street
London N7 9BH

Project Editor: Carine Tracanelli
Art Director: Sharanjit Dhol
Designers: Linda Henley, Ian Hunt, James Lawrence, Bruce Low
Photographers: Nick Bailey, Colin Bowling, Paul Forrester,
Andrew Sydenham, Laura Wickenden, Chas Wilder

Creative Director: Richard Dewing
Publisher: Oliver Salzmann

Typeset in Great Britain by
Central Southern Typesetters, Eastbourne
Manufactured in Hong Kong by Regent Publishing Services Ltd.
Printed in Hong Kong by Midas Printing Ltd.

Material in this book previously appeared in:
Decoupage by Lesley Player, *Decorative Tiling* by Paul Henry,
Decorative Painting by Sally Richmond, *Picture Framing* by Fay Boon,
Toleware by Ann Witchell, *Beadwork* by Sara Withers,
Stencilling by Jamie Sapsford and Betsy Skinner,
Batik by Joy Campbell, *Fabric Painting* by Melanie Williams

CONTENTS

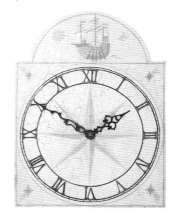

Decoupage

Decorate everyday objects in your own personal style
using this fascinating yet simple craft

INTRODUCTION

The fascination of decoupage lies in its ability to transform old items of battered furniture or uninteresting household articles into attractive and eye-catching pieces that will enhance any room. Once you have been captured by the potential of the technique, you will want to try it on almost everything in your home. Every junk shop, charity shop, jumble sale and car boot sale will seem like an Aladdin's cave, brimming with articles ready for you to practise your skill. The joy of decoupage is that it enables you to decorate objects in such a variety of ways that you can personalize them for yourself and to suit your own home or in the styles that your family and friends like best.

Whenever we visit craft fairs and craft shops we see the treasures that people have made from everyday objects. The purpose of this book is to show how easy it is to take the first steps on the way to being able to effect these transformations yourself.

Provided that the surfaces are correctly prepared, decoupage can be used on metal, wood, terracotta and pottery, glass, plastic and cardboard. As you experiment you will find that different approaches and techniques can be applied to achieve a variety of results, so that whether you are renovating an old piece or simply decorating an everyday object such as a waste paper bin or plant pot you will be able to adapt the basic methods to suit your own purposes.

Always make sure that something is worth rejuvenating before you begin. Decoupage can give worn and rusty pieces a new lease of life, but if you do not like the underlying shape or proportions of an item, no amount of hard work will change these or create an attractive object from something that is inherently unappealing.

There is hardly anything that cannot be wholly transformed by this basically easy craft. Experiment on simple objects to begin with and follow the guidelines explained on the pages that follow, and you will soon be able to give a new life and personal style to every kind of household object.

MATERIALS AND EQUIPMENT

The materials and equipment needed for decoupage could hardly be simpler, and, apart from the actual illustrations you will use, you will probably already have many of them in your home tool box.

MOTIFS AND PICTURE SOURCES

It can be great fun collecting suitable pictures to use. Some of the illustrations used in the projects in this book appear on pages 39-40 to help you get started, but as your skill and interest in decoupage grows you will begin to regard all kinds of printed material in a new light.

The recent revival in interest in the craft has meant that there are several books available that reprint interesting and amusing Victorian illustrations, which can be photocopied and coloured. You will also find that gift-wrapping paper is a wonderful source of motifs, as are greetings cards. You can photocopy photographs, old prints, sheet music, letters and stamps, which can be made to look as if they are antique by a simple ageing process. Even magazines and newspapers contain illustrations that can be used – look out for fashion and computer magazines, which often contain stunning and colourful pictures. Old books, which turn up at jumble sales and in charity shops, can be an unexpected source of illustrations – old history books, for example, often contain interesting maps.

If you are using modern magazines, greetings cards or gift-wrapping paper you can, of course, simply cut out the motifs you want. It is, however, probably better to photocopy illustrations from books, and most libraries and many stationery shops now have photocopiers, many of which have enlargement and reduction facilities. The great advantage of photocopying is that you can repeat a motif as often as you wish, and you can also photocopy onto coloured or textured paper. Colour photocopying is more expensive, and although there may be occasions when you prefer to have a coloured copy, it is certainly less expensive and

> ### TIP
>
> - Try not to use original source pictures because you will not be able to repeat a successful design. Most libraries and stationers have photocopying facilities, and colouring black and white copies is part of the pleasure of decoupage. Remember always to make the photocopies from the original for the best results.

often more satisfying to hand-tint a black and white photocopy.

CUTTING EQUIPMENT

You will need a large pair of scissors for general cutting out, a smaller pair for cutting out motifs from gift-wrapping paper or magazines and a pair of nail scissors for cutting out intricate shapes.

A craft knife or scalpel can be useful, especially if you have to cut out especially delicate shapes. Remember to rest your work on a cutting mat. The special rubberized mats that are sold in art shops are best because they are not damaged by score lines. Kitchen chopping boards can be used, but the best kinds will quickly blunt your blades while the cheaper kinds will eventually become marked. Kitchen boards are useful when you apply adhesive, however, because they are easily wiped clean.

SEALANTS

Paper must be sealed before it can be used for decoupage in order to prevent it from absorbing paint or varnish, to stop discolouration and to inhibit colours from running. In addition, when a water-based adhesive such as PVA is used with paper, the paper tends to stretch when it is applied to a surface, causing wrinkles and air bubbles. Sealing the paper beforehand helps to avoid this.

I prefer to use a sanding sealer or button polish, which I apply to both sides of the image. This gives the paper a slightly crisp feel, and it makes intricate cutting out easier. If you want an aged or antique look, use shellac, which is honey-coloured.

Sanding sealer, button polish and shellac are available from most hardware and do-it-yourself stores and from many craft and art shops. They are all spirit based and dry quickly.

You can also use spray fixatives, water-based varnishes or PVA adhesive, which should be diluted to the consistency of paint. Again, coat both sides of the image, and remember that water-based preparations take longer to dry than spirit-based ones.

ADHESIVES

All the projects illustrated in this book were decorated with motifs glued with PVA (polyvinyl acetate) adhesive. This water-based adhesive is white when it is wet and transparent when it is dry. It can be thinned with water and used as a varnish. When it is dry it has a hard, "plastic" feel. When

you use it to apply individual motifs, always wipe away any excess adhesive from around the edge of the design with a damp cloth. PVA adhesive is available in craft and art shops and in all hardware and do-it-yourself stores.

PAINTS

Water-based emulsion (latex) and acrylic paints are easy to use because they dry reasonably quickly and you can wash the brushes in water and detergent. (If you wish, use a hair-drier to speed up drying times.) The projects in this book were painted with matt emulsion (latex) paint.

Artists' paints can be used to colour or decorate objects. Acrylic paints, which can be bought in tubes, cannot be used to bring out the cracks in a crackle varnish, however, because they are water-

based and the paint will adhere to the second coat of crackle varnish, which is also water-based, and will smudge when you try to wipe it off. You can use artists' acrylic paints to tint white emulsion (latex) paint both to create a background colour or add lines and details to finished objects.

Artists' oil paints are used in an antique glaze or to bring out the cracks when crackle varnish is used. The paint is applied by dampening a cloth

with white spirit, squeezing a small amount of paint onto the cloth and rubbing it over the surface of the decoupaged item once the second-stage varnish is dry and the cracks have appeared. Raw umber is often used to enhance the cracks after the second stage of crackle varnish, while burnt umber creates reddish-brown cracks.

PRIMERS AND UNDERCOATS

Use a red oxide metal primer on metal. Clean your brushes in white spirit.

If you are decorating untreated wood, use acrylic primer followed by white acrylic undercoat.

VARNISHES AND FINISHES

When you have stuck down the motifs and when the adhesive is absolutely dry, you must apply several layers of varnish. The aim is to "lose" the edges of the motifs in the varnish, and some people apply up to twenty coats while others find that three or four coats are sufficient. However many coats you apply, you should leave each one to dry thoroughly, then rub it down very lightly with the finest grade sandpaper before applying the next. Do not sand the final coat. Make sure that you remove any dust adhering to the surface of the object before applying varnish.

The kind of varnish you will use will be largely determined by the use to which the object will be put. Trays and table mats, for example, will need a tough, heat-resistant, gloss surface that can be wiped clean. A lamp, on the other hand, will look

attractive if the light reflects from a smooth satin finish, and some pieces of furniture need a wax polish over a matt varnish. If you do not like your first choice and if you have not applied a wax polish, you can sand the surface gently with fine sandpaper and apply a varnish with a different finish.

As we have already noted, PVA adhesive can be diluted and used as a varnish. There are, however, several other kinds of varnish that you might prefer to use.

ACRYLIC VARNISH

This water-based varnish is especially easy to use. You can wash your brushes in water, it does not have a strong, pungent smell, it dries fairly quickly, it is waterproof when it is dry, and it does not yellow with age. Acrylic varnish can be bought in hardware and do-it-yourself stores and in art shops, and it is available in matt, gloss and silk finishes.

WATER-BASED VARNISH

A water-based varnish takes only 10–15 minutes to dry, making it especially useful when you are trying to build up several layers to blur the edges of your cut-out motifs as quickly as possible. It is available from good art shops in gloss, matt and satin finishes. I use it because it dries so quickly.

POLYURETHANE VARNISH

Polyurethane wood varnish is available in all do-it-yourself stores, and it comes in matt, gloss and satin finishes and in a range of tints, including clear. It does have a tendency to yellow slightly with age, and so it can be used when you want to give an "aged" effect to your work. Many people prefer polyurethane varnish to acrylic varnish, which has a rather hard appearance.

SHELLAC

You can use shellac to seal most surfaces, including paper and new wood, but it is not heat resistant and you must apply a coat of varnish to finish off. Shellac is honey-coloured and is often used to "age" pieces. It is also useful as an insulating layer between two incompatible paints or varnishes. Clean your brushes in methylated spirits.

WHITE POLISH

Like shellac, of which it is a rather more refined version, white polish is spirit-based. It gives a transparent finish that will dissolve in methylated spirits, even when it is dry. Use it when you do not want an antique effect.

CRACKLE VARNISH

Also sometimes known as cracklure, crackle varnish is sold in a two-stage pack from good art shops. The first coat is oil-based, and it continues to dry under the second, faster drying, water-based layer, which causes the top coat to crack. It is a fascinating varnish to use because the results are always unpredictable.

Drying times vary, depending on the thickness of the varnish and on the temperature and humidity of the room in which it is applied. You can speed up the second stage by using a hair-drier, set to medium, held about 60cm (2ft) away from the surface. When it is dry, the cracked varnish can be aged with artists' oil paints to reveal the cracks to best effect. If you do not like the results, you can wash off the second coat and try again.

You can buy a wholly water-based crackle varnish, which is available in some art shops. It is simpler to use and gives more predictable results than oil-based cracklure. You can choose from a variety of "cracking" effects and sizes, which do not depend on temperature or humidity, and you may want to experiment with this type of crackle varnish until you feel confident enough to tackle the oil-based version.

Because new kinds of crackle varnish keep coming onto the market, make sure that you read the manufacturer's instructions before you begin. If

Crackle varnish–first, oil-based coat

Crackle varnish – second, water-based coat

Oil-based varnish tinted with raw umber

Antique colored wax

you are in doubt, ask the advice of the art shop in which you bought the varnish.

The placemats demonstrate the different kinds of crackle varnish and illustrate the effects that can be achieved with each kind (see pages 12-16).

CRACKLE GLAZE

Use crackle glaze between two different colours of emulsion (latex) paint to produce a cracked or crazed second colour, through which the underlying colour can be seen. This is available in art shops.

WAX

Ordinary furniture wax can be used to give a polished sheen to an object that has been finished with matt varnish. Apply this with a damp cloth, and get into the habit of polishing the object every time you walk past it so that you not only have a beautifully gleaming finish but also have that lingering scent that only wax polish gives to a room.

ANTIQUING GLAZE

Use this when you want to produce really beautiful objects, and as you gain experience and confidence you may want to make your own glaze with white spirit and artists' oil paint. Mix them to a

creamy consistency in a small glass jar and apply the glaze with a soft cloth to give a soft "aged" appearance.

SANDING

You will need a selection of sandpapers, ranging from coarse to the finest you can buy. Not only must you prepare the surface of the object to be decorated, but finishing the decoupaged article with very fine sandpaper gives a smooth, professional-looking finish.

BRUSHES

In order to complete the projects shown in this book you will need a selection of brushes. Good brushes are expensive but, as long as you look after them well, they will last far longer than less expensive brushes. However, there may be times when it it more convenient to use a cheaper brush, which you can discard when it is unusable.

After applying emulsion (latex) paint, wash your brushes thoroughly in water and detergent. It is a good idea to have separate brushes for oil paints and varnishes. Clean them with white spirit or a proprietary cleaner.

Design brushes

Craft Knife

Sponge

Decorating brush

Varnish brush

Synthetic bristled brush

House-painter's brush

VARNISH BRUSHES

These flat brushes can be synthetic or pure bristle. They are available in different widths. When you are using water-based varnishes and paints, synthetic brushes tend to give better results because they give a better flow and do not leave brush marks. If you use crackle varnish, use two separate varnish brushes and label them for the appropriate stages because it is important that the two varnishes are not mixed when they are wet or the crackle will not work. Always clean the brushes immediately after use.

DECORATING BRUSHES

Look out for a variety of widths in do-it-yourself stores. If possible, choose the more expensive brushes, which do not shed hairs as much as cheaper ones. It can be extremely annoying to find that you have not noticed a stray hair until the paint or varnish has dried.

Use cheap brushes for shellac because methylated spirits tends to spoil them. Do not use white spirit to clean brushes used for shellac.

WATERCOLOUR BRUSHES

Use artists' paintbrushes to add fine details and for touching up. You will find a range of widths and qualities in art shops, and the most useful for acrylic paints are sizes no. 4, no. 6 and no. 9. I used a flat-edged oil paintbrush for the edges of the table mats because it is easy to control.

ADDITIONAL EQUIPMENT

In addition to the above, you will need one or two other items to complete the projects.

SPONGES

Natural sponges produce the best and softest effects when you are sponging on paints, but if you use a synthetic sponge, tear rather than cut off small pieces so that they have slightly rough edges. All types of sponges are available in art shops.

ROLLER

A small rubber roller (sometimes called a brayer) or a small plastic roller of the kind sold in do-it-yourself stores for smoothing the edges of wallpaper is useful for pressing over glued images to remove all air bubbles and to ensure even

adhesion. You can use the back of a spoon instead in small areas, and when you are applying motifs to large, flat surfaces, such as furniture, you may be able to use your pastry rolling-pin. Press down with a firm, smooth motion, pushing air bubbles and excess glue from the centre to the edges of the motif. Do not use your fingers, or you will tear the paper.

If the surface to which you are applying a motif is uneven, use a slightly dampened sponge, pressed evenly from the centre outwards.

CLEANING MATERIALS

Use methylated spirits to dilute shellac and button polish and to clean the brushes with which you apply these substances.

White spirit can be used to clean the surface of an object before decoupage motifs are applied. Use it also to dilute oil-based paints and varnishes and to clean brushes.

Clean brushes used for emulsion (latex) paint and water-based varnishes with detergent and water. Work a small amount of neat detergent into the bristles first, then rinse them thoroughly with clean water.

TECHNIQUES

Decoupage is a very simple craft, and once you have mastered the few simple rules you will be able to apply them to complicated projects. One of the most important rules, however, is to prepare the surface carefully and thoroughly before you even begin to think about the motifs you are going to use.

PREPARING SURFACES

NEW WOOD

Seal new wood with an acrylic primer/undercoat or with a shellac sanding sealer. Then apply a coat of emulsion (latex) or oil-based paint. If you prefer, stain the wood before sealing with a coloured wood stain.

VARNISHED WOOD

Use medium grade sandpaper to rub down the surface to provide a key to which the paint can adhere. You must make sure that you remove all flaking and loose varnish with sandpaper. If the sanding exposes bare wood, apply a primer/ undercoat or a layer of shellac before painting.

PAINTED WOOD

If an article has been previously painted with a water-based paint, it can generally be painted over quite easily with either oil- or water-based paint. It must be well sanded, using medium sandpaper, working down to fine grade, to provide a key for an acrylic primer undercoat. If you are re-painting wood that has been previously painted with oil-based paint it may have dried out sufficiently over the years for you simply to apply emulsion (latex) paint after rubbing it down lightly to provide a key. This can be done to achieve a distressed effect by rubbing down to reveal the old paint beneath.

MEDIUM DENSITY FIBREBOARD (MDF)

MDF is available from large timber merchants and most do-it-yourself stores, which will often cut it to the size you need. Treat it exactly as you would ordinary, untreated wood.

METAL

Use a wire brush to remove loose rust, and paint on a rust inhibitor such as red oxide (available from motor accessory shops) if the rust is deeply engrained. You must apply a base coat of metal primer; if you do not, the metal will stain through any top coat of metal or oil-based paint you use.

CERAMICS

Lightly sand the surface to create a key, then simply apply a coat of acrylic primer/undercoat.

SEALING PAPER PRINTS

Always coat both sides of gift-wrapping paper or photocopies with shellac. This not only protects the paper from the adhesive and varnish (which will cause the image to discolour) but strengthens the paper and makes it easier to cut out. Use methylated spirits to clean your brush.

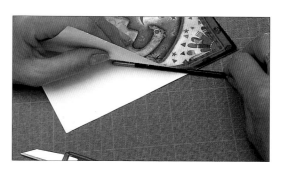

SEPARATING PICTURES

Most of us have kept greetings cards that we are reluctant to throw away but are not sure what to do with. Decoupage could be the answer. The images are, however, sometimes printed on thick card, and because the aim of decoupage is to lose the edges of the paper and "sink" the image in coats of varnish until it appears to be part of the original article, the picture needs to be separated from the card backing.

Paint the picture side of the card with a coat of shellac. Carefully insert a craft knife between the picture and the card, making sure that the picture has a reasonable backing. It will be more difficult to separate if it is too thin. Peel back the picture from the card, working slowly and carefully, and use a paintbrush or ruler to hold the card as you gently lift the picture from its backing. When you have separated the picture, apply a coat of shellac to the back of the image to protect and thicken it.

PLACE MATS

These mats illustrate the different kinds of crackle varnish that can be applied and the different results that can be achieved. The motifs appear on page 40.

You will need
◊ pieces of MDF, each 30 x 25cm (12 x 10in)
◊ acrylic primer/undercoat
◊ fine sandpaper
◊ emulsion (latex) paint (we used cream for the background and maroon for the edging line)
◊ decorating brush
◊ flat-edged, stiff-bristled paintbrush
◊ photocopied motifs
◊ watercolour paints (light brown, maroon and green for colour washing the motifs)
◊ watercolour brush
◊ hair-drier
◊ shellac
◊ nail scissors
◊ craft knife or scalpel
◊ PVA adhesive
◊ sponge or roller
◊ crackle varnish (see below)
◊ artists' oil paint (raw umber)
◊ oil-based varnish (gloss or satin finish)

1 Seal the MDF with acrylic primer/undercoat. When the primer is dry, apply two coats of cream-coloured emulsion (latex) paint, allowing the first coat to dry thoroughly and sanding lightly before applying the second coat.

2 Use the flat-edged paintbrush to paint a maroon line around the edge of each mat. Leave to dry.

3 Age the photocopied motifs by covering the whole image with watered-down dark gold or light brown (use tea if you prefer). Make sure that you do not allow the motif to become too wet and mop up any excess liquid with kitchen towel.

4 When the background is dry, colour the knights' cloaks (we used red but you could use green), but do not use too strong a colour or you will not get the "aged" effect. Use a hair-drier to speed up the drying process.

5 When the paint is dry, apply a coat of shellac or white button polish to the back and front of the paper. Use a hair-drier for speed.

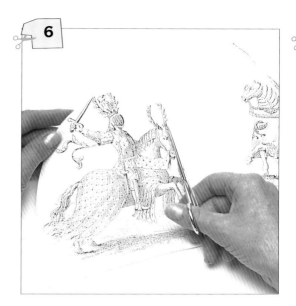

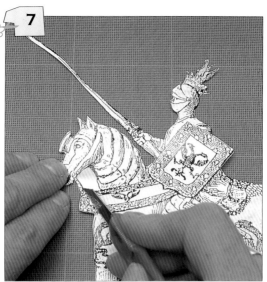

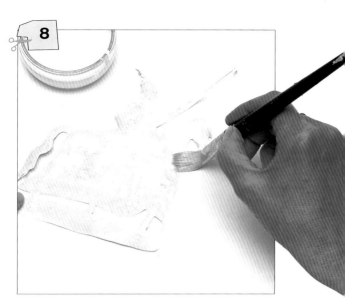

6 When the shellac is completely dry, cut neatly around the image with sharp nail scissors.

7 Use a craft knife or scalpel to cut out the intricate shapes, then place the motif on the mat, lightly marking the position with a pencil.

8 Apply a fine layer of PVA adhesive to the back of the motif, working from the centre outwards to cover the shape evenly.

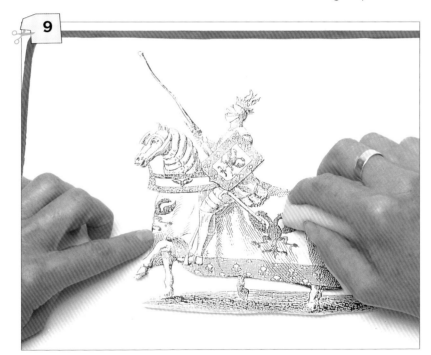

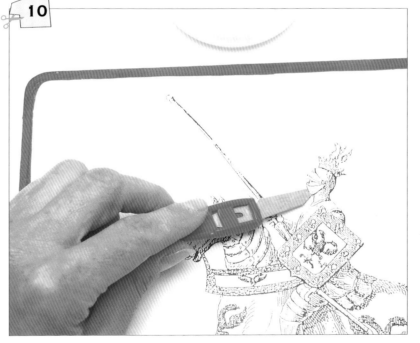

9 Place the motif on the mat, making sure it is correctly positioned, and press it down firmly with a damp sponge or roller.

10 Allow to dry, then check for air bubbles and lifting edges. Air bubbles in the centre can be pierced and cut with the point of your craft knife, which can then be used to insert a tiny amount of adhesive. Use the point of your craft knife to add minute amounts of adhesive under any lifting edges. Press them down firmly but gently.

APPLYING
CRACKLE VARNISH

This kind of varnish is used to give an interesting "antique" effect. The cracks can be large or small, but they are rarely consistent, which makes it almost impossible to produce two identical items. This inconsistency and unpredictability does help to give a feeling of age and authenticity to objects, and we have used the place mats to illustrate the differences between oil-based crackle (cracklure) and water-based crackle varnishes.

You will need

◊ two-stage oil-based or water-based crackle varnish
◊ varnishing brushes
◊ hair-drier (optional)
◊ artists' oil paint (raw umber)
◊ white spirit
◊ varnish
◊ fine sandpaper

TIP
• Hold the items you are varnishing up to the light to check that you have completely covered the surface and have not missed any small patches. Holding the object to the light will also help you see the crackles, which can be difficult to detect until you have worked over the surface with artists' oil paint.

WATER-BASED
VARNISH

OIL-BASED
VARNISH

OIL-BASED CRACKLE VARNISH

Cracklure or oil-based crackle varnish is affected by the atmosphere because the second coat is water-based and therefore absorbs moisture. If the second stage crackle effect is not to your liking, you can simply wash it off and start again without damaging the paint and decoupage below the original first coat.

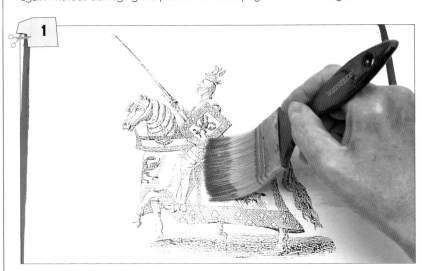

1 Use a flat varnishing brush to apply the first, oil-based crackle. Apply the varnish sparingly, beginning in the centre and spreading it outwards before reloading the brush.

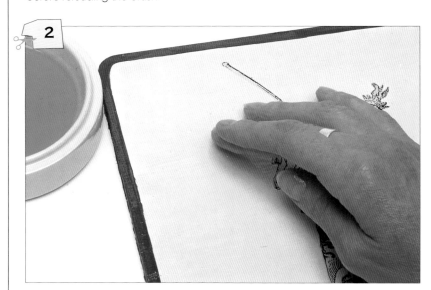

2 Leave the varnish to dry. This can take between 1 and 2 hours, depending on the humidity in the atmosphere. When the varnish is ready for the second stage it feels smooth and dry when stroked, but tacky when gently touched with the finger tips.

3

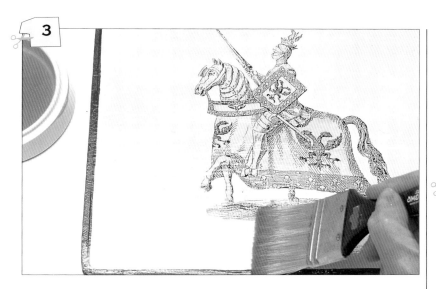

3 Use a well-cleaned brush or a different one to apply the second coat of water-based varnish. Make sure you cover the entire surface and brush it in so that it adheres well to the first coat. Leave to dry for at least 1–4 hours, but preferably overnight. The cracks will begin to appear as soon as the varnish begins to dry, but they will not be visible unless you hold it to the light. Using a hair-drier, set on medium and held at a distance from the surface of the varnish, will encourage cracks to appear.

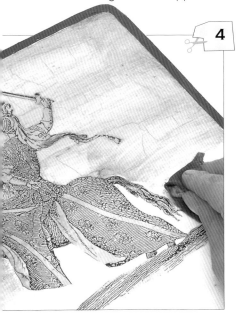

4

4 Squeeze about 2cm (¾in) of artists' oil paint into a dish and add a small amount of white spirit to soften the paint. Use a soft cloth or piece of kitchen towel to spread paint all over the surface of the varnish. Wipe off the excess paint with a clean cloth, leaving the crackle-effect enhanced by the darker oil paint

5 Leave to dry for abut 24 hours then apply three or four coats of varnish, allowing the varnish to dry between coats and sanding each coat gently. Gloss varnish is hard wearing and effective for table mats, and you might find a heat-resistant varnish in your local hardware or do-it-yourself store.

WATER-BASED CRACKLE VARNISH

If you buy this two-stage varnish from a good art shop you will be able to choose between large or small cracks. This kind of varnish is easy to use, and the results are always good. Although the cracks tend to look fairly predictable, you can achieve a good ageing effect by rubbing artists' oil paint over the surface.

1

1 The first stage is a milky white fluid, which takes about 20 minutes to dry, when it becomes clear. If you want small cracks, apply a second coat of the stage-one fluid, which should be left to dry for a further 20 minutes.

2

2 When the stage one varnish is dry, apply the second stage. Make sure that the base coat is completely covered. Check by holding your work up to the light. Leave to dry for 20 minutes, and when the second stage is completely dry, cracks will have appeared over the whole surface.

3 Use a soft cloth, dampened with white spirit, to rub artists' oil paint over the surface of the varnish. Leave this to dry, which can take up to 24 hours.

4 Apply four coats of gloss, heat-proof polyurethane varnish, sanding with fine sandpaper between each coat.

CERAMIC LAMP

The base of this lamp was bought in a car boot sale, but you can find similar, plain bases
in most do-it-yourself and home furnishing stores. This kind of lamp is suitable for Victorian
animal illustrations – we used lizards, which we enlarged on a photocopier and
colour washed.

You will need

◊ ceramic lamp base
◊ medium and fine sandpaper
◊ emulsion (latex) paint (yellow)
◊ decorating brushes for emulsion (latex) paint
  and varnish
◊ photocopied motifs
◊ watercolour paint (olive green)
◊ scissors and craft knife
◊ PVA adhesive
◊ sponge
◊ oil-based crackle varnish
◊ hair-drier (optional)
◊ artists' oil paint (raw umber)
◊ white spirit
◊ polyurethane varnish (satin finish)

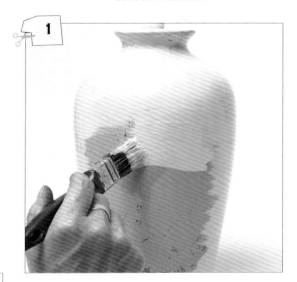

1 Rub over the lamp base gently with sandpaper
to provide a key for the paint, then apply two coats
of emulsion (latex) paint.

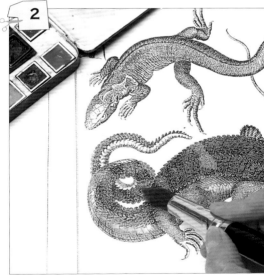

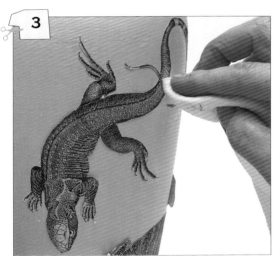

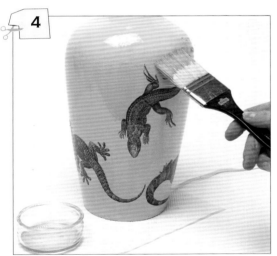

2 While the paint is drying, apply olive green
watercolour to the lizards. Use the paint thinly to
give an aged appearance. When the paint is dry,
apply shellac to both sides of the motifs and leave
to dry before you cut them out.

3 Use PVA adhesive to stick the lizards to the
base of the lamp. Press the motifs down firmly and
evenly on the surface of the lamp and wipe away
the excess glue.

4 When the adhesive is dry, apply the first stage
of the crackle varnish. Leave it to dry until it feels
smooth when stroked but sticky to the touch.

5 Apply the second stage of the crackle varnish, making sure that the whole surface is covered.

6 Leave the lamp to dry. This will depend on the temperature and humidity of the room in which you are working, but after a couple of hours you can use a hair-drier to encourage the crackles to form.

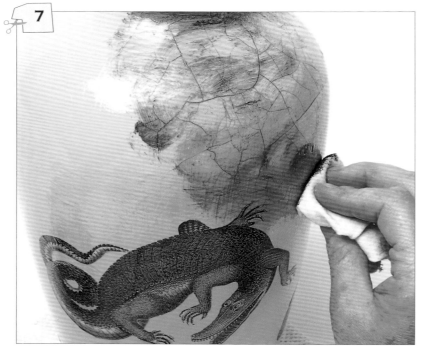

TIP

• Always clean away any glue from around the motifs because the adhesive will show up as lighter patches on the finished object if you apply crackle varnish over it.

7 Mix some artists' oil paint with white spirit and apply it to the surface of the lamp with a cloth.

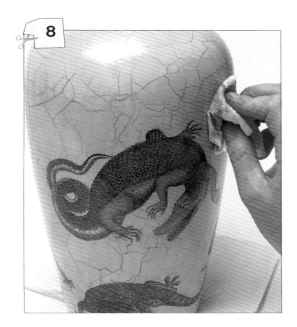

8 Rub the mixture into the cracks with a circular movement and remove the excess with a clean cloth. Leave to dry for about 2 hours.

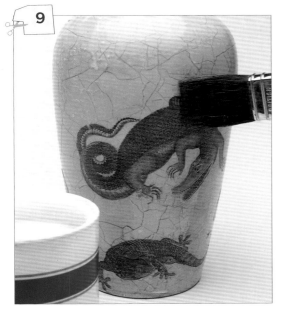

9 Apply four or five coats of satin-finish varnish to "lose" the edges of the paper. A polyurethane varnish gives a slightly translucent finish, which is appropriate for a lamp. Finally, paint the shade with dark green emulsion (latex) paint to match the green of the lizards.

METAL TRUNK

This old metal trunk had been stored in a garage for years. It had seen better days, when it was used by an aunt to ship her possessions back and forth to Africa. There was a small area of rust, which was easily removed, then turning the trunk into a useful storage space that does double-duty as a coffee table was a straightforward matter.

You will need
◊ metal trunk
◊ medium and fine sandpaper
◊ rust remover
◊ inexpensive brushes for rust remover, iron oxide paint and shellac
◊ iron oxide, rust-resistant paint
◊ white spirit
◊ primer/undercoat
◊ emulsion (latex) paints
◊ decorating brushes for paint and varnish
◊ gift-wrapping paper with appropriate motifs
◊ shellac
◊ methylated spirits
◊ scissors and craft knife
◊ masking tape
◊ PVA adhesive
◊ sponge or roller
◊ polyurethane varnish (matt)
◊ artists' oil paint (raw umber)
◊ wax polish

1 Wash the trunk to remove all dirt and grease, then dry carefully. Rub away any loose paint or rust with medium sandpaper, brushing away all dust with a soft, dry brush. Apply rust remover to any areas affected by rust, remembering to treat the inside of the trunk as well. As you apply the rust remover, white appears on the affected areas. Apply further coats until no more white appears.

2 Paint the trunk, inside and out, with red oxide rust-resistant paint. Clean your brush thoroughly in white spirit.

3 Paint the trunk with primer/undercoat. When the primer is dry, apply two coats of emulsion (latex) paint. Apply the coats in opposite directions – cross-hatching – to give a surface that has an old, rough appearance, rather like linen.

4 Use a narrower brush to pick out the handles and edging strips in a contrasting colour.

5 Apply shellac to both sides of the gift-wrapping paper and clean your brush in methylated spirits. When the shellac is dry, carefully cut out the motifs you want.

6

7

6 Arrange the motifs on the trunk, using masking tape to hold them in place until you are satisfied with their position. Mark the positions lightly with pencil. Remove the tape and apply an even coat of PVA adhesive to the back of the motifs, pressing them down with a sponge or roller. When the adhesive is dry, apply a coat of matt polyurethane varnish to prevent too much oil paint accumulating around the edges of the decoupage.

7 Use a soft cloth to apply a mixture of artists' oil paint and white spirit unevenly over the surface of the trunk. For example, we made the edges and corners darker and applied more oil paint around the locks and other areas where a well-travelled trunk would be expected to gather dust. Leave to dry overnight before applying three or four further coats of varnish, leaving each coat to dry and rubbing it down lightly with fine sandpaper between coats. Finally, build up several layers of wax polish to create a deep, lustrous sheen.

KEY BOX

This unpainted key box was found, almost by accident, in a furniture shop. It is worth looking in large do-it-yourself stores, which often stock a range of inexpensive, unpainted shelves and small cupboards that are ideal subjects for decoupage.

You will need

◊ unpainted wooden key box
◊ fine sandpaper
◊ white spirit
◊ shellac or acrylic primer/undercoat
◊ brushes for shellac, varnish (you will need two), and emulsion (latex) and watercolour paints
◊ emulsion (latex) paint (rust, blue and two shades of cream)
◊ wax candle
◊ photocopied coat of arms and keys
◊ watercolour paints
◊ hair-drier (optional)
◊ scissors and craft knife
◊ PVA adhesive
◊ sponge or roller
◊ fine wire wool
◊ water-based crackle varnish
◊ artists' oil paint (raw umber)
◊ white spirit
◊ oil-based varnish (matt)

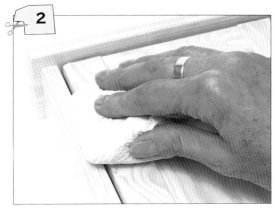

1 Gently rub down the surface of the box with fine sandpaper.

2 Use white spirit on a clean cloth to remove any dust and grease from the surface of the wood, then seal the box. We used shellac sanding sealer rather than white primer so that the grain of the wood showed through when the box was rubbed down to give a distressed effect.

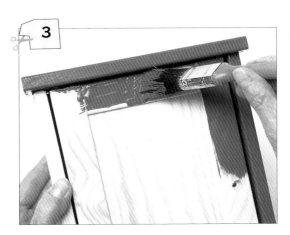

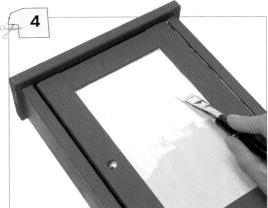

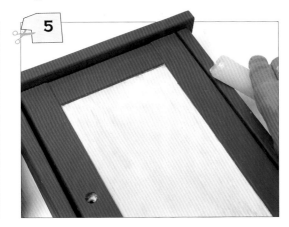

3 Paint the outer panels, the top and bottom and inside the box with two coats of rust or brick red emulsion (latex) paint.

4 Give the front panel two coats of cream-coloured emulsion (latex) paint. Making the first coat slightly darker than the second and allowing it to show through streaks in the second coat will help give depth to a flat surface.

5 When the paint is dry, rub the areas you would like to look distressed with a wax candle. The usual places are near the knob and on the edges of the door, and the wax makes it easier to remove the contrasting colour with wire wool.

6 Paint the door surround with blue emulsion (latex) paint.

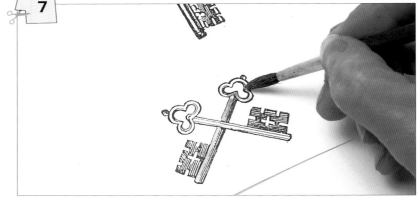

7 While the paint dries, colour the motifs. Use a hair-drier to speed up the drying process if you wish.

8 When the motifs are dry, cut them out and apply shellac to the front and back.

9 Apply PVA adhesive evenly to the back of the motifs and place them on the front of the central panel, pressing them down firmly and carefully with a damp sponge or roller.

10 When the adhesive is dry, use fine wire wool to distress the areas you have previously rubbed with the candle wax. Remove all traces of dust with a dry paint brush.

11 Apply the first stage of the crackle varnish and leave to dry for about 20 minutes.

12 Apply the second stage of the crackle varnish, then leave it to dry thoroughly.

13 Rub artists' oil paint into the cracks with a soft cloth dampened with white spirit. Wipe away any excess paint.

14 Leave overnight for the paint to dry, then apply two or three coats of matt varnish.

WOODEN BOX

These round wooden boxes are sold in some large do-it-yourself stores, and
they are sometimes sold through mail order, so it is worth looking in handicraft magazines.
They are not expensive and are available in a range of sizes, so they are ideal for
personalizing to give as a gift.

You will need

◊ wooden box
◊ shellac
◊ emulsion (latex) paint (black)
◊ brushes for applying shellac, emulsion
  (latex) and watercolour paints and varnish
◊ photocopied motifs
◊ watercolour paint
◊ masking tape
◊ PVA adhesive
◊ gift-wrapping tape (optional)
◊ acrylic varnish

1 Seal the surface of the box with a coat of shellac. When it is dry, apply a coat of black emulsion (latex) paint, which will dry to charcoal grey.

2 While the box dries, paint the photocopied motifs with watercolours. We used lions from an old history book and painted them yellow. When the paint is dry, apply shellac to both sides of each motif.

3 Arrange the motifs around the side of the box, using masking tape to hold them in place. When you are satisfied with the arrangement, remove the tape and glue the motifs in place with PVA adhesive.

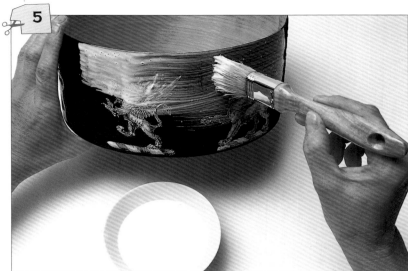

4 If you wish, decorate the rim of the box lid with a strip of narrow gift-wrapping tape.

5 When the adhesive is dry, apply at least five coats of quick-drying acrylic varnish.

WATERING CAN

These watering cans are sold in hardware stores and garden centres. If you are careful, you can use the can after you have decorated it. You must protect the decoupage with many coats of varnish and take care when you fill the can that you do not knock it against the tap and chip the varnish.

You will need
◊ galvanized iron watering can
◊ vinegar
◊ iron oxide, rust-resistant paint
◊ inexpensive decorating brushes for rust-resistant paint and shellac
◊ emulsion (latex) paint (pale blue)
◊ decorating brush
◊ gift-wrapping paper or suitable motifs
◊ shellac
◊ scissors and craft knife
◊ masking tape
◊ PVA adhesive
◊ sponge or roller
◊ watercolour brush
◊ acrylic paints
◊ artists' oil paint (raw umber)
◊ white spirit
◊ quick-drying varnish
◊ polyurethane (gloss)

1 Carefully wipe the metal with a solution of one part vinegar to one part water to remove all traces of grease. If your watering can is an old one, clean it as shown for the trunk (see page 20).

2 Apply a coat of red oxide, rust-resistant paint to the watering can. Use an inexpensive brush.

3 When the rust-resistant paint is dry, apply two coats of emulsion (latex) paint. Leave to dry.

4 While the paint dries, prepare the motifs by applying shellac to both sides. When the shellac is dry, carefully cut out the motifs.

5 Arrange the motifs on the watering can, holding them in place with small pieces of masking tape until you are satisfied with their position. Draw in their positions lightly with a pencil. Remove the tape and glue the motifs in position with PVA adhesive. Press them down carefully and evenly with a damp sponge or small roller.

6 While the adhesive is drying, use a watercolour brush to paint the edges of the can. Use tubes of artists' acrylic paint, which are ideal for small areas such as this.

TIP

• You will find a small number of acrylic paints useful because you can mix the colours with white emulsion (latex) paint to make a range of colours that can be used for touching up images, highlighting edges or painting lines.

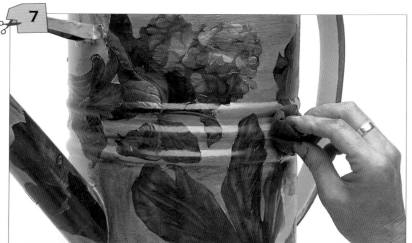

7 When the adhesive and paint are completely dry, mix a small amount of raw umber with white spirit and use a clean cloth to rub it over the surface of the can to "age" the surface. Add extra antique glaze to areas that you would expect to accumulate dirt over the years.

8 Apply at least four coats of a quick-drying varnish to "lose" the edges of the motifs. Give a final coat of hard-gloss polyurethane. If you want to use the can, you will need to apply at least five coats of varnish to seal and protect it. Handle the finished can carefully so that no water gets under the surface of the varnish.

PAINTED TABLE WITH CRACKLE EFFECT

Once you have started to use decoupage to transform old furniture, nothing will escape your attention. This old table had stood outside for many years, but it needed only sanding to remove the surface and remains of the old varnish and to provide a key for the under-coat before it was ready to be decorated for its new life.

You will need

◊ small wooden table
◊ medium and fine sandpaper
◊ acrylic primer/undercoat
◊ decorating brushes for primer/undercoat, crackle glaze and emulsion (latex) paint
◊ emulsion (latex) paint (mauve and yellow)
◊ crackle glaze
◊ flat-edged brush
◊ gift-wrapping paper or suitable motifs
◊ shellac
◊ scissors and craft knife
◊ masking tape
◊ PVA adhesive
◊ sponge or roller
◊ quick-drying acrylic varnish

1 Prepare the surface of the table by rubbing it down with medium, then fine, sandpaper. Brush away any dust and apply a coat of acrylic primer.

2 Paint the surface of the table with emulsion (latex) paint. Choose a colour that you want to show through the cracks in the glaze. When the paint is dry, apply a coat of crackle glaze.

3 When the glaze is dry – after about 30 minutes – apply the second coat of emulsion (latex) paint. Load your brush well and cover the surface of the table in one movement. If you apply two coats, the crackle effect will not work. As the paint dries, you will see the cracks appearing.

4 Use a flat-edged brush to highlight the edges of the table with the first colour of emulsion (latex) paint.

TIP

• Apply as many coats of varnish as necessary to "sink" the edges of the motifs. When it is completely dry it can be finished with a coat of oil-based satin varnish.

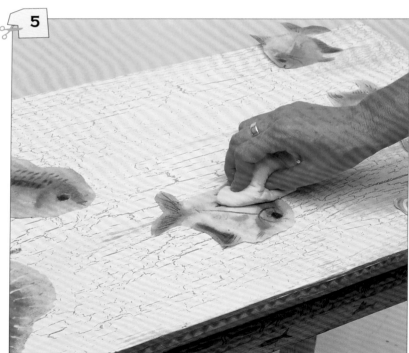

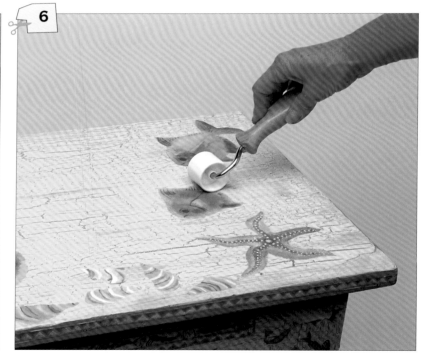

5 While the paint is drying, apply shellac to both sides of the motifs and, when it is dry, carefully cut out the motifs. Arrange the motifs over the table, holding them in place with masking tape until you are happy with the arrangement.

6 Use PVA adhesive to glue the motifs in place, pressing them in place with a damp sponge or roller. On a large area such as a table, you could even use a rolling pin.

7

7 Use a damp sponge to press the motifs into awkward corners.

8

8 When the adhesive is completely dry, apply four or five coats of a quick-drying acrylic varnish.

GALVANIZED IRON BUCKET

This old galvanized iron bucket was found in a skip, but it was such an unusual shape that we decided to give it a new life as a container for dried flowers. You could use a similar container in the kitchen to store bread. It needed a lot of work to remove patches of rust and to clean it up before it could be decorated.

You will need

◊ iron bucket
◊ medium and fine sandpaper
◊ rust remover
◊ inexpensive brushes for rust remover and iron oxide paint
◊ iron oxide, rust-resistant paint
◊ primer/undercoat (optional)
◊ crackle glaze
◊ 3cm (1¼in) decorating brushes for glaze and paint
◊ emulsion (latex) paints (sea green and dark blue)
◊ gift-wrapping paper or suitable motifs
◊ shellac
◊ scissors and craft knife
◊ adhesive tak (optional)
◊ PVA adhesive
◊ sponge or roller
◊ artists' oil paint (raw umber)
◊ white spirit
◊ quick-drying varnish (matt)
◊ soil-based varnish (matt)
◊ wax polish

1 Remove as much dirt as you can with a stiff brush then use medium sandpaper to remove patches of rust. Paint rust remover on all affected areas, continuing to apply the remover until it stops turning white. Remember to treat the inside and the lid. Paint the bucket inside and out with rust-resistant paint.

2 Because we wanted the colour of the red oxide paint to show through the cracks, we left this as the base coat. If you prefer, apply a coat of primer in the colour of your choice. When the base coat is dry, apply a coat of crackle glaze, making sure that you completely cover the surface of the bucket.

3 When the glaze is dry, apply a coat of emulsion (latex) paint. Use a well-loaded brush but do not go over areas that have already been painted because this will prevent the cracking effect. As the second coat begins to dry, cracks will appear. Leave until it is quite dry.

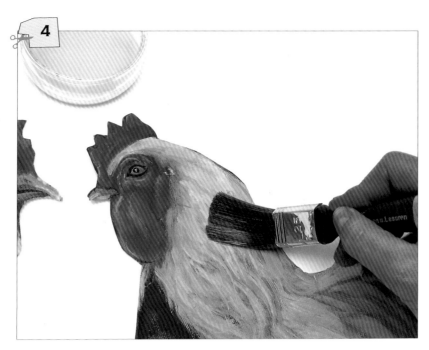

4 Apply shellac to both sides of the motifs or gift-wrapping paper. The honey-coloured shellac will have a slightly ageing effect on the motifs.

5 Cut out the motifs when the shellac is dry and use PVA adhesive to stick them to the sides of the bucket, using a damp sponge or roller to press them down evenly.

6 Use the point of your craft knife to check that all the edges are firmly stuck down, adding tiny amounts of adhesive if necessary. Remove air bubbles by making a small slit in the paper and inserting a little adhesive on your craft knife.

7 Soften a small amount of artists' oil paint in a little white spirit to make an antique glaze and use a soft cloth to apply it all over the surface of the bucket.

9 Apply five coats of a quick-drying varnish to "lose" the edges of the motifs. It is milky white when it is wet, but it dries clear.

8 Use a paintbrush to apply extra antique glaze in the areas you would expect dirt to accumulate. Dip your cloth in the glaze and add extra to the corners and edges.

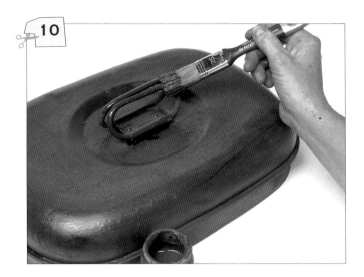

10 At this stage you can stand back to admire your handiwork before you apply the final coats of varnish. We decided to add contrasting blue to the handle of the lid.

TIP
• Because there are so many different varnishes on the market, always read the manufacturer's instructions before you begin.

11 Apply a final coat of oil-based satin-finish varnish and, when it is dry, polish with wax to give a warm sheen to the finished bucket.

WASTE-PAPER BIN

This bin has been decorated with a collage of illustrations cut from comics and computer magazines. The bin was going to be placed in a boy's room, and so he chose and cut out the images himself.

You will need

◊ metal waste-paper bin
◊ acrylic primer/undercoat
◊ emulsion (latex) paint (red)
◊ paint and varnishes brushes
◊ comics and magazines
◊ scissors and craft knife
◊ shellac
◊ PVA adhesive
◊ quick-drying acrylic varnish
◊ acrylic varnish (gloss)

1 Paint the inside and outside of the bin with acrylic primer, then apply two coats of emulsion (latex) paint so that a bright colour will be visible if there are any gaps in the collage.

2 While the paint is drying, cut out the images from the magazines. Coat both sides of each one with shellac. You may find it easier to do this before cutting the shapes from the magazines.

3 Beginning with the large, background pictures, use PVA adhesive to stick the images over the surface of the bin.

4 When the adhesive is completely dry, apply five coats of acrylic varnish then finish with a coat of gloss varnish.

MOTIFS

Decorative Tiling

Achieve perfect tiling results and create beautiful
and original projects for the home

INTRODUCTION

Tiles are attractive to look at, permanent, easy to maintain and extraordinarily versatile. They are also one of the oldest forms of decorative surface, familiar to us all, whether it is from illustrations of ancient Babylonian gateways or from Victorian public houses. Although they are usually seen on large, flat surfaces, especially on walls in kitchens and bathrooms, there is no reason why they should not be used in other areas of the home or to produce decorative objects in their own right. They have been widely used for many years in warm countries, especially those around the Mediterranean, but even in cooler countries, now that central heating is becoming so widespread, there is no reason that tiles cannot be used throughout the home in all kinds of ways. This book has been designed to show how tiles can be used relatively easily to produce a variety of ornamental objects. Once you have mastered the techniques involved, you will be able to use the ideas on the pages that follow to inspire you to try tiles in other, more adventurous and imaginative ways.

MATERIALS AND EQUIPMENT

Ceramic tiles are widely available from countless suppliers in an enormous range of styles and sizes. In fact, choosing tiles can be quite a daunting experience. Once you have made your selection, however, the skills needed are straightforward and easy to learn, and you are likely already to have most of the tools you will need in your standard household tool kit.

If there is one near to you where you live, it is probably worth visiting a specialist tile shop. Not only will you be able to look at a vast range of tiles, but you will also be able to ask for advice about using them in the best possible ways.

TIP
• Check carefully whether the tiles you are using are sized in metric or imperial units. Sometimes the slight difference is unimportant, but it could ruin a project. Measure before you begin – it is easy to adjust measurements before cutting, impossible afterwards.

BELOW: **It is worth investing in a tile cutter for accuracy and convenience.**

TILES

At their most basic, ceramic tiles are flat slabs of fired clay, usually covered with a glaze to protect the surface or with a decoration of some kind. They are hard and brittle but extremely durable. They range in size from mosaic pieces about 15mm (¾in) square to floor tiles that are 30cm (12in) square; floor tiles are often, but not always, larger than wall tiles. Rectangular tiles are becoming increasingly popular, although they have always been successfully used in public areas such as underground railway stations. Interlocking shapes are also sometimes used for floors. Tiles may be plain coloured, screen printed, hand painted or decorated by a combination of techniques. Raised images are sometimes incorporated, especially to give a period or traditional appearance to an area.

WALL TILES

There are practically no limits to the size, colours and designs of wall tiles, but they are most often 10cm (about 4in) or about 15cm (6in) square, with the 15cm (6in) squares being most widely used. You will, therefore, find the greatest range of designs and colours in this size.

TIP

- All the quantities and dimensions are given in both metric and imperial units. The measurements are not interchangeable, however, and you should keep to one system or the other.

MOSAIC TILES

Small tiles are generally known as mosaics, and they were used in the past for large, decorative panels in churches and other public buildings. Although they may be made of ceramic, they are often made of glass, and they are usually sold in sheets of a single colour. Most are square, although interlocking shapes are also available. Ceramic mosaics are hard-wearing and can be used for floors in entrance halls, where they can be arranged to create images or even names. Glass mosaics are more often used on walls or in swimming pools, and they are not available in such a wide range of colours as the ceramic equivalents.

BORDER TILES

There are few better ways of enlivening a room than by introducing some of these brightly coloured strips, which are enjoying something of a revival. They are usually available in lengths of 15cm (6in) or 20cm (8in), in almost every possible width, and they can be used to edge any other size of tile.

EMBOSSED OR RAISED TILES

Although these tend to be slightly more expensive than plain tiles, they are widely available and they are worth using to give an extra special finish.

TIP

- Cut tiles have surprisingly sharp edges, so take care that you do not nick your fingers as you handle them. Clear away any broken pieces immediately to avoid accidents.

TOOLS

Only a few tools are needed for tiling, and they are all readily available from local hardware shops, do-it-yourself stores or tile shops.

You will need:

◊ Tile cutter (see below)
◊ Steel rule both to measure and to guide the hand-held cutter
◊ Waterproof pen to write on glazed surface of tiles

◊ Tile nippers (sharp, pincer-type tools) to nibble away small pieces from a tile
◊ Carborundum stone to smooth away sharp edges and to help ease the fit; always use a carborundum stone with water for best results

You must have a good tile cutter, and two kinds are generally sold – plier-cutters and bench-cutters. A plier-cutter has a diamond or tungsten carbide tip or wheel, which is used to scribe lines. The other end of the tool, which has plier jaws, is used to snap the tile carefully along the scribed line. Unfortunately, these tools do not have very long lives, and you should make sure you have some spare tips before you embark on any large projects. A bench-cutter is useful if you are cutting a large number of right angles or a batch of similar shapes. The tool is used to scribe the tile, which then, with downward pressure, can be snapped quite easily. This kind of cutter is useful if you are using heavy tiles or if you cannot exert much pressure with your hands.

TILE CEMENT

Premixed cement is probably the easiest kind to use, and it is available in non-slip and waterproof versions. You will usually need about 1 litre (1.75pt) of adhesive for each square metre (10.75sq ft) of tiles. Spreading combs are often supplied with the cement, but make sure that you use one that feels comfortable in your hand and that is not too large for the area to be tiled.

GROUT

It is probably best to buy grout in powder form and to mix it with water as you need it. Recently an all-in-one adhesive and grout has become available which does double duty and which you may prefer to use. Always read the manufacturer's instructions before you begin.

TILE SPACERS

Small plastic crosses are the most popular kind of tile spacer, which are used to make sure that all the tiles are evenly spaced, and they are left between the tiles and grouted over. You can use matchsticks instead.

OTHER EQUIPMENT

The projects in this book also require the use of some other tools. Even if you do not already have them in your existing tool kit, you will find them in all DIY stores and general hardware shops.

◊ Small hammer
◊ Selection of panel pins, both sunk-head copper pins and fine steel frame pins
◊ Hand or power drill with a selection of bits suitable for wood
◊ PVA-based wood glue; choose a quick-drying kind if you can
◊ Sandpaper; you will need various grades
◊ Paint and paintbrushes; both oil- and water-based paints are used in different projects
◊ Steel rule and pencil for measuring and marking wooden frames and battens
◊ Spirit level; essential for fixing the batten for the first row of tiles but useful in other projects, too
◊ Fine tenon saw and mitre box to give frames true right-angled corners
◊ Small frame clamps (cramps)

BASIC WALL TILING

It is not the purpose of this book to explain all about wall tiling – there are plenty of good
do-it-yourself guides available – but here are the key points.

You will need
◊ Spirit level
◊ Pencil
◊ Batten
◊ Ruler or measuring tape
◊ Hammer and pins
◊ Tiles
◊ Tile cement and comb
◊ Spacers
◊ Grout

TIP

• Always make sure that the surface to
be tiled is sound because tiles are
considerably heavier than most other
forms of wall covering. Wash the
surface with warm water and
detergent before you begin to tile.

1 Use a spirit level to establish a horizontal line and
fix a batten on the wall at the level of the first full row
of tiles. This might not be the base of the wall but,
because it is better to finish with a complete, uncut
row of tiles, do some preparatory measuring.

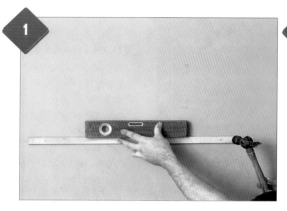

2 Use a notched comb to spread tile cement over
the wall. Do not cover more than about 0.5sq m
(about 5sq ft).

3 Press each tile firmly to the cement with a slight twisting action
to make sure that there is full contact between the tile, the cement
and the wall.

4 Place spacers at each corner to make sure that the grout lines are even,
pressing the spacers firmly against the wall because they will be left in place and
grouted over.

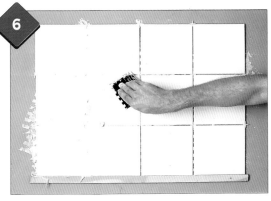

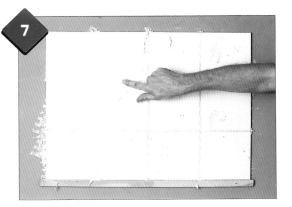

5 Continue to fix tiles in place, cleaning off any cement that is left on the front of the tiles before it dries and becomes hard to remove.

6 Leave the cement to dry, preferably overnight, then spread grout into the gaps between the tiles.

7 Smooth the joins with a finger and add more grout if necessary.

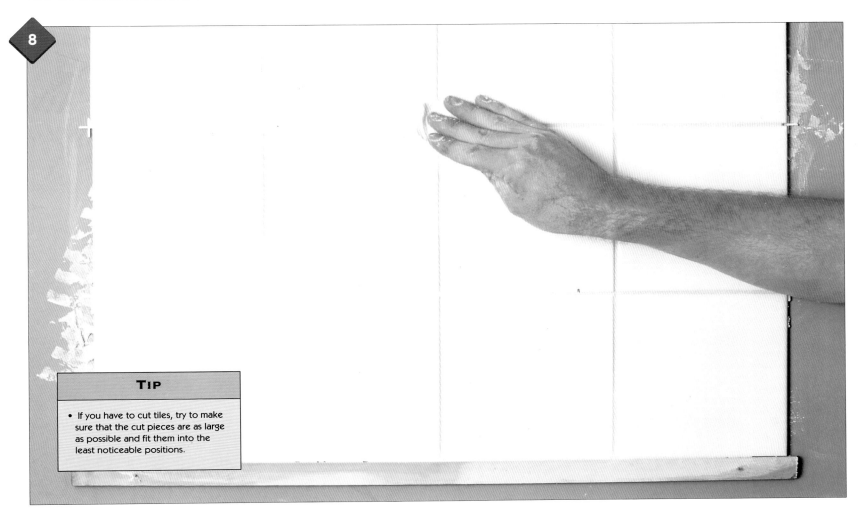

TIP

• If you have to cut tiles, try to make sure that the cut pieces are as large as possible and fit them into the least noticeable positions.

8 When the grout is set, polish the tiles with a clean, dry cloth.

Stencilled Flowers

If you feel like a change of decor but don't have sufficient funds to allow you to re-tile a whole wall with patterned tiles, a semi-permanent solution is to use enamel paints to decorate some plain tiles or even to give existing tiles a new lease of life.

You will need

◊ Plain tiles
◊ Stencils (cut out from the templates on page 80)
◊ Masking tape
◊ White tiles for mixing colours
◊ Cold ceramic paints – red, yellow and green
◊ Stencil brushes
◊ Craft knife
◊ Tile cement and comb
◊ Border tiles
◊ Grout

1 Use masking tape to hold the stencil in position on a tile.

2 Mix a range of greens from the yellow and green on a spare white tile. The different shades will enhance the overall appearance of the motifs.

3 Carefully apply the green paint with an upright stencil brush. Use only a little paint at a time. If you overload the brush, the paint will smudge around the edges.

TIP

• A range of cold enamel paints has been specially produced for use on ceramics, but although the paints will last for several years if treated with care and cleaned gently, they are not permanent. You can clean them off completely with a solvent and paint on new decorations if you wish. They are not suitable for use on tiles in places where they are likely to become wet – in showers, for example – although you can use them in other areas of the bathroom that do not become wet.

4 Mix red and green to make brown for the stem and apply as before.

5 Leave the paint to dry for a few moments before lifting the stencil.

TIP
• Do not mix too much of any one colour at a time because the paint dries quickly.

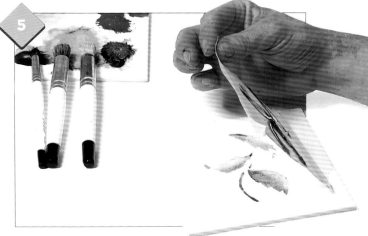

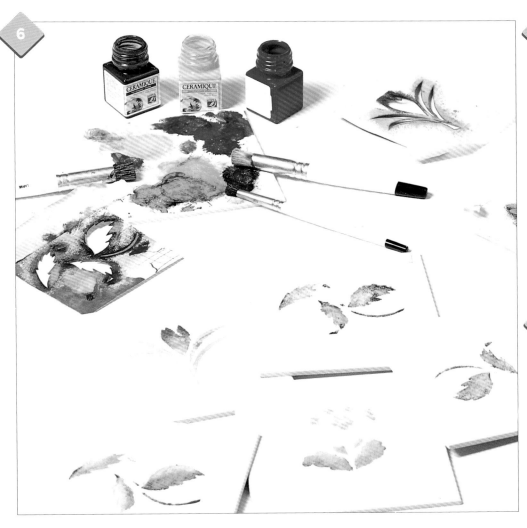

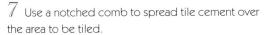

7 Use a notched comb to spread tile cement over the area to be tiled.

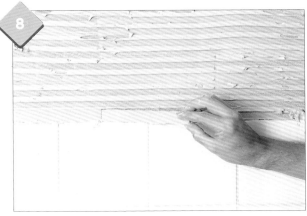

6 Use the other designs to decorate as many tiles as you need. You can remove any smudges of paint with a craft knife before the paint is set, then leave overnight for the paint to dry completely.

8 Fix the border tiles to the wall. Stagger the joins for best results.

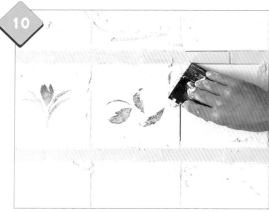

9 Add the decorated tiles above the row of border tiles, making sure that they are pressed firmly against the wall. Add another row of border tiles before fixing any additional plain tiles that are required Leave the tile cement to set overnight.

10 Spread grout into the spaces between the tiles, trying to avoid getting grout on the decorated areas. Make sure that the joints are completely filled, adding more grout if necessary.

11 Leave the grout to dry, then polish with a clean, dry cloth.

DECORATING A TILED WALL

- You can work directly onto an already tiled wall. Make sure that the surface is completely clean, and just before you begin stencilling, wipe it over with methylated spirits to remove any traces of grease. Take great care when you apply the colours not to overload your brushes, and leave each colour to dry before you apply a new shade to avoid smudging.

TRADITIONAL HALL PANEL

Many Victorian and Edwardian houses in Britain have decorative tiled panels on each side of the front door. There is no reason these panels should be confined to porches, however – they would be ideal in a conservatory or a bathroom or even set into a tiled wall as a special feature.

You will need

◊ 2 sets of decorative picture tiles – i.e.,
   10 15 x 15cm (6 x 6in) tiles
◊ Additional tiles and border strips to
   complement the picture tiles
◊ Tile cutter
◊ Spirit level
◊ Batten, hammer and pins
◊ Tile cement and comb
◊ Sponges
◊ Grout

1 Measure the area to be tiled and lay out the various tiles on a large flat area so that you can double-check the measurements. Cut tiles to size if necessary.

2 Use a spirit level to establish a horizontal line and fix a batten to the wall.

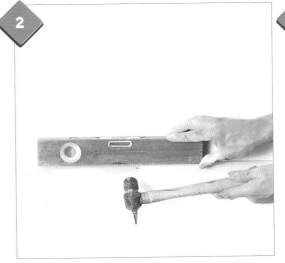

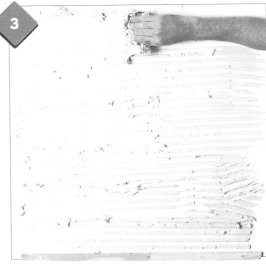

3 Spread tile cement over the area to be tiled with a notched comb.

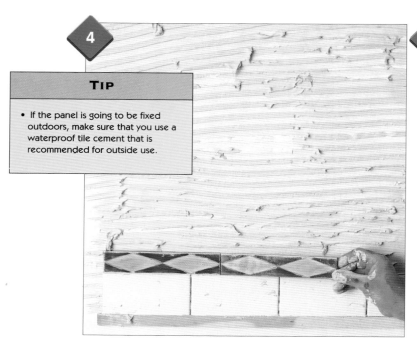

TIP

• If the panel is going to be fixed outdoors, make sure that you use a waterproof tile cement that is recommended for outside use.

4 Beginning with the bottom tiles in your design, press each tile firmly to the cement with a slight twisting action.

5 Work upwards in horizontal rows to ensure that the joins are even. It is more difficult to make fine adjustments if you apply the tiles in vertical rows.

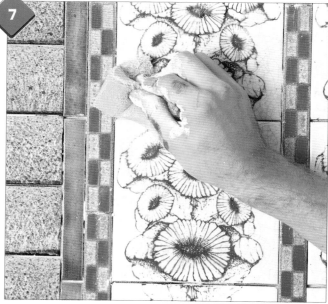

6 As you apply each picture tile, check that it is the right way up. It is all too easy to position tiles the wrong way round and not to notice until it is too late!

7 Continue to position the tiles, using a sponge to remove any cement from the front of the tiles before it sets.

8 When the tile cement is dry, carefully remove the batten and make good the surface. Spread grout over the entire pattern, taking care that all the joins are filled. Wipe off the surplus with a damp sponge, checking that all the joints are smooth.

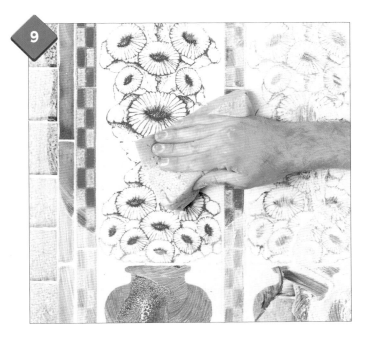

9 Leave the grout to dry, then polish the surface with a clean, dry cloth to remove any remaining traces.

CHESS BOARD

This board is the perfect foil for a special set of chessmen, although it can, of course, also be used for draughts. Alternatively, it could be used as a stand for plants. The project is ideal for beginners because none of the tiles needs to be cut and only basic wood-working skills are required.

You will need

◊ 1 square of 6mm (¼in) plywood, 40 x 40cm (16 x 16in)
◊ Drill with fine bit
◊ 4 wooden knobs for feet
◊ Screws
◊ Wooden edging strip, 2m (6ft) long
◊ PVA wood adhesive
◊ Panel pins
◊ Tile cement and comb
◊ 64 mosaic tiles (32 of each colour), each tile 5 x 5cm (2 x 2in)
◊ Grout
◊ Wood stain

TIP

• If you cannot find mosaic tiles, cut small squares from larger tiles. Do this slowly and carefully because it is vital that each cut tile is absolutely square.

1 Mark the positions for the feet, slightly inset from the corners of the plywood square, and drill locating holes with a fine bit.

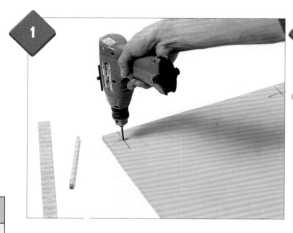

2 Attach the feet with screws through the locating holes.

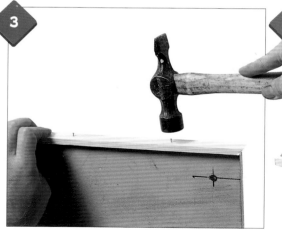

3 Measure and cut lengths of edging strip and attach them to the sides of the plywood with wood adhesive and panel pins. The bottom edge of each strip should be flush with the base of the board.

4 Use a notched comb to spread tile cement over the board, making sure that you apply the cement right up to the edges.

5 Beginning with a light coloured tile in the bottom right-hand corner, lay the tiles alternately. When you have filled the board, press each tile firmly down.

6 Leave the tile cement to set, then spread grout over the surface.

7 Wipe off any surplus grout with a damp sponge, making sure that the joins are smooth and well filled and that there is no grout on the wood.

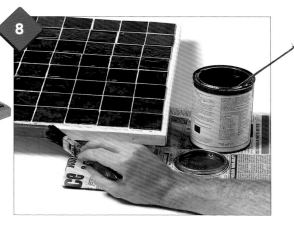

8 Leave the grout to dry before painting the edging strip and feet with wood stain to protect them.

TABLE STAND

Tiles are often used because they are durable, but they are also heat-resistant, which makes them ideal for use as stands for hot pans and teapots. Rather than using a single old tile, why not make a frame for an attractive tile so that you can place it on the dining table.

You will need

◊ 38 x 38mm (1⅛x 1⅛in) wooden moulding, 1.5m (5ft) long
◊ Saw
◊ PVA wood adhesive
◊ Clamps
◊ 1 decorative tile, 20 x 20cm (8 x 8in)
◊ 4 x 20mm (¼ x ⅞in) wooden strip, 80cm (32in) long
◊ Hammer and pins
◊ Base colour paint and picture frame rubbing gold
◊ Paintbrush
◊ Silicone sealant

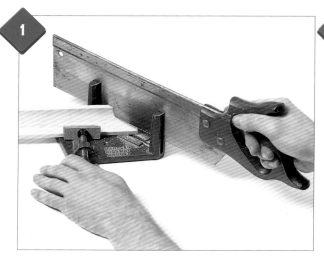

1 Cut the moulding into four pieces with mitred corners so that each has an internal length of slightly more than 20cm (8in) to make fitting the tile easier.

2 Glue a corner and hold the frame pieces together with clamps, using small off-cuts of wood to prevent the clamps from marking the frame.

3 Use a damp cloth to wipe off any surplus adhesive and leave to dry.

4 Repeat steps 2 and 3 on the other three corners. This may take some time.

5 Place the tile on a flat surface and turn the frame upside down over the tile. Mark on the frame the level of the tile as a guide for positioning the support.

6 Cut the wooden strip into four lengths to fit inside the frame. Glue and pin the lengths to the frame so that the upper edges are flush with the marked line.

7 Check that the tile rests firmly on the supports.

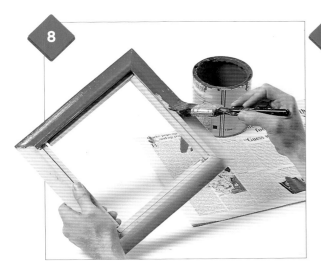

8 Remove the tile and paint the frame with the base colour of your choice. Allow to dry.

9 Use your fingers to apply an even coat of frame rubbing gold to the external sides of the frame.

10 Leave the rubbing gold to dry, then carefully rub it back with a dry sponge to reveal traces of the base coat.

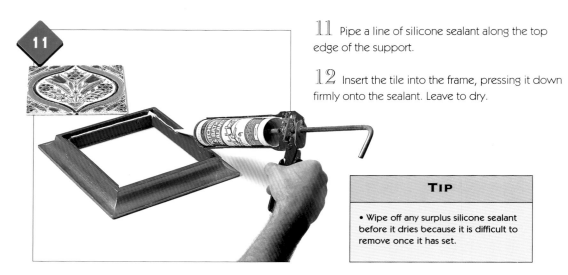

11 Pipe a line of silicone sealant along the top edge of the support.

12 Insert the tile into the frame, pressing it down firmly onto the sealant. Leave to dry.

TIP

• Wipe off any surplus silicone sealant before it dries because it is difficult to remove once it has set.

Small Tray

Small trays are always useful, whether it is for serving drinks, for a few mugs of coffee and a plate of biscuits or for arranging sandwiches or savoury snacks. You can make the tray as large as you wish, but remember that the tiles themselves are relatively heavy, and this factor will limit the final size.

You will need

◊ 3 decorative tiles, each 15 x 15cm (6 x 6in)
◊ Approximately 1.5m (5ft) of wooden moulding
◊ Saw
◊ PVA wood adhesive
◊ Clamps
◊ 1 piece of 4mm (⅛in) plywood, approximately 46 x 16cm (18½ x 6¼in)
◊ Water-based paints in 2 colours
◊ Craquelle varnish
◊ Silicone sealant
◊ Hammer and panel pins

1 Measure the moulding against a tile and mark the positions of the mitres.

2 Cut the wood so that you have two pieces with inside edges of 15cm (6in) and two pieces with inside edges of 45cm (18in). These sizes are only approximate: you must base the cutting marks on the dimensions of the tiles you are actually using.

3 Glue together the cut edges of a long piece and a short piece with PVA wood adhesive.

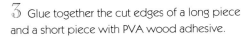

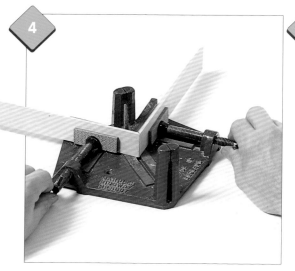

4 Clamp the two pieces together, using off-cuts of wood to stop the clamps marking the moulding. Wipe off any surplus adhesive before it sets, then leave to dry.

5 Repeat steps 3 and 4 at the other three corners, leaving the adhesive to dry each time. Trim the plywood base so that it fits exactly into the base of the frame.

6 Paint the entire frame and one side of the base in base colour and allow to dry. Apply a coat of craquelle varnish and leave to dry, preferably overnight.

7 Apply a coat of the second colour, painting it on in quick, confident strokes so that you do not disturb the craquelle. Leave to dry.

8 Turn the frame upside down and pipe a line of silicone sealant along the edge of the rebate.

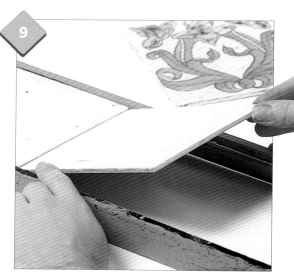

9 Carefully insert the tiles, face down and in the correct order, into the frame, pressing them down firmly onto the sealant. Remove any surplus sealant from the surface of the tiles, then leave to dry.

TIP

• When you paint a frame, make sure that you also paint the inside rebate in case it shows around the outside edges of the tiles.

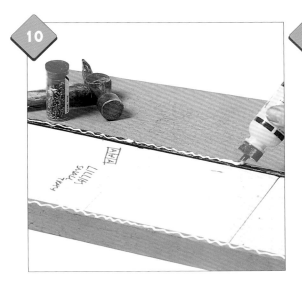

10 Apply a wavy line of wood adhesive to the edge of the frame.

11 Position the base board over the frame, wiping away any surplus adhesive before it dries.

12 Use small steel pins to fix the edge of the base board to the frame.

FRAMED PANEL

Hand-painted tiles can be used with plain tiles when you are covering a wall, but you may be unwilling to stick such pretty tiles in place permanently. One solution is to frame them and use them as a picture so that you can move them around, either if you move house or simply to change the decor of a room. The materials quoted here are for a 12-tile panel, but they can be simply adjusted to accommodate the tiles of your choice. Because the frame itself is so light, no special fixing method is necessary, which is an additional advantage.

You will need
◊ 2.5 x 2.5cm (1 x 1in) wooden strip, 3.3m (11ft) long
◊ Saw and mitre box
◊ PVA wood adhesive
◊ Clamps
◊ 12 decorative tiles, each 15 x 15cm (6 x 6in)
◊ Hammer, nails and panel pins
◊ 2 pieces of 6mm (¼in) plywood, each 45 x 10cm (18 x 4in)
◊ Silicone sealant
◊ Grout and spreader
◊ Hockey stick moulding, 2.2m (7ft 6in) long
◊ Liquid wood wax
◊ 2 screw eyes and wire or string for hanging

1 Using the mitre box, cut two strips of wood, each 45cm (18in) long on the longest edge, with both ends mitred in opposite directions. Then cut two strips of wood, each 60cm (24in) long on the longest edge, with both ends mitred in opposite directions. Cut two strips of wood, each 55cm (22in) long, with square ends.

2 Glue the mitred corner of one short piece to the mitred end of a long piece, clamping them in the mitre frame until the adhesive is set. Repeat with the remaining mitred corners to make a frame, leaving the adhesive to dry completely each time. The frame should have the exact measurements of the outside dimensions of the tile panels.

3 Use one of the tiles to mark on the short sides of the frame the position of the centre of the two vertical struts.

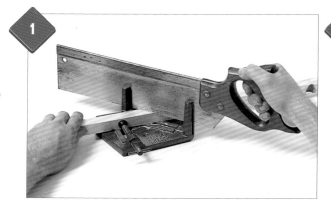

4 Position the two vertical pieces on the pencil marks before gluing and nailing into place.

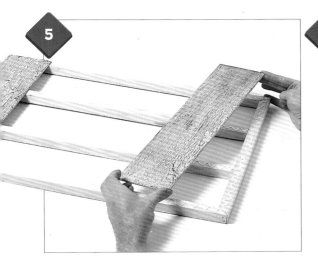

5 Apply a line of wood adhesive along the shorter ends of the two rectangles of plywood and glue them to the ends of the frame.

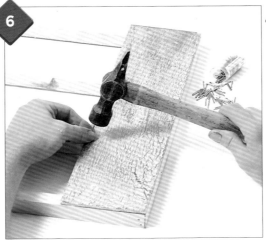

6 Pin the plywood to the underlying struts to give additional stability to the frame. Leave to dry overnight.

7 Apply the silicone sealant in wavy lines to the top side of the frame.

8 Begin to position the tiles on the sealant. When all the tiles are in place, adjust the spacing if necessary. Do not use tile spacers, which would leave too great a gap between each tile. Remove any surplus sealant from the surface of the tiles and leave to dry for at least 4 hours.

9 Apply grout to the joins with a spreader and leave for about 10 minutes so that it dries slightly. Clean off the grout, using a finger to press the grout between the joins, and use a damp sponge to remove all traces of grout. This can take several attempts.

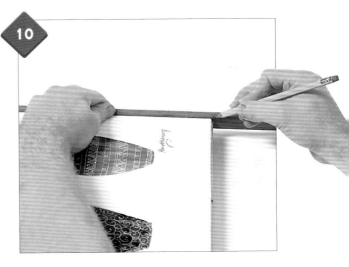

10 Measure the hockey stick moulding against the outside edge of the frame to get an exact fit.

11 Cut the moulding to length, mitring the corners and making sure that the mitred cuts are in opposite directions at each end of each piece.

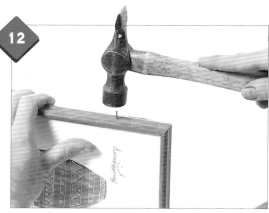

12 Apply a line of adhesive to the edge of the frame, then use small panel pins to tack the moulding to the frame.

13 Seal the moulding with liquid wax, taking care not to get the wax on the face of the tiles. When it is dry, buff it with a dry cloth.

14 Turn over the panel and fix two screw eyes to the frame, about one-third of the way down from the top, before attaching the wire or string.

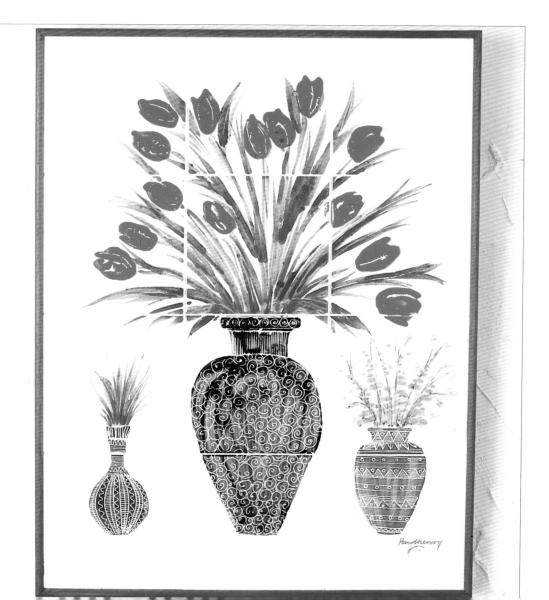

GAUDI-STYLE PLANTER

The Spanish architect Antonio Gaudi (1852–1926) is probably best remembered for his work in Barcelona, especially the garden he created at Guell Park, which was constructed from thousands of broken tiles. Even if we had the space, such a project is far too ambitious for most of us, but these planters can be made to pay homage to Gaudi's individual style and to act as a reminder of Spain. It is also an ideal way of using broken tiles. It doesn't matter if they are patterned, but they must have a distinct colour.

You will need
◊ 1 30cm (12in) terracotta flowerpot
◊ Metal rule and felt-tipped pen
◊ Selection of broken tiles
◊ Sacking or hessian and heavy hammer
◊ Tile cement for exterior use and spreader
◊ Rubber gloves
◊ Tile nippers

1 Turn the flowerpot upside down and mark on the base four equidistant points. Midway between the four original points, mark four more points on the bottom of the rim.

2 Join the marks to create a series of triangles. Make sure that the triangles around the flowerpot are clearly drawn in.

3 Wrap several tiles, all of the same colour, in a piece of sack and hit them with a heavy hammer. You need fairly small pieces, none larger than about 5cm (2in) in any direction.

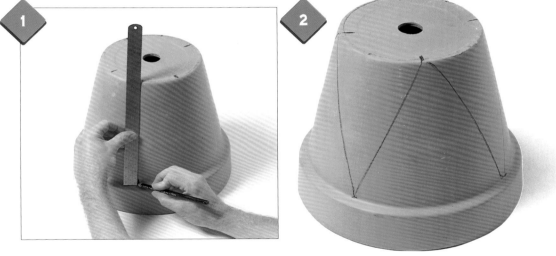

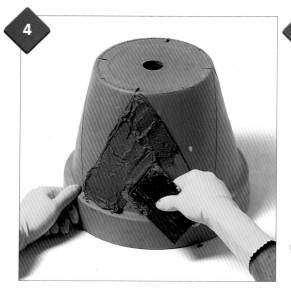

4 Apply tile cement to one of the triangles. Make sure you wear rubber gloves because the cement may irritate your skin.

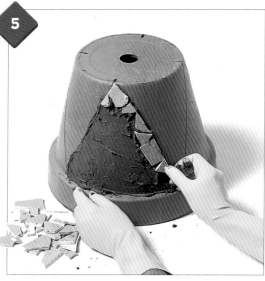

5 Begin to position the tiles, placing the straight edges along the sides of the triangles.

6 Continue to fill the triangle. You may need to cut small pieces to fit into the apex.

TIP

• Keep the same colours together when you break the tiles, otherwise you will spend a lot of time sorting them out.

TIP

• Do not be tempted to try to use large pieces of tile. The cement will not cushion them and the surface of the finished planter will be jagged and difficult to handle without cutting yourself.

7 Complete two or three sections, using different colours in each, then use a spreader to cover the tile pieces with a layer of cement. This will fill in any gaps and act as a grout.

8 Use a wet sponge to remove the surplus cement, checking that all the gaps are completely filled.

9 Continue to work around the flowerpot. Pay particular attention to the points at what will be the base. The tile pieces must not protrude or the flowerpot will not be stable when it is turned the right way up.

10 Check that all holes are filled, using extra cement as necessary, then use a damp sponge to remove all surplus cement. Take care to clean off any cement from the terracotta pot – it is difficult to remove when it has hardened. Leave for 24 hours for the cement to harden completely.

SUN AND MOON PANEL

Tiled rooms can sometimes appear very plain, especially if a limited budget has meant that you have used tiles of a single colour for quite a large area. This project, which would be ideal for a kitchen or bathroom, uses just a few coloured tiles to create an eye-catching feature. The quantities quoted are for one sun and one moon, but you could use several motifs in the same room.

You will need
◊ 8 white tiles, each 15 x 15cm (6 x 6in)
◊ 3 yellow tiles, each 15 x 15cm (6 x 6in)
◊ 1 orange tile, 15 x 15cm (6 x 6in)
◊ Pair of compasses and felt-tipped pen
◊ Tile cutter
◊ Tile nippers
◊ Carborundum stone
◊ Cold ceramic paint – brown
◊ Stencil brush
◊ Tile cement and comb
◊ Grout

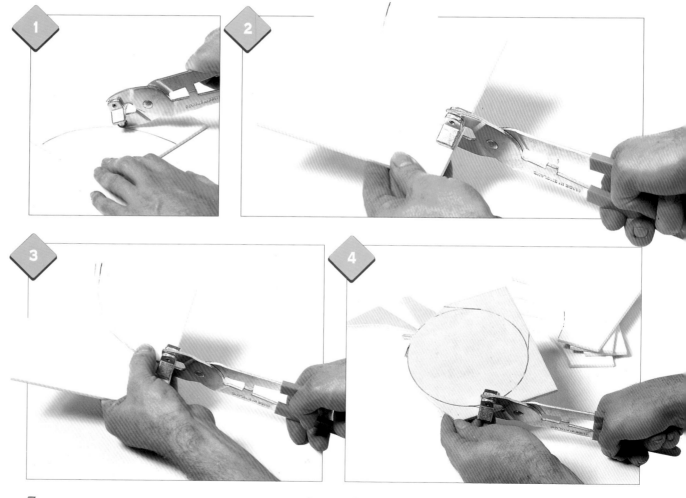

1 Lay four tiles in a square and, using the centre point, draw a circle with a radius of 6.5cm (2´in) so that each tile has a quadrant of the circle marked on it. Scribe the line on each tile, pushing the cutter away from you so that you can see clearly the line you are following. Turn over the tile and tap it roughly along the line you have scribed. This will help the tile snap along the line.

2 Gently squeeze the tile cutter to crack the tile. You can often hear the sound of the tile beginning to crack.

3 Snapping a tile along a curved line can be difficult, so be patient. Repeat on all four tiles, but with a radius of 6.5cm (2⅛in) for the moon.

4 Using the template on page 79 trace a circle on a yellow tile. Scribe the outline of the circle, and cut away the pieces from the edge.

5 Use tile nippers to snap off the protruding edges to give a neat outline.

6 Smooth the edge with a carborundum stone. Make a second yellow circle in the same way for the moon.

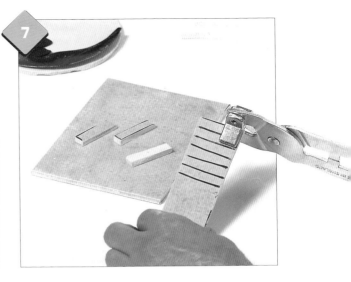

7 Cut strips 2.5 x 1cm (1 x 3/8in) from orange and yellow tiles.

8 Stencil the moon's face onto one of the yellow circles using the special cold ceramic paint. Stencil the sun's face onto the other yellow circle. Leave the ceramic paint to harden overnight or the colour will rub off at the next stage.

9 Lay out the pieces of the design on a flat surface to make sure that all the elements fit together. If necessary, trim the strips cut in step 8 so that they fit neatly around the sun's face.

10 Fix the white tiles with the cut-out sections to the wall, making sure that they form even circles.

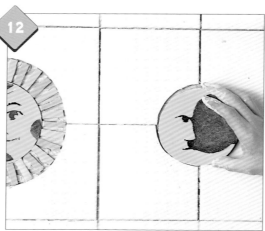

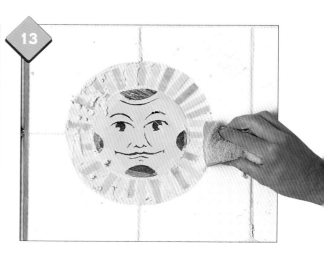

11 Position the sun in the centre of the appropriate space. Carefully place alternate strips of orange and yellow around the sun's face, pressing each piece firmly against the wall.

12 Fit the moon's face into the other space.

13 Use grout to fill the spaces between the sun's rays and also all other exposed joins. Apply the grout with a sponge because you will need quite a lot to fill all the spaces. Do not use your fingers – there are too many sharp edges and you could easily cut yourself. The spaces between the rays will be slightly below the surface of the tiles when you have finished. Although the ceramic paint is fairly hard-wearing, try to avoid getting grout on the painted surfaces.

ART DECO FISH

Simple designs can be cut from tiles of contrasting colours to form interesting panels or borders. The process is time consuming, although it is much less expensive than buying specially decorated border tiles. Large and small geometric patterns can look extremely effective, but we have used a fish, which would be ideal in a bathroom.

You will need
◊ Tracing paper and pencil
◊ Cardboard
◊ Felt-tipped pen
◊ 2 white tiles, each 15 x 15cm (6 x 6in)
   2 black tiles, each 15 x 15cm (6 x 6in)
◊ Tile cutter
◊ Tile nippers
◊ Carborundum stone
◊ Tile cement and comb
◊ Narrow border tiles
◊ Grout

1 Transfer the fish pattern (see page 80) to a piece of cardboard, and use it to transfer the outline to the white tiles.

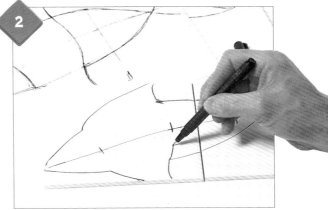

2 Join up the register marks by hand.

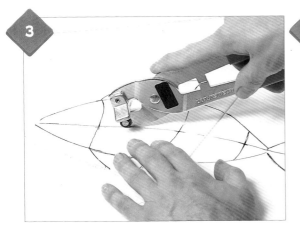

3 Carefully scribe along the marked lines, beginning with the longest cuts. Try to cut in one smooth action and avoid jerky movements.

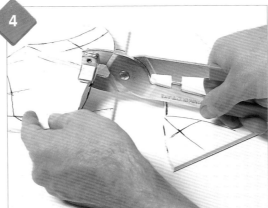

4 Tap the underside of the tiles and break along the scribed lines. If some cuts are not successful, you can always cut odd pieces from other tiles. Sometimes it seems as if tiles will not break just as you want them to.

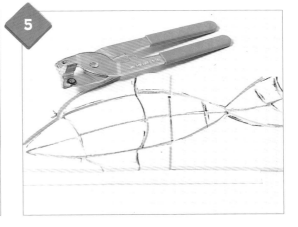

5 Lay out the pieces on top of the tracing to avoid confusion later on.

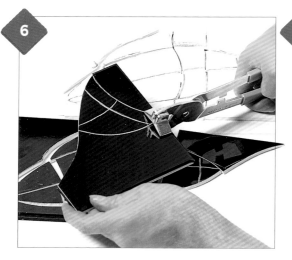

6 Repeat steps 1–5 inclusive with the black tiles.

7 Re-arrange the black and white pieces to create a chequered design.

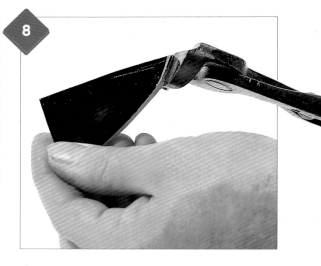

8 Use your tile nippers to remove any protruding pieces of tile.

9 Smooth the rough edges with a carborundum stone and make sure that the pieces fit neatly together. Remember to use water with the carborundum stone to prevent the edges from chipping.

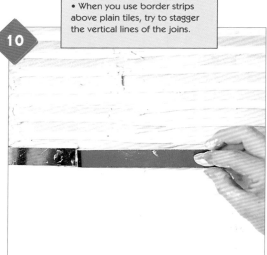

10 Apply tile cement to a small area of the wall with a toothed scraper or comb, then start to position the tiles, beginning with the bottom row of border tiles.

11 Working from the left-hand side, position the mosaic pieces.

12 Continue to fix tile pieces, building up the motifs from left to right.

13 Finish off with another row of border tiles. Make sure that all the surfaces are flat and that all the pieces are firmly pressed to the cement. Check that the spaces between the tile pieces are even, then clean any surplus cement from the surfaces of the tiles. Leave overnight for the cement to dry.

14 Use a sponge to apply the grout. Remove surplus grout from the surface of the tiles before it dries, making sure that all the joins are completely and neatly filled. When the grout is dry, clean the surface with a slightly damp sponge.

WINDOW BOX

A window box is a wonderful way of brightening up a dull windowsill, and this planter could be used indoors or out. We have used tiles with a fairly traditional floral pattern, but it would look equally stunning with geometric or abstract patterns. Although it is rather time-consuming, this project is well worth the effort.

You will need

◊ Saw and mitre box
◊ 2.5 x 2.5cm (1 x 1in) wooden strip, 4.5m (15ft) long
◊ PVA wood adhesive
◊ Hammer and panel pins
◊ Clamps
◊ 1 piece of 6mm (¼in) plywood, 165 x 25cm (5ft 6in x 10in)
◊ Hockey stick moulding, 1m (3ft) long
◊ 50 x 12mm (2 x ⅜in) wooden strip, 4.5m (15ft) long
◊ Drill
◊ 8 small wooden knobs
◊ 18 x 4mm (¾ x ¼in) wooden strip, 2m (6ft) long
◊ Sandpaper
◊ Oil-based paint for exterior use
◊ Silicone sealant
◊ Grout

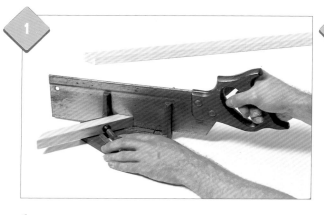

1 Use the saw and mitre box to cut the length of square wooden strip into two pieces, each with an inside length of just over 60cm (24in), and two pieces, each with an inside length of just over 15cm (6in).

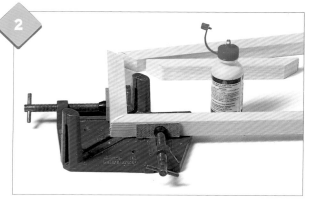

2 Check that the angles at each end of each piece run in opposite directions, then glue one short piece to one long piece with wood adhesive.

3 Clamp them together until the adhesive is dry, then use insert pins diagonally across the corners for extra strength. Repeat steps 2 and 3 until the frame is complete.

4 Cut a piece of plywood to the exact dimensions of the frame. Glue and pin it to the frame then leave to dry. Make a second frame with a plywood cover in exactly the same way. These are the two long sides of the window box.

5 From the remaining plywood cut two squares, each 20 x 20cm (8 x 8in), and from the 2.5 x 2.5cm (1 x 1in) wooden strip cut four lengths, each 15cm (6in) long. Glue and pin a strip along two opposite sides of each plywood square, positioning the strips in the centre of the edges. These pieces form the two short sides.

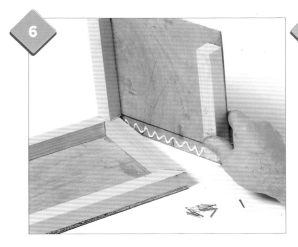

6 Glue and pin both short sides to a long side. Leave to dry.

7 Glue and pin the second long side to the short sides to create a box. Leave to dry.

8 Cut four pieces of hockey stick moulding, each 20cm (8in) long, and glue and pin a length of moulding to each vertical corner edge.

9 Use the saw and mitre box to cut the 50 x 12mm (2 x 3/8in) wooden strip into two pieces, each with an inside length of just over 60cm (24in), and two pieces, each with an inside length of just over 15cm (6in). Make sure that the angles at each end face in opposite directions. Making sure that the inside edge is flush with the inside of the box, glue and pin the pieces along the top edge of the frame to create a decorative ledge. Repeat to make an edging around the foot of the box.

10 Drill through the corners of the top ledge to make seating holes for the knobs. Glue a knob in each corner. Repeat at the four bottom corners to make feet.

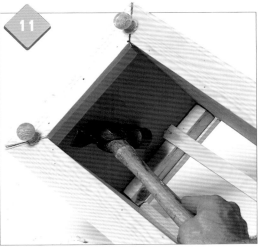

11 From the 18 x 4mm (¾ x ¼in) strip cut two lengths, each 65cm (26in) long. Glue and pin the strips to the inside bottom ledge to provide supports for the pots.

TIP

• The materials quoted here are for a window box with four 15 x 15cm (6 x 6in) tiles along each of the long sides. Larger or smaller versions can be easily made in the same way, however, by increasing or reducing the dimensions of the basic frame.

12 Smooth any rough surfaces with sandpaper and paint the entire box, inside and out, with several coats of an oil-based paint, which will protect the box if it stands outdoors. You need not paint the panels at the front, back and sides that will be covered by tiles.

13 Apply silicone sealant to one long side and firmly place four tiles in position. Leave to dry, then repeat on the other long side. Leave to dry.

14 Spread grout along the joins between and around the tiles, cleaning off any surplus grout before it dries hard. Leave to dry before using a clean, dry cloth to polish the tiles and remove the final traces of grout. Use an exterior grout if the window box is to be used outside.

TEMPLATES

The templates on the following pages are used to complete the Stencilled Flowers, Sun and Moon and Art Deco Fish projects.

If you are using a different sized tile from those listed in this book or if you would prefer to create your own designs from patterns and motifs that you have seen in a magazine, you may need to adjust the size. The easiest way of enlarging or decreasing the size of an outline is by photocopying, and many libraries, office supply shops and stationers have photocopiers that can enlarge or reduce in a range of percentages.

If you do not have access to a photocopier, use the grid method. Use a sharp pencil and ruler to draw a series of evenly spaced, parallel lines horizontally and vertically across the image you wish to copy. It is usually easier if at least some of the grid lines touch the edges of the original shape. On a clean sheet of paper draw a second grid, but this time with the lines spaced at a proportionately greater distance – for example, if you wanted to double the size of the image, the lines on your first grid might be 2.5cm (1in) apart on the original and 5cm (2in) apart in your second grid. It is relatively simple to transfer the shapes in one square of the original grid to the corresponding square in the second grid. If the outline you want to copy is complicated, a smaller grid might be easier to use – 1cm (½in) squares in the original and 2cm (1in) squares in the larger version.

CUTTING STENCILS

When you are happy with the size of your image, go over the outlines with a fine felt-tipped pen. Then use either tracing paper or carbon paper to transfer the outline to stencil card.

Working on a special cutting mat or on a spare piece of thick cardboard, use a craft knife or scalpel to cut through the lines. Work slowly and carefully so that the cut lines are neat and accurate.

Carefully made stencils can be used time and again, especially if you take care to wipe away any paint that is left on them, using water or a solvent as appropriate, and then allow them to dry flat, away from direct heat.

Sun and Moon Panel

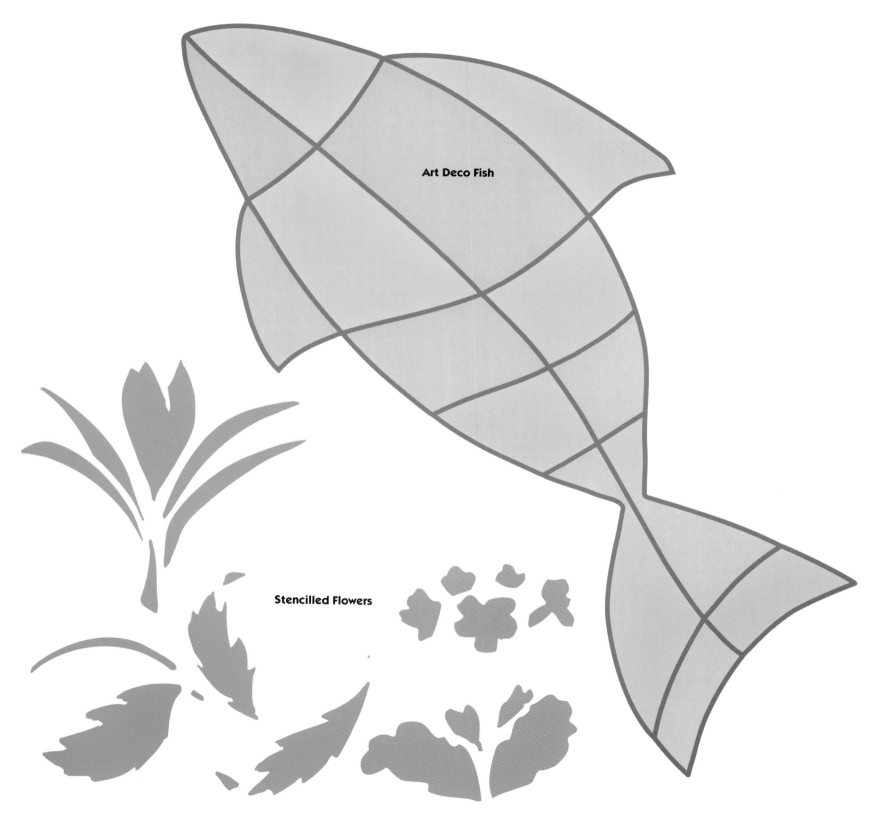

Art Deco Fish

Stencilled Flowers

Decorative Painting

Transform pieces of furniture to beautiful effect
with this individual and challenging pastime

INTRODUCTION

A close colleague and I have a favourite saying: "If it will stand still for long enough, paint it."

Paint is an exciting medium with endless potential, and it can be used to transform rather plain, rather unexciting or battered items into unusual, pretty things. If you are already interested in painting you are likely to have come across different kinds of articles that you would like to decorate but are not quite sure how to begin.

There are several different types of paint that can be used, and different paints are suitable for different surfaces. However, once you know what paint is appropriate, you will be able to experiment and transform practically every room in your home. Junk-shop finds will become family heirlooms, and familiar, every-day items will become unrecognizable. Remember, though, that an object that is inherently unattractive will always be unattractive, no matter what you do to the surface. Do not waste time trying to transform an object that you will never want to have in a room with you. On the other hand, pieces of furniture and ornaments that are just a bit tattered or worn or rusty but that are elegant or pleasingly proportioned are well worth rejuvenating.

This book explains how to prepare a variety of surfaces so that they will accept decorative paint and it will show, by working through a range of articles, how different techniques and finishes can be applied.

MATERIALS AND TECHNIQUES

PAINTS

Artists' acrylic paints, which come in tubes, are available in a huge variety of colours from most shops supplying artists' materials. All the colours can be intermixed, and because acrylics are water-based, they can be dissolved in, and mixed with, water. When they are dry they are waterproof and can only be removed with methylated spirits (de-natured alcohol). They are fast drying and are, therefore, ideal for design work because there is little danger that you will smudge them. Acrylic paints can be used on water- or spirit-based paints, and they can sometimes be made to adhere on top of oil-based paints if you add a tiny amount of washing-up detergent to them. Clean your brushes in water.

Artists' oil paints, which are also available in tubes and can be found in art shops, look much like acrylic paints. They contain linseed oil, however, and are, therefore, classified as oil-based. Like other oil-based products, they can be dissolved with turpentine or white (mineral) spirit, which should be used to remove the paint when it has dried and to clean your brushes. They can be used on almost any surface.

Water-based acrylic varnish

Emulsion (latex)

Enamels

Ceramic paint

Casein paint

Shellac

Metal paint

Artists' acrylic and oil paints

Emulsion paint (latex) is water-based, and it is probably most often associated with home decorating. All DIY stores and shops selling home decorating materials will stock emulsion paints, and many of the larger stores have colour-mixing machines, which are invaluable because so many of the standard paints are in pastel shades. You may find it useful to buy a small range of dark colours and white and to mix your own colours. Look out for the small, trial-size pots, which are ideal for furniture and small items and which are often made in unusual colours.

Emulsion paint needs a porous surface to adhere to, although it will also cover spirit-based paints and varnishes. Clean your brushes in water. When emulsion paint is dry it is waterproof and can then be removed only with methylated spirits (de-natured alcohol).

Acrylic primer/undercoat, which is also water-based, is widely available in DIY and home decorating stores. It is similar to emulsion paint but has an acrylic binder, which makes it stronger. Use it to seal and prime bare wood. It is only available in white, so you will need to use shellac as a primer if you are planning to use a dark top coat. Clean your brushes in water.

Casein or buttermilk paint, which is made from a by-product of cheese-making, is another water-based paint but it remains water-soluble when it is dry. It is a soft paint, which can be polished by burnishing to give a very smooth finish. It is available from art shops and some specialist paint suppliers. Apply it to a porous surface or over a coat of a spirit-based paint. Clean your brushes in water.

Several types of **ceramic paint** are available, and they can be either water- or oil-based. They are available from art shops and from many craft suppliers. Check before you buy, because some kinds have to be baked in the oven to make them set. Follow the manufacturer's instructions for use and for cleaning brushes.

Metal paints are very hard wearing and will adhere to most surfaces. They are available in both spray and brush-on forms, although if you use spray paint make sure you work in a well-ventilated room or, preferably, outdoors. Some types can be used to isolate rust, while other kinds should be applied only when the rust has been treated and isolated. When they are dry they can be dissolved with methylated spirits or the appropriate solvent, such as xylene, acetone or toluene, recommended by the manufacturer. Also follow the manufacturer's instructions for cleaning brushes.

Enamel paints, which are available in art shops, some craft suppliers and in DIY stores, are oil-based and can be used on metal, glass, ceramics, plastics and wood. Dilute the paint with turpentine or white (mineral) spirit, which should also be used for cleaning your brushes.

Acrylic varnish, which is water-based, is now widely available in shops that sell other household paints. It is quick-drying and non-yellowing, and although it looks milky when you apply it, it dries clear. Check the durability before you buy because some are tougher than others. The varnish can be tinted with artists'

acrylics, gouache and universal stainers, which need to be diluted with water before they are added to the varnish. Some of the better makes will adhere to non-porous surfaces, but others need to be treated as emulsion paints. The varnish is waterproof when it is dry, but you should wash your brushes in water.

Shellac is available through specialist suppliers, some DIY stores and from builders' merchants. It comes in a wide variety of grades and stages of refinement, all of which are quick drying, and it is also obtainable in flakes, which can be dissolved in methylated spirits (de-natured alcohol) even when they are dry. Shellac button polish or sanding sealer should be used for the projects described in this book. Shellac can be used to seal bare wood, and it will adhere to most surfaces. It is often used to form an isolating layer between two incompatible paints. Wash brushes in methylated spirits (de-natured alcohol).

White polish, a more highly refined form of shellac, gives a transparent finish. It dissolves in methylated spirits (de-natured alcohol), even when it is dry, and you should clean your brushes in methylated spirits. It is available from the same sources as other shellac products.

Oil-based varnish contains resins and oils that usually cause it to yellow as it ages. Normally the stronger the varnish – yacht varnish, for example – the more yellow it becomes. It is, however, very durable, waterproof and widely available from stores selling household paints and varnishes. It will adhere to most surfaces, and can be tinted with artists' oil paints, which should be diluted with white (mineral) spirit before being added to the varnish. Clean your brushes in white (mineral) spirit.

Crackle varnish, which is sometimes sold as cracklure, is a two-part product. The first, slow-drying coat continues to dry under the second, fast-drying coat, causing the top coat to crack. It can be unpredictable, and drying times vary considerably depending on the thickness of the coat, the circulation of air around the painted item, the humidity and so on. The varnish has to be patinated with artists' oil tube paints or powders to reveal the cracks to best effect. It is usually supplied as one oil-based and one water-based varnish, although wholly water-based versions are available. Brands that have an oil-based first coat can be used on most surfaces. Check the manufacturer's instructions before you begin. You will find crackle varnish in specialist paint shops and in some art shops.

Wax is widely available in clear form or in different wood colours. It is useful for antiquing surfaces, and it can also be tinted with artists' oil paints or with shoe polish. Wax should always be the final finish: do not attempt to varnish over it. Although the surface is waterproof, you will need to re-wax regularly. Use white spirit to clean your brushes.

Antiquing fluid can be bought ready made, or you can mix your own with artists' oil paints and white (mineral) spirit. The consistency can range from thick cream to a runny liquid. Earth colours – raw umber, burnt umber, green umber and Payne's grey, for example – are normally used.

Crackle varnish – first, oil-based coat

Crackle varnish – second, water-based coat

Oil-based varnish tinted with raw umber

Antique coloured wax

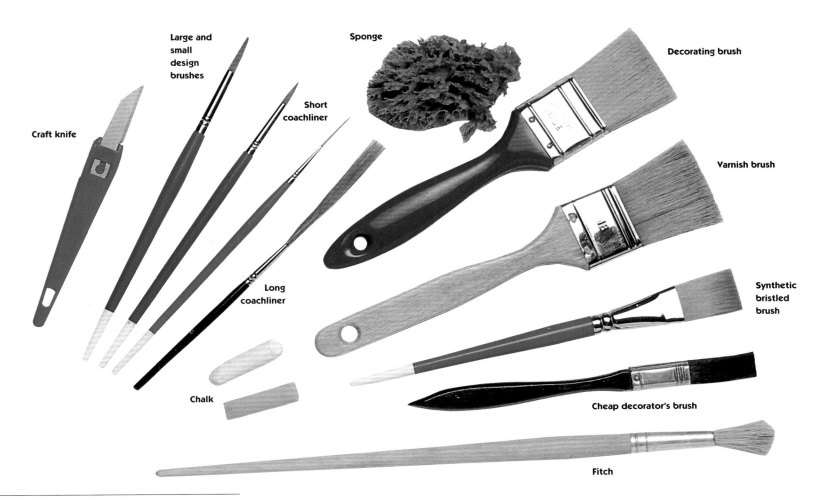

Craft knife

Large and small design brushes

Short coachliner

Sponge

Decorating brush

Varnish brush

Long coachliner

Synthetic bristled brush

Chalk

Cheap decorator's brush

Fitch

BRUSHES

You will need a selection of brushes to complete the projects described in this book. The best brushes are expensive, but if you take care of them they will last for many years. Cheaper brushes are available, and if you are not intending to do a lot of painting you may find they are adequate. Do not expect them to last, however. Always try to use the appropriate brush for the type of project and the paint you will be applying.

Varnish brushes are flat and are available in a variety of widths and kinds, ranging from pure bristle to synthetic fibres. When you apply water-based paints and varnishes, the synthetic brushes are generally better because they give a better flow and tend not to leave brush marks. They are not essential, however. You can use a varnish brush for paint as well as for varnish, especially when you are

decorating small items, but in general it is best to keep separate brushes for paint and for varnish and for oil- and water-based products.

Decorator's brushes have much thicker heads than varnish brushes, although they, too, are available in a variety of widths and types. When you are applying paint, use the largest brush you can, simply because it will give you quicker coverage. If you are planning to work on small articles only, you will probably not need a decorator's brush, and a selection of varnish brushes will be sufficient. It is, however, worth buying one or two small, cheap brushes to use with shellac, because the methylated spirits (de-natured alcohol) in it will ruin your brushes.

Fitches are used for oil painting, and they are available in art shop and some craft suppliers. They generally have long handles and short, stiff bristles, and they are made in various sizes and shapes.

Fitches are useful for spattering and for mixing paints and varnishes, but they are not essential.

Also available from art shops, **design brushes** are made in a range of sizes and different kinds of hair. Really good brushes can be expensive, and if you are working with acrylics it is better to use a synthetic brush. In fact, top quality, sable watercolour brushes should not be used for any of the projects described in this book. The most useful sizes to begin with are no. 4, no. 6 and no. 9.

Brushes known as **coachliners** are used for painting free-hand lines. They look rather daunting, but they do make lining easier. They have long hairs, all the same lengths, which are tear-shaped, so that the line is the same width throughout. They are available with long or short hairs and in a variety of widths. The short ones are for painting curves and short lines, and for the projects in this book you will find a short, no. 1 brush most useful.

OTHER EQUIPMENT

In addition to paints and a good selection of brushes, you will also use some or all of the following to complete the projects.

◊ Natural marine sponge: the frilly outer edge gives a varied pattern when it is used for sponging. Always squeeze out in water before use to soften the sponge and never leave it soaking in harsh solvents. Synthetic sponges are not a suitable substitute.
◊ Craft knife: these are always useful to have, and cheap, disposable ones are widely available. Dispose of used blades safely.
◊ Wire wool: you can buy a range of grades. The finest, grade 0000, is used for burnishing.
◊ Sandpaper: you will use a range of grades of ordinary sandpaper or of wet and dry paper.
◊ Chalk: blackboard chalk is useful for planning designs on furniture and other large items. Be careful if you use coloured chalk because it may stain your work.
◊ Graphite tracing-down paper: wax-free paper is used to transfer designs to most surfaces, and it is easy to remove with a damp cloth. It is available in a variety of colours and is invaluable if you are going to trace a lot of designs. An alternative would be to use a soft pencil to outline the reverse of your design before tracing over the front with a sharp, hard pencil. Ordinary carbon paper is slightly waxy, and not only resists being painted over but is likely to stain.
◊ Tracing paper: the see-through film is readily available and ideal for transferring designs.
◊ Drawing pens: most drawing pens have fine, fibre tips, but you should test them before use to make sure that they will not smudge when varnished. For the projects used in this book you will need alcohol-proof pens, which are available from art shops and good stationery shops.

Graphite tracing-down paper

Drawing pen

Pencil

Tracing paper

TECHNIQUES

PREPARING SURFACES

Bare Wood
Bare wood must be sealed, usually with an oil- or water-based priming paint or with shellac/sanding sealer. There are practically no limitations to the paints or varnishes that can be used, and bare wood can be stained before sealing.

Varnished Wood
Before applying emulsion (latex) paint, sand down with medium to coarse sandpaper to create a key to which the paint can adhere. If the sanding exposes a lot of bare wood, apply a coat of acrylic primer/ undercoat or a coat of shellac/sanding sealer. Any types of paint or varnish can be used over the emulsion (latex).

The surface must be sound before a coat of oil-based paint or varnish is applied. Flaking or loose varnish must be removed, and you will have to sand lightly with fine to medium grade sandpaper to create a key for further coats of paint to cling to. Only oil- or spirit-based products can be used over oil-based base coats.

Painted Wood
If something is already painted with a water-based finish, as long as the finish is sound you can paint over it with any kind of paint you wish. If the existing paint is oil-based, it may still be possible to use a water-based paint, especially if the existing surface was applied some time ago, because the water-resistant oils will have tended to dry out. You may find that you need only give the surface a light sanding to provide a key for the new paint. You would also prepare the surface in this way if you were planning to use oil-based paint.

An alternative approach is to sand the surface lightly and then to apply an isolating coat of shellac, which is compatible with both oil- and water-based paints.

If the original coat is chipped, you must repair the chips with a primer. If the existing paint has been badly applied and has run, you will probably find it easier to strip the paint completely before you begin. There are several good proprietary paint removers on the market – always read the manufacturer's instructions before you begin – or, if the piece can be easily transported, have it stripped for you by a professional firm.

Medium Density Fibreboard (MDF)
You should treat this as you would ordinary wood.

Metal
Use a wire brush to remove any loose rust, and then use a rust remover to stop the metal from corroding further. Apply a coat of metal primer before giving a top coat of metal or oil-based paint.

Some paints are available that do most of this work for you, so all you need do is remove the loose flakes of rust. Read the manufacturer's instructions.

BRUSH STROKES

In the tradition of folk painting, most designs on painted furniture are very stylized. If you look at traditional Scandinavian, European and North American furniture and barge and caravan painting, you will see that the designs tend to be built up with single brush-strokes. This style was not only quick to execute, but it gave a feeling of spontaneity and sense of movement that could never be achieved simply by colouring in shapes. It takes a little time and effort to master the technique, but it is well worth practising on scrap paper before you begin.

Practise the movements described below until you get a feeling for how and when to twist the brush. For the strokes to look good, they will have to be done fairly quickly and in a single movement, but it may be helpful to work through the strokes in "slow motion" before you begin. The same rules apply whether you are left- or right-handed. The handle of the brush should always turn towards the inner edge of the curve, so for strokes facing the opposite way, turn the handle clockwise.

The brush strokes illustrated here are a guide only. If you master them you will be able to paint easily and quickly every time. This is not, however, the only way to paint, and if you have a style and method with which you feel comfortable and achieve the results you want, that is fine. No two artists work in exactly the same way, and that is what makes this such an individual and challenging pastime.

RIGHT: **Paint each rose from start to finish, keeping the paint wet to blend the colours**

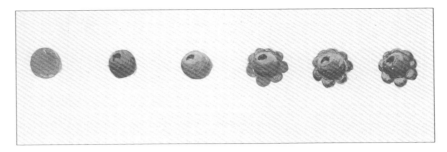

Free-hand Lining

Use a coachliner or a sword liner because the length of the hairs will help you achieve a straight line that is the same width along its length. Load the whole brush, drawing it through the paint without twisting the hairs. Place the whole length of the brush down, just keeping the metal ferule clear of the surface. Always draw the brush towards you because your arm will naturally move in an arc if you paint from side to side. If you are painting close to an edge, place your little finger on the edge to support your hand and help to maintain a straight line. Always have a straight edge – a ruler, for example – about 2.5cm (1in) from the line you are drawing so that your eye can use it as a guide, but never use a ruler to paint against. Small wobbles and uneven lines can be rectified by going over the line once it is dry. As you near the end of the line, begin to lift the brush. Keep a damp cloth at hand so that you can wipe off any mistakes.

Roses

Complete each rose before moving on to the next because the paint must be kept wet to blend the colours. Mix a light, mid- and dark tone of the same colour on your palette before starting. When you are painting anything that is to look three-dimensional you must decide on the position of an imaginary light source and then be consistent in the placing of highlights and shadows. In the examples illustrated, the light source is from the top left-hand side.

Use the mid-tone to paint a ball. Add shade to the lower right with the dark tone and make a dark dot in the top left to represent the heart of the flower. Add highlights to the top left with the lightest tone, then use the mid-tone to paint the petals. Shade the petals at the bottom right of the rose before highlighting the petals on the top right and top left of the rose.

Curves and Petals

Use a round-ended design brush and press the whole brush down firmly, twisting it anticlockwise as you slide it sideways (**A**). Gradually lift the brush as you draw the arc, still twisting the hairs to give a clean point.

To paint a tear-shaped petal (**B**) use a round-ended design brush and push the brush down then lift, while turning the handle anticlockwise to bring the hairs to a fine point.

Use a pointed design brush to paint a curved line (**C**). Place only the tip of the brush on the surface, gradually pressing it down as you move the brush to increase the width of the stroke. Then twist the handle anticlockwise while drawing it up again to make a point.

Paint a leaf with two strokes of the brush (**D**). Work in the same way as for the tear-shaped stroke, but make a gentle S-shape. Make the second stroke as a tear next to the first.

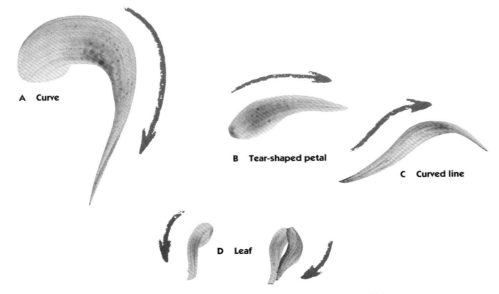

A Curve

B Tear-shaped petal

C Curved line

D Leaf

TOY BOX

This is a simple project to get you started, and it requires no special artistic skill to complete. Remember that you want the box to look hand-painted, so do not worry unduly if the lines are not absolutely straight. It will loose its charm if it looks machine-printed.

You will need

◊ Rectangular box – ours was 48 x 30 x 24cm (19 x 12 x 9in)
◊ Acrylic primer/undercoat
◊ Sandpaper
◊ 2.5cm (1in) flat varnish brush
◊ Emulsion (latex) paint – yellow
◊ Ruler and chalk
◊ Emulsion paint (latex) or artists' acrylics – pink and green
◊ Saucer or plate (for mixing paint)
◊ Coachliner
◊ Water-based varnish and varnish brush

1 Prepare the box. If the wood is untreated, seal it with acrylic primer/undercoat and, when dry, sand it lightly (see Preparing Surfaces, page 86). Apply a coat of yellow emulsion and leave to dry. Find the centre of each side and mark it with chalk, then use a small amount of pink and dilute with water. Use a flat varnish brush to paint in the pink lines. Do not overload the brush with paint and use the width of the bristles to give the width of the lines. If you prefer, draw in all the lines with chalk before you begin.

2 Allow the pink paint to dry, then dilute the green paint. Work in the same way but at right angles to the pink lines. The gap between the green lines should be narrower than the gap between the pink lines.

3 Use a coachliner and pink to paint two parallel lines between the wide pink lines, then use green to paint one line between the wide green lines. Finish the outside of the box by painting the moulded edge with undiluted green emulsion. Give the inside a coat of primer before applying green emulsion.

4 Cover the whole box with a coat of water-based varnish. Because the box may have to withstand a fair amount of wear and tear, use a durable floor varnish and apply three or four coats, allowing each coat to dry completely before you apply the next.

WATERING CAN

This simple yet pretty watering can will brighten the chore of watering your indoor or conservatory plants. We chose a design based on motifs drawn from a garden pond – goldfish and dragonflies – and the outlines are easily traced on and coloured in, so no special artistic skills are required.

You will need

◊ Metal watering can
◊ Metal paint – blue (we used a paint with a hammered finish)
◊ Brush for metal paint
◊ Solvent to clean brush (see manufacturer's instructions)
◊ Tracing paper
◊ Graphite tracing-down paper
◊ Pencil
◊ Masking tape
◊ Artists' acrylic paints – white, cadmium red, cadmium yellow, phthalocyanine turquoise and phthalocyanine blue
◊ Saucer or plate (for mixing paint)
◊ Design brush – no. 4
◊ Varnish and varnish brush

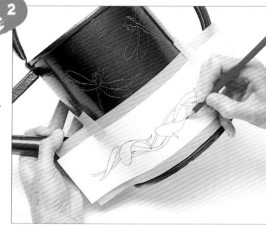

1 Cover the watering can with a coat of metal paint. Some metal paints are very thick and form dribbles and runs while they dry. Keep your brush handy and watch the can until the paint is dry.

2 Transfer the fish design (see page 120) to tracing paper and place the paper around the bottom edge of the can, using masking tape to hold it in position. Insert the tracing-down paper and use a sharp pencil to go over the design. Copy and transfer the dragonflies (see page 120) in the same way.

3 Use two shades of acrylic blue to paint the wavy lines between the fish to suggest water.

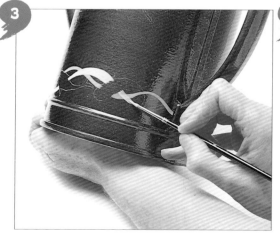

4 Mix red and yellow to give a rich orange colour and paint in the goldfish. Highlight the top edge of each fish with a fine yellow line.

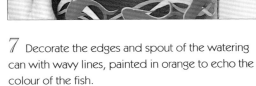

5 Block in the dragonflies with white paint. This is necessary because the background colour is dark and they would not otherwise show up.

6 Allow the white paint to dry before applying a wash of turquoise. Simply mixing turquoise and white would have given a pastel shade, but overpainting the turquoise on white gives a vibrant colour.

7 Decorate the edges and spout of the watering can with wavy lines, painted in orange to echo the colour of the fish.

8 Give the watering can several coats of varnish, allowing each to dry before you apply the next.

TIP

• Some of the solvents recommended for cleaning brushes used for metal paints are very expensive. You may find it more economical to use a cheaper brush and to discard it after use.

MIRROR FRAME

This pen-work frame looks like inlaid wood, but the intricacy of the design belies its simplicity, for the motifs are traced on and painted around. Choose a frame that is made of pale wood and that has a simple profile.

You will need

◊ Wooden frame
◊ Ruler and pencil
◊ Shellac and cheap decorator's brush
◊ Sandpaper
◊ Tracing paper
◊ Graphite tracing-down paper
◊ Masking tape
◊ Spirit- or alcohol-proof drawing pen
◊ Small design brush
◊ Artists' acrylic paint – black
◊ Methylated spirits (de-natured alcohol) (to clean brush)
◊ White polish
◊ Fine wire wool – grade 0000

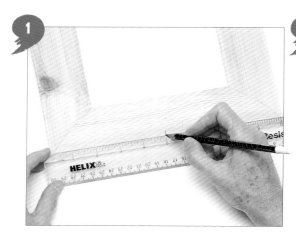

1 Use a ruler and pencil to mark the centre of each side of the frame.

2 Apply a coat of shellac to the frame to seal the wood. When it is dry, lightly sand the frame to remove the roughness of the raised grain.

3 Transfer the motif (see page 120) to tracing paper and position it centrally along the side of the frame, using the marks made in step 1 as your guide. Hold the tracing in place with masking tape and slide under the tracing-down paper. Use a sharp pencil to go over the outlines.

4 Go over the traced lines with a drawing pen. You may need to adjust the position of the corner motifs if your frame is a different size from the one we used. Alternatively, add leaves or make the stems longer so that the design will fit, but make sure that you keep the overall proportions the same. You may want to redraw the motifs onto clean tracing paper before transferring the outlines to the frame.

5 Using a small design brush and black acrylic paint, carefully block in the background so that the design shows in relief. You will probably need two coats to give good coverage, so remember to allow the first coat to dry before applying the second

6 When the whole frame is painted and completely dry, apply a coat of white polish. Leave to dry for about 15 minutes.

7 Gently burnish the frame with wire wool to give a smooth finish. Apply several coats of white polish allowing each to dry before burnishing. Do not burnish the final coat.

TRAY

Naive art has a wonderfully refreshing simplicity. The style was originally used to record events and objects that were important in everyday life, and because the paintings were not executed by great artists, they have a beguiling and often humorous charm. Prize livestock was a popular subject and is appropriate for a kitchen tray. We chose a sheep and finished off the design with some free-hand lines.

You will need

◊ Tray (ours was wooden; if you use a different kind of tray, turn to Preparing Surfaces, page 86, before you begin)
◊ Shellac and brush
◊ Fine sandpaper
◊ Emulsion paint – dark blue-green
◊ Tracing paper
◊ Pencil
◊ Masking tape
◊ Graphite tracing-down paper
◊ Artists' acrylic paints – white, raw umber and black
◊ Design brushes – No. 8 or 9 and No. 4
◊ Saucer or plate (for mixing paint)
◊ Short coachliner
◊ Varnish and varnish brush

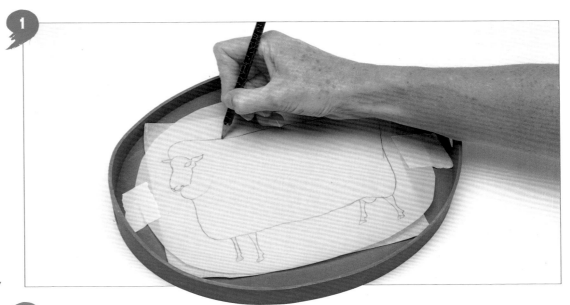

1 Seal the tray with a coat of shellac. Sand it lightly to smooth the surface before applying a coat of blue-green emulsion. Transfer the design (see page 120) to tracing paper, hold it in position with masking tape, and use tracing-down paper to transfer the outline to the tray.

2 Mix white acrylic paint with a little raw umber in a saucer or plate to create an off-white colour and use it to block in the sheep's body. Because the background is dark, you will probably not achieve a perfect cover with one coat.

3 When the first coat of paint is dry, use the same off-white to stipple on a second coat very thickly to give the texture and impression of the fleece.

4 Add more raw umber to the original colour and shade the sheep's body, adding shadow to the belly, along the back and around the neck to create a three-dimensional effect.

5 Use raw umber mixed with a little white to paint the details of the face – eyes, nose and ears – and to add more shadow under the chin. Use black acrylic for the pupils of the eyes and for the legs.

6 Add a sparkle to the eyes and highlights to the hooves with white acrylic paint.

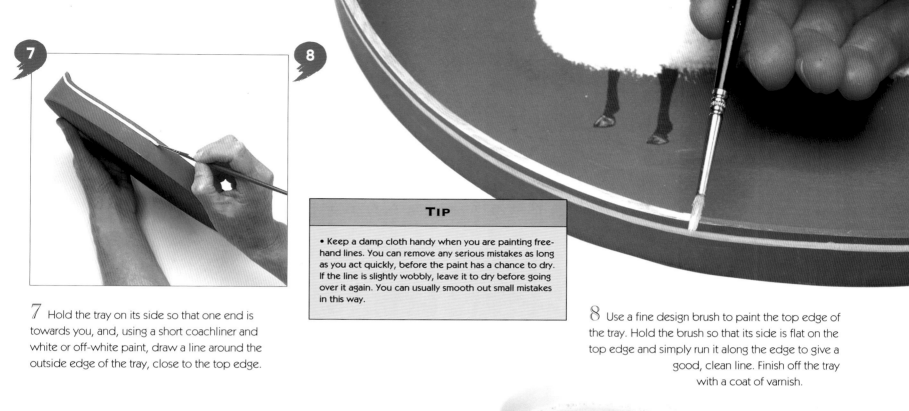

7 Hold the tray on its side so that one end is towards you, and, using a short coachliner and white or off-white paint, draw a line around the outside edge of the tray, close to the top edge.

8 Use a fine design brush to paint the top edge of the tray. Hold the brush so that its side is flat on the top edge and simply run it along the edge to give a good, clean line. Finish off the tray with a coat of varnish.

CHAIR

Most of us have pieces of furniture that have seen better days but that we would be sad to part with. As long as the underlying shape is attractive, there are all kinds of ways in which we can turn these battered items into beautiful objects. The finish described here would suit a period setting and would blend in well with other antiques.

You will need
◊ Chair
◊ Coarse sandpaper
◊ Acrylic primer/undercoat
◊ Decorator's brush – 2.5–4cm (1–1⅛in)
◊ Emulsion (latex) paint – white and dark blue-green
◊ Methylated spirits (de-natured alcohol)
◊ Kitchen paper or old cloth
◊ Chalk
◊ Tracing paper
◊ Pencil
◊ Graphite tracing-down paper
◊ Masking tape
◊ Artists' acrylic paints – Hooker's green, phthalocyanine blue and white
◊ Saucer or plate (for mixing paint)
◊ Design brush – no. 4
◊ Varnish and varnish brush

1 This worn and scuffed chair still had the remains of its original varnish, which, because of the chair's age, would probably have been shellac. Because the chair will receive several coats of paint, use coarse sandpaper to remove the old finish. Work outside if possible because this is a messy job; if you have to work indoors wear a face mask and make sure that your working area is well ventilated.

2 When the chair is back to the bare wood, seal it with acrylic primer or undercoat. Begin by painting the legs and support rails, then paint around the turned rails. If the legs are not turned, follow the grain of the wood and paint up and down. The chair can then be turned the right way up and the top half painted.

3 Apply three coats of white emulsion, allowing each coat to dry completely before adding the next. Paint as neatly as you can because the brush marks will show when the chair is finished. When the white emulsion is dry, apply a coat of dark blue-green emulsion diluted in the proportions of 1 part paint to 5 parts water. Leave to dry.

4 Wet some kitchen towel or an old rag with methylated spirits and carefully rub over the chair, working on one section at a time. Methylated spirits is a solvent for dry emulsion paint, so work carefully because it will remove not only the pale blue-green but may also remove sufficient white to reveal the wood beneath. You are aiming for a grainy look with the blue-green sitting in the brush marks and the white showing through.

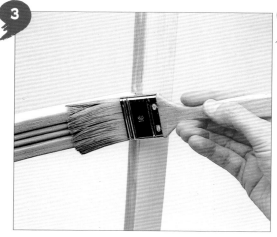

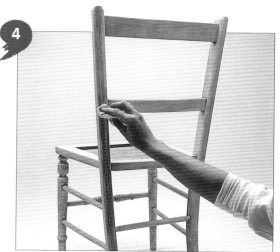

5

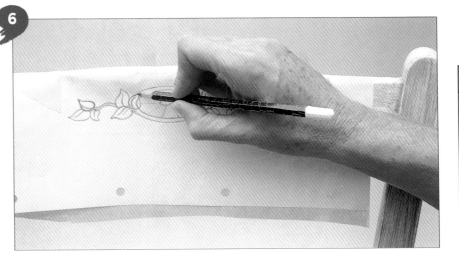

6

TIP

• If you inadvertently remove too much paint with the methylated spirits, apply more blue-green emulsion and allow it to dry before proceeding.

5 On all turned areas, mouldings or carvings rub across the indentations so that the blue-green is not removed and the crevices remain quite dark. On raised areas, remove more of the blue-green so that they appear lighter than the main body of the chair. This will help to highlight the details of the chair's shape.

6 Use chalk to mark the centre of the back rail. Transfer the design (see page 120) to tracing paper and place it centrally on the back rail, holding it in place with masking tape. Use tracing-down paper and a sharp pencil to transfer the design to the chair.

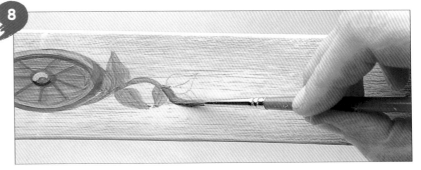

8

7

9

7 Mix the green and blue acrylic paints with a little white and use it to block in the central oval. To give the design depth, it needs to be shaded and highlighted. Decide on an imaginary source of light and use darker green to add shade. We assumed that light was coming from the top left, and added shade under the oval, on the right-hand side of the curve and the top left-hand side of the inner curve, where the imagined roundness of the outside moulding of the oval would have cast a shadow. Paint dark lines radiating from the centre to the inner edge. Mix more white into the original colour and highlight the facets that are towards the light source – in our case this was the top left-hand side, the bottom right inner edge of the oval and the left- hand side of the central oval.

8 Use a slightly greener shade to block in the stems and leaves at the sides of the oval.

9 With a still darker green, shade the leaves, observing the same imagined light source as in step 7. Also add shade to the underside of the stem by painting in a fine dark green line. Add a highlight to the opposite side.

10

10 When the paint is completely dry, apply the varnish. Because chairs are usually subjected to a good deal of wear and tear, you should apply two or three coats, allowing each coat to dry before applying the next.

BOOK-SHAPED BOX

It's always good to be able to personalize items, especially if you are going to give them as a gift. This box was already shaped like a book, which made us think of an illuminated initial letter, but that would have limited the use of the design. The pattern is, therefore, one in which different initials can be inserted. It is possible to find books with different styles of lettering, which you can adapt as you wish.

You will need

◊ Box
◊ Shellac or acrylic primer/undercoat
◊ Brush for shellac
◊ Sandpaper
◊ Emulsion (latex) paint – blue
◊ 2.5cm (1in) brush
◊ Emulsion (latex) or artists' acrylic paint – white, blue, yellow, Venetian red, black and Hooker's green
◊ Saucer or plate (for mixing paint)
◊ Natural sponge
◊ Small stiff-bristled brush such as a fitch
◊ Pencil and ruler
◊ Short coachliner
◊ Tracing paper
◊ Masking tape
◊ Graphite tracing-down paper
◊ Design brush – no. 4
◊ Varnish and varnish brush

1 Seal the box with acrylic primer/undercoat and sand it lightly when dry. Apply a coat of blue emulsion, then mix two shades of blue, one lighter and one darker than your base colour, diluting each with approximately 5 parts of water. Use a brush to put some paint on the dampened sponge. Do not dip the sponge in the paint or you will overload it.

2 Use a light dabbing movement to sponge the surface of the box. From time to time, turn the sponge in mid-air (not on the surface of the box) so that the pattern is varied. Repeat with the second colour, filling in any spaces.

3 Mix another shade of blue (or a completely different colour if you prefer) and use a stiff-bristled brush to spatter the surface, running your finger through the bristles to make tiny speckles.

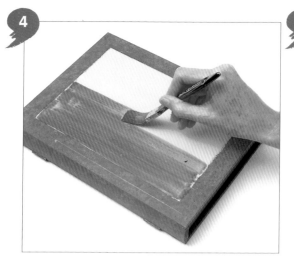

4 Use a ruler and pencil to mark on the front of the box a rectangle that is about 2.5cm (1in) smaller all round than the box. Paint this area yellow and leave it to dry. Then paint it red, diluting the paint a little to allow the yellow to show through. Paint carefully so that the brush marks do not show.

5 Use the coachliner to outline the rectangle with green paint, then paint another green line, about 10mm (⅜in) outside the rectangle. Between the two green lines, paint two yellow lines, leaving blue showing between them.

6 Trace the lettering, using the outlines on page 120 if you wish, and position them so that they are centred near the top of the box. Hold it in place with masking tape and use tracing-down paper to transfer the letters. Do the same with the initials of your choice.

7 Block in the letters in black using a small, fine brush.

8 Highlight the letters with yellow before varnishing the box to protect it.

COMMEMORATIVE PLATE

A hand-painted plate to mark a special occasion is a wonderfully personal way to show that you have thought about the event. You could use the same basic idea to make a house-warming gift, when you might replace the child's name with the new address. We have used an inexpensive enamel plate and based the design on traditional barge-ware. The same technique could be used on other enamel items.

You will need

◊ White enamel plate
◊ Coloured chalk
◊ Enamel craft paints – red, white, light green and dark green
◊ Design brush – no. 4
◊ White (mineral) spirit (for cleaning brush)

1 Use chalk to indicate the position of the letters of the name, making sure they are evenly spaced. Paint the name in light green paint.

2 Shade the letters with dark green, remembering that you must determine your imaginary light source. In our example the light source was from the top left-hand side, and the shading was, therefore, applied to the right-hand side and the bottom of the letters.

3 Sketch the central motif with chalk, indicating the positions of the leaves and main branch. If you want to use traditional roses, see Brush Strokes (page 87). Use light green to block in the leaves.

4 Shade the leaves to give a three-dimensional appearance, again bearing the imaginary light source in mind as you work. Mix a little red with the green to create a brown for the branch.

TIP

• Enamel items decorated in this way will withstand occasional gentle washing, but they are not suitable for everyday use.

5 Load the brush with red and drop paint onto the plate to form round blobs to represent the berries. Take care not to overload your brush and test the amount of paint you need on the side of the plate. You can wipe it off with kitchen towel soaked in white spirit before it dries.

6 Allow the berries to dry a little, then paint in the highlights with white paint to make them look round and shiny.

7 Hold the plate so that the name is at the top and find the centre of the bottom. Allow sufficient room for the word and date, chalking the characters in so that they are evenly and symmetrically placed. Paint in the letters and numbers.

8 Paint a line around the border in red. Most enamel plates already have a blue edge, and you can paint over this. Leave the paint to dry for about 24 hours, although it will be dry to the touch after about 6 hours.

CLOCK FACE

A piece of medium density fibreboard (MDF) was used for the face, and battery-operated hands are widely available in various styles. Although it looks complicated, the ship design is traced and the central compass is drawn with ruler and compasses. Perhaps the most difficult feature are the free-hand lines, and you should practise these on scrap paper before you begin. The face has been given an "antique" finish by a final coat of two-stage crackle varnish.

You will need

◊ Clockface and hands and movement
◊ Acrylic primer/undercoat
◊ Sandpaper
◊ Brushes for base coat and varnish –
   2.5–4cm (1–1⅛in)
◊ Emulsion (latex) paint – yellow
◊ Square of card, 25 x 25cm (10 x 10in)
◊ Pair of compasses
◊ Ruler and pencil
◊ Protractor
◊ Scissors
◊ Artists' acrylic paint – Payne's grey, raw sienna,
   Venetian red and white
◊ Design brush – no. 4
◊ Short coachliner – no. 1
◊ Tracing paper
◊ Masking tape
◊ Graphite tracing-down paper
◊ Crackle varnish (optional)
◊ Oil-based varnish
◊ Artists' oil paint – raw umber
◊ White (mineral) spirit

1 Seal the MDF with a coat of acrylic primer/undercoat and, when it is dry, sand it lightly. Apply a coat of yellow emulsion paint. If you prefer, use two coats of emulsion only, sanding between each one.

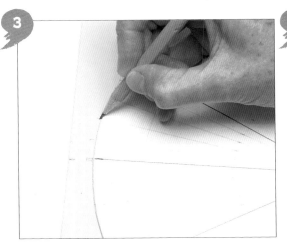

2 Use a pair of compasses to draw a circle, 25cm (10in) in diameter, on the card. Draw a line through the centre of the circle, place your protractor on the line and mark off sections every 30 degrees. Join up the marks across the centre to give 12 sections. Subdivide some of the sections by marking off 6 degrees to give the minutes. Cut out the card.

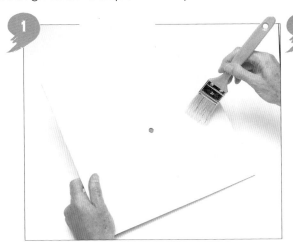

3 Measure and mark the central points of each side of the clock face. Position the card dial centrally on the clock face, making sure that the points that will be 3, 6, 9 and 12 o'clock are correctly aligned. Draw around the card and transfer the hour and minute measurements to the clock face.

4 Use Payne's grey and a short coachliner to paint in the circle. Paint a second circle, about 3mm (⅛in) outside the first, and between the two circles paint in the minute and hour marks, differentiating between the two.

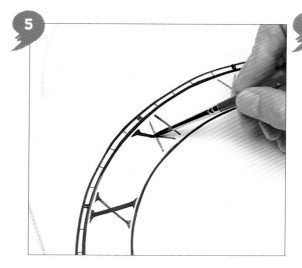

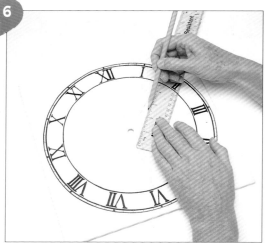

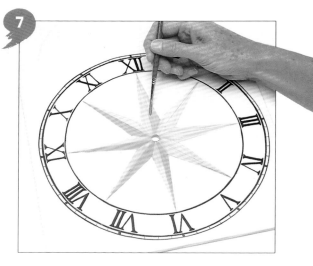

5 Draw in the numerals with pencil before painting them in. Make the line starting at the top left of the Xs and Vs as thick as the upright line of the Is, while the lines starting at the top right should be finer.

6 In the centre of the dial draw a pencil line running horizontally from 9 to 3 and a vertical line running from 12 to 6. Place your protractor at the intersection of these lines and mark off 45 degrees between each line. Join these points through the centre. Find a point about 2.5cm (1in) from the centre on each of these lines and join this point to the top of the adjacent lines to form an eight-pointed star.

7 Use raw sienna to paint in the star compass, diluting the paint with water to make the first coat fairly light. Use a stronger tone of the same colour to add shade, remembering to identify the imaginary light source before you do so. We assumed a light source at the top left, so the two sections facing the light at 11 o'clock were left pale, while the two opposite section were shaded. The remaining sections alternated between light and dark.

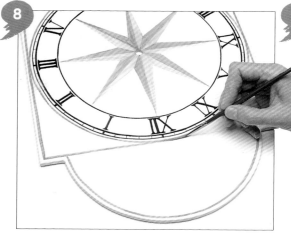

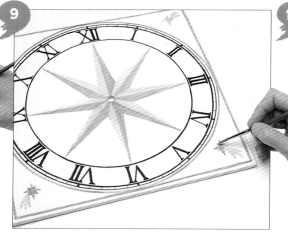

8 With a coachliner and raw sienna, paint another circle outside the dial. Outline the whole clock face, too, following the arc at the top and joining the lines between the top corners.

9 Trace the ship and shooting star motifs (see page 120) and use tracing-down paper to transfer them to the clock face. Paint in the shooting stars in each corner, making the stars darker than the tails.

10 Use diluted raw sienna to paint in the ship, moon and sun. Paint the sails in white and add shadows with a little Payne's grey.

11 Mix a little Venetian red into the raw sienna and make the paint a little thicker before adding the details of the windows and so on and to add more shadows to the ship. Leave the paint to dry.

12 If you do not want a crackle finish, apply a coat of varnish. If you use crackle varnish, apply the first, oil-based coat. Use the varnish sparingly, spreading it out from the centre before reloading your brush. Leave to become tacky, which can take from 1 to 4 hours.

13 Test the varnish by pressing it lightly with your fingers. If should feel almost dry but your fingers will feel a slight tackiness. Apply the second, water-based coat, which will dry fairly quickly. Make sure that the second coat covers the whole surface. While this coat is still wet, massage it lightly with your fingers to encourage it to adhere to the first coat. Stop massaging when the varnish begins to pull against your fingers and feels almost dry.

14 Leave to dry for at least 30 minutes but preferably overnight. The second coat of varnish is water soluble, so take care that it does not come into contact with water and that you do not leave it in a damp atmosphere. Apply gentle heat to encourage the varnish to crack – you should be able to see the cracks when you hold the clock face up to the light.

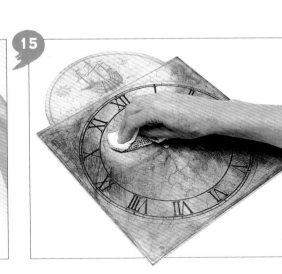

15 To patinate the clock face squeeze about 10mm (⅛in) of oil paint onto the surface. Do not use acrylic paint, which will remove the finish. Dampen a piece of kitchen towel with a little white spirit and use a circular motion to spread the paint over the whole clock face and to encourage it into the cracks. Use a clean piece of kitchen towel to wipe off any excess.

TIP
• If the crackle varnish does not turn out as you hoped, remove the top, water-based coat by washing it off. You can then start again with the first coat of varnish without damaging the underlying painting.

16 Different pigments in oil paints dry at different rates. Raw umber dries in about 24 hours, but some colours take longer. When you are sure that the paint it dry, seal the surface with an oil-based varnish.

GAMES BOARD

This could be the ideal present for someone who has everything. The board was cut from a piece of medium density fibreboard (MDF), although the same idea could be used to decorate a table-top.

You will need

◊ Square of MDF, 46 x 46cm (18 x 18in), or a suitable table
◊ Shellac and brush
◊ Methylated spirits (de-natured alcohol) (to clean brush)
◊ Sandpaper
◊ Emulsion (latex) paint – dark red
◊ Decorator's brush
◊ Long ruler and pencil
◊ Artists' acrylic paints – black, gold, burnt umber and raw sienna
◊ Design brush – no. 8 or 9
◊ Coachliner
◊ Chalk
◊ Varnish and varnish brush
◊ Black felt and all-purpose adhesive to back board
◊ Craft knife

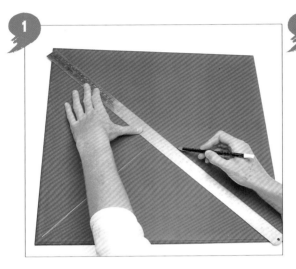

1 Prepare the board by sealing it with a coat of shellac. When it is dry, sand it and apply a coat of dark red emulsion. Leave to dry. Find the centre of the board by drawing two diagonal lines.

2 Measure from the intersection of the two diagonals the eight by eight squares needed for the standard games board.

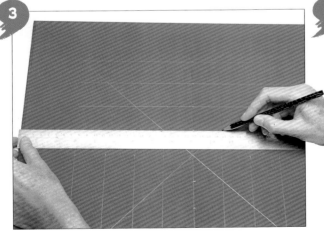

3 Mark the positions for the 64 squares. Our squares measured 3.75cm (1½in), giving an overall area of 30 x 30cm (12 x 12in).

4 Check that the width of the outside border is the same on all sides before drawing in the squares.

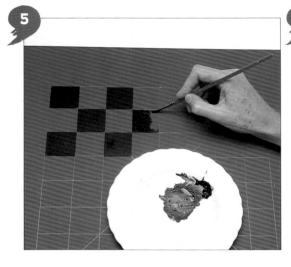

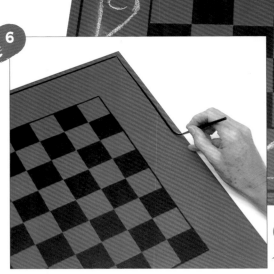

5 Use black acrylic paint to colour alternate squares. Because it is so easy to go over a line, begin with your brush inside the line, move it up to the line and draw it in again before you lift it from the surface.

6 Use a coachliner and black acrylic to paint a line around the squares and just inside the edge of the board.

7 Draw a chalk line about 10mm (⅜in) in from the outer border and, working from the centre, draw in symmetrical wavy lines, using the chalk line as a guide for the base of the wavy lines.

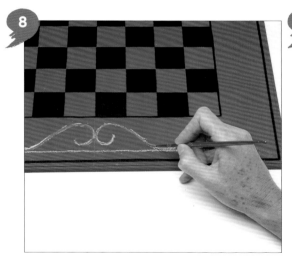

8 Use a fine design brush or short coachliner to paint over the wavy chalk lines with raw sienna. When the paint is dry, wipe away the straight chalk lines with a damp cloth.

9 Use a single stroke to chalk in the leaves, positioning them so that they grow from the centre towards the corners. Vary the size of the leaves for interest. Paint the leaves in raw sienna with a single stroke (see Brush Strokes, page 87).

10 Go over the design painted in raw sienna in gold acrylic paint, again using single brush strokes for the leaves. Going over the pattern twice will ensure that it stands out against the dark background.

TIP

- If you have difficulty finding shellac, use two coats of emulsion paint, sanding the surface lightly between coats.

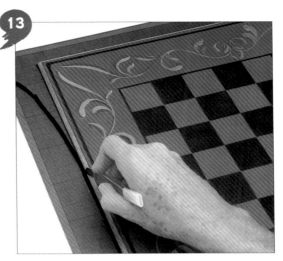

11 Use burnt umber to shade the design, remembering to make the shadows consistent with a single imagined light source. When the paint is dry, apply two or three coats of varnish.

12 If you have made a board, coat the underside with an even layer of all-purpose adhesive, using a small piece of card to spread the glue, and place the felt over it, smoothing it down.

13 Turn over the board and use a craft knife to trim away the excess felt.

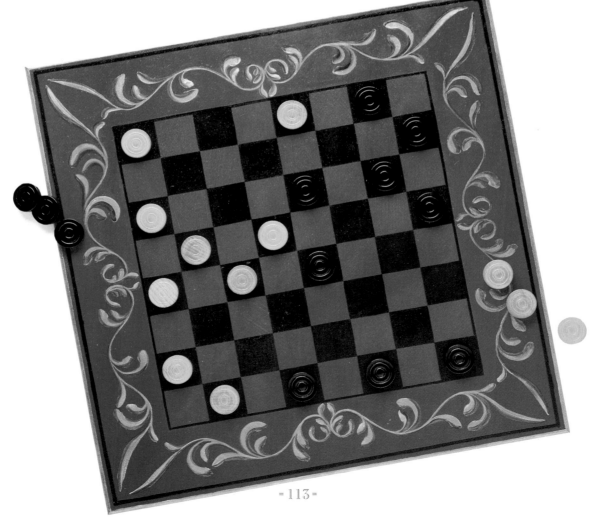

CHEST OF DRAWERS

This miniature chest of drawers has been prettily decorated so that it is perfect for storing jewellery or all the other odds and ends that otherwise accumulate on a dressing table. This method could be used to decorate a full-size chest of drawers, and the same design could be scaled up to make it appropriate for a larger piece of furniture.

You will need

◊ Miniature chest of drawers
◊ Acrylic primer/undercoat
◊ Decorator's brush
◊ Sandpaper
◊ Emulsion (latex) paint – turquoise
◊ Chalk
◊ Artists acrylic paints – Hooker's green, cadmium red, cadmium yellow and white
◊ Design brush – no. 4
◊ Antiquing fluid (use raw umber artists' oil paint mixed with white (mineral) spirit to give a runny consistency)
◊ Oil-based varnish and varnish brush

1 Seal the chest of drawers with acrylic primer/undercoat and sand lightly when it is dry. Apply a coat of turquoise emulsion. So that the drawers do not stick, do not paint the inside, but take the paint just around the top and sides of the drawers and just inside the drawer openings.

2 Replace the drawers and mark the design in chalk on the front, aligning the drops of the garlands on each drawer. Indicate the positions of the roses by simply drawing circles. Do not worry about the leaves at this stage.

3 Paint in the roses one by one because the paint must be wet to allow you to blend in the colours (see Brush Strokes, page 87). Mix three shades of coral pink with the red, yellow and white. When you paint the roses remember to apply shadow consistently.

4 Paint in the rosebuds by making a small oval with coral paint. Then use green to paint the sepals around the bud. Starting at the stem end, push the brush down and then up to form the sepals so that they are thick at the base and taper to a point.

5 Paint in the leaves so that they just peep from behind the roses. Shade them on one side, using the same imagined light source as for the roses. Keep the design balanced, filling in any obvious gaps with leaves.

6 Paint in the stems for the garland and drops with green. The garland should emerge from the roses at a point just above the centre so that it looks as if it is supporting the roses.

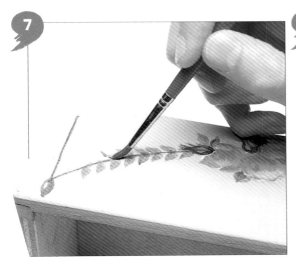

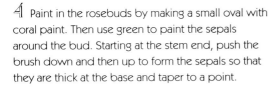

7 Paint in the leaves along the garland (see Brush Strokes, page 87), remembering to make them look as if they are growing from the centre outwards. The leaves on the drops point downwards and end in a single leaf.

8 Add darker green to the leaves in the garlands, keeping the shadows consistent with the shading added around the roses.

9 Chalk in an oval on each side and on the top of the chest, drawing around an oval plate if you have one that is a suitable size. Paint the leaves on the sides so that they appear to grow from the bottom, up each side and meet at the top.

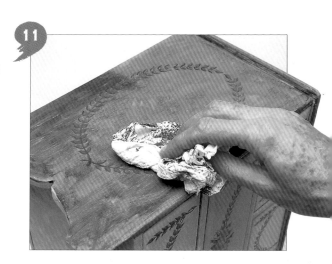

10 Paint over the whole chest and drawers with antiquing fluid. Do not worry if you do not like the effect because it can be removed with white spirit without harming the underlying paint.

11 Use clean, dry kitchen towel to wipe off the excess antiquing fluid. How much you remove is a matter of choice, but it is a good idea to wipe off more around the main design while leaving the edges slightly dirtier. Leave to dry for 24 hours before sealing with oil-based varnish.

PIANO STOOL

This piano stool was found in a second-hand shop, and although it looked very battered, it was such a pretty shape that it was well worth painting. It still had some of its original shellac varnish on it, which was removed with coarse sandpaper before the wood was sealed with acrylic primer/undercoat (see also the Chair, page 98).

You will need
◊ Piano stool
◊ Acrylic primer/undercoat
◊ Emulsion (latex) paint – coral
◊ Decorator's brush
◊ Chalk
◊ Ruler
◊ Tracing paper and pencil
◊ Masking tape
◊ Graphite tracing-down paper
◊ Artists' acrylic paints – white, raw umber and burnt umber
◊ Design brush – no. 4
◊ Coachliner
◊ Coloured varnish and varnish brush

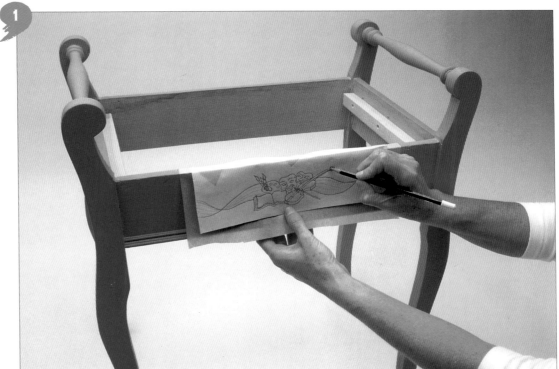

1 Apply a coat of coral emulsion to the primed piano stool and, when it is dry, use chalk to mark the centre of the back and front panels. Copy the design (see page 120) and hold the tracing paper in position with masking tape. Use tracing-down paper to transfer the design.

2 Block in each element of the design separately, bearing in mind that you must have a consistent imaginary light source. Use white paint for the book, and shade the pages where they bend by blending in some raw umber. The artist's palette and brushes are painted in the same way, but they are slightly darker to make them stand out against the book.

3 Mix burnt umber with a little white to paint the violin. The side of the violin and the details are painted in burnt umber only. The masks are painted white and shaded in the same way as the book, with burnt umber used to pick out the features.

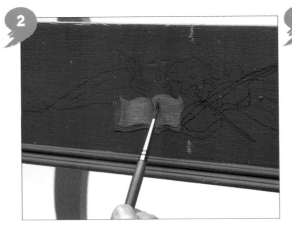

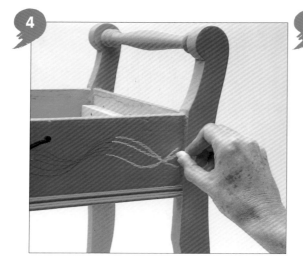

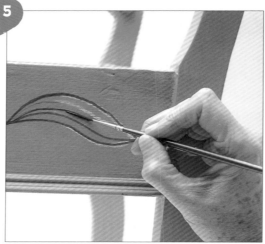

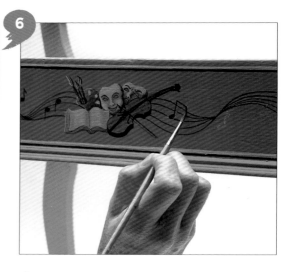

4 If the lines of the staves of music are not long enough for your piano stool, use chalk to draw in longer lines. You can easily wipe off chalk lines with which you are not satisfied. Try to balance the design by making the curves in the lines symmetrical.

5 Use a coachliner and burnt umber to paint in the lines of the staves.

6 Plan the position of the notes in chalk before painting them in with a fine brush.

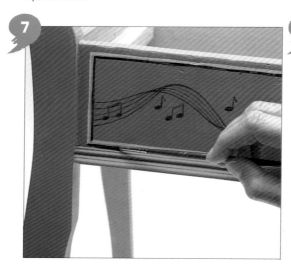

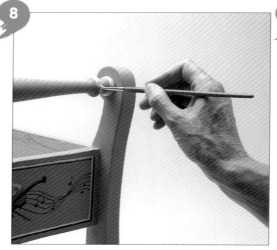

7 Make a border around the whole pattern by painting a thick white line with a coachliner. Use raw umber to draw in lines inside the top and left-hand white lines and outside the bottom and right-hand white lines to give the effect of a moulded panel.

8 Pick out the mouldings in white. Take care not to paint right up to the angle where it joins a straight section because it is very difficult to avoid a ragged edge.

9 Use either a coloured varnish or make your own, by mixing clear varnish with a little raw umber. If the varnish is oil-based, use artists' oil paint; if the varnish is water-based, use artists' acrylic paint diluted with appropriate solvent before adding to varnish.

TEMPLATES

This book belongs to

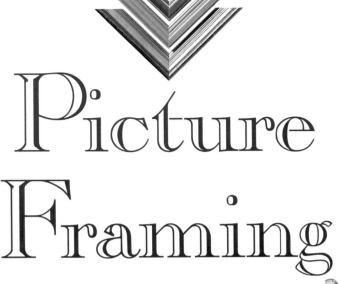

Picture Framing

**Make your own frames in which to display
your favourite paintings and photographs**

INTRODUCTION

Framing is a wonderful craft, and one of its great appeals is that it takes so little time to learn how to make a simple frame. With only a couple of pieces of wood and some glass you can make a present for a friend or a frame for a favourite photograph that is ready to hang on the wall within minutes.

Once you have mastered the basic techniques, you will find that there are endless possibilities, and the time taken perfecting the various aspects of the craft is very satisfying. The frame is important because any picture needs to be confined within a clearly defined area. When there is no frame, the eye tends to wander and it is difficult to focus on the image and to appreciate it properly. It is essential that the frame enhances the picture without overpowering it. The finishing edge – that is, the mount and the frame – should complement the picture but they must never be so intrusive that they are the first thing you look at. The frame is there to protect the work and to give it its own space within its surroundings. The finishing edge must ensure that the eye travels easily to the focal point of the picture.

There are no hard and fast rules that must be observed when you are choosing colours for the mounts and mouldings. Some people seem to have a knack for selecting the perfect combinations of shades; others learn as they go along. You may find it helpful to visit art galleries, museums and shops to look at the ways different frames and mouldings can be used to create different effects and how the various materials can be used to enhance the pictures they surround. If you look at Victorian watercolours, for example, you will see how the overall balance is maintained by the use of light ivory or cream-coloured mounts, often decorated with wash lines, together with a fairly dark wooden or deep gold frame. In general, a dark mount will look best with a lighter frame. Photographs, for instance, look good in smaller, darker mounts, with a narrow aluminium or silver-coloured frame. Traditional framing has a long and rich history, but new products, which make techniques such as gilding and distressing so much easier than they used to be, have changed people's attitudes to the craft and encouraged new fashions. For example, at present a wood and paint finish is popular, and this technique is explained later in the book.

EQUIPMENT AND TECHNIQUES

You need only a few tools to get started and you can even begin, as I did, by working on the sitting-room floor. If you are lucky, you will find that you already have most of the tools and equipment you will need in your household tool cupboard. There are, however, two items that you will probably have to buy – a mitre box or clamp and a mount cutter – but, in general you should think about buying new tools only as you need them, rather than acquiring them all at once.

FRAMING

To make the frames described in this book you will need the following:

◊ Pin hammer
◊ Tenon saw
◊ Screwdriver
◊ Pincers/pliers
◊ Nail punch
◊ Set square
◊ Hand drill and bits

◊ Panel pins
◊ Mitre box or clamp
◊ Metal ruler
◊ Plastic ruler and pencil
◊ Craft knife
◊ Wood glue

MOULDINGS

There is an enormous range of mouldings available to the amateur framer these days, but the main problem is finding shops that supply what you need and want. Some manufacturers operate a mail-order service, and you will find their names and addresses in craft magazines. A timber merchant may keep a few mouldings in stock, and your local picture framer may also be persuaded to help. When you are choosing a moulding, consider the size of the picture and such aspects as whether it is boldly coloured or finely drawn.

Because hard wood has become much scarcer in recent years, plastic mouldings have been introduced. These have the great advantages that they do not warp or suffer from woodworm. They also take gilding and coloured finishes well, although they do not, of course, have the wonderful smell and feel of real wood.

MOULDING FORMULA

- This simple formula can be used to work out fairly accurately how much moulding you will need. Add together:

  The height of the picture x 2
  The width of the picture x 2
  The width across the top of the frame (ie of the moulding) x 8

You need the additional width of the moulding for the mitre cuts that are made at the ends of each of the four pieces.

For example, say that you are framing a picture measuring 31 x 25cm (12 x 10in) and that the depth of the moulding is 1cm (⅓in):

  31cm (12in) x 2 = 62cm (24in)
  25cm (10in) x 2 = 50cm (20in)
  1cm (⅓in) x 8 = 8cm (4in)
              = 120cm (48in)

Add an extra 5cm (2in) to be on the safe side, and this means that you will need 125cm (50in) in total.

USING THE CLAMP AND SAW

When your saw is new you may find that a little oil will make it run smoothly when you are cutting moulding. Try not to put a lot of pressure on the saw when you are cutting. Aim to use short, light, even strokes and to let the saw do the work. When it is not being used, always keep the saw in its cover to protect the teeth.

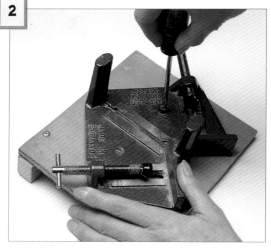

1 The clamp needs to be fixed to a wooden base. You will need a piece of 1cm (½in) plywood measuring about 20 x 18cm (8 x 7in). Cut a length of 3.5 x 2.5cm (1½ x 1in) timber to 20cm (8in) and screw it along the longer side of the piece of plywood to form a lip that will butt up against the edge of your working surface.

2 Screw the metal mitre clamp on to the plywood base so that the lip is on the other side.

3 Before you use a clamp for the first time, you may find it helpful to draw a line on the rubber insert of the base of the clamp to indicate the central cutting line.

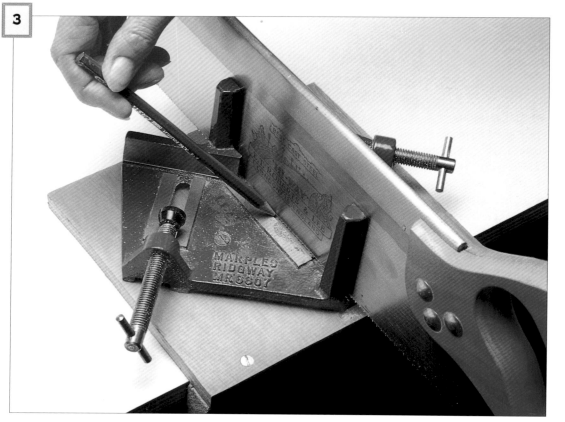

USING CORNER CLAMPS

Frame corner clamps held with a cord are available, although they can be rather fiddly and awkward to work with. They can be useful, however, especially if you are making small or very narrow frames that are difficult to pin.

Take the four cut pieces of the frame and glue the ends of the long sides. Lay the frame on your working surface in the correct position and put the four corner clamps in place. Pull up the string until it is very tight, clean off any glue that has seeped out from the joints and put to one side until the glue is dry. There are several different types of frame corner clamps available.

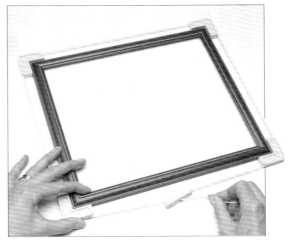

MOUNTING

Your choice of mount can affect the final appearance of the painting even more than the frame itself. If the mount is too small it can appear to squeeze and confine the picture, so, at least at first, you should always make the mount slightly larger than you had originally planned.

You will need the following equipment to make the mounts described in this book:

◊ Cutting mat
◊ Mount cutter with ruler
◊ Compasses
◊ Pencil
◊ Adhesive tape
◊ Plastic ruler and pencil
◊ Scissors
◊ Craft knife
◊ Mapping pen and paint brush

You must make sure that the blade of your mount cutter is sharp. Keep a supply of spare blades and replace the worn one as often as necessary, but certainly every 5 or 6 mounts. Dispose of the old blade carefully.

Remember that the bottom edge of the mount is usually deeper than the top and sides, which should be the same depth. For example, if the top and sides were 8cm (3½in) deep, the bottom should be 10cm (4in) deep. This difference helps to lead the eye into the picture.

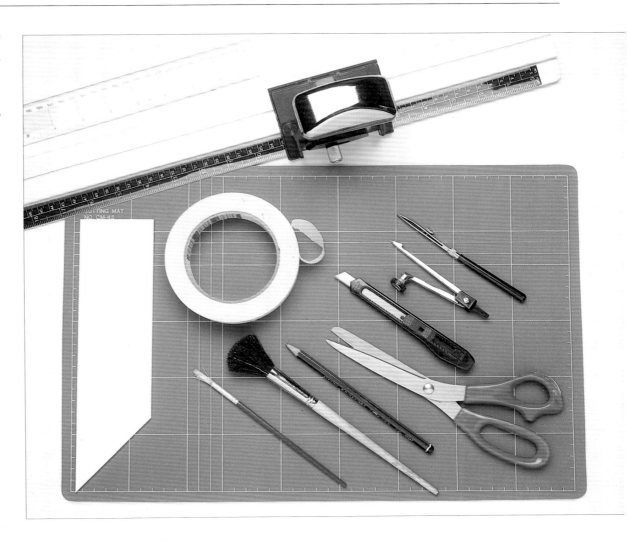

There is a huge range of mounting boards and cards available – the selection is so wide, in fact, that it can be rather confusing.

In general you should choose a light colour, especially if you are framing a watercolour painting. Pick an appropriate colour from the painting itself and match the tone of the colour with a light green, soft brown, ivory, cream and so on. If the colour seems too bland when it is surrounding the picture, wash or crayon lines can be added to draw the eye to the painting. A brightly coloured painting may look best with a pale mount but with a more vividly coloured frame.

There are several kinds of mount, and it is important to select the appropriate kind for the image you are framing. The different types are:

◊ A normal window mount
◊ A double mount, in which about 1cm (⅜in) of the colour of the underlying mount can be seen around the edge of the top mount
◊ A float, in which the picture lies on a coloured mount with 2–3cm (about 1in) of the mount showing all round the edge of the picture
◊ A float and mount combined, in which the picture lies on the lower mount while the window in the top mount is cut to reveal 1–2cm (about ⅜in) of the bottom mount around the picture
◊ Fabric covered mounts, when silk or hessian is used over the mount
◊ Paper-covered mounts
◊ Wash mounts

These are just a few of the possible mounting methods and materials. If you take care with the mount, choosing it thoughtfully and cutting it precisely, it will make all the difference to the final look of the picture.

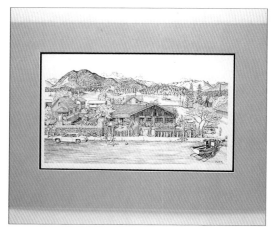

Being sepia, this photograph has been treated like a drawing, and so has a large mount. Generally, however, they can often look swamped if the mount is too large, and they generally look best in small, dark mounts.

Prints require special treatment. If they are original, they will have a plate mark impressed on the paper, all around the image. The window of the mount should be sufficiently large for the plate mark to be visible, which usually means leaving a margin of white about 1cm (⅜in) wide around the actual printed image.

TIP

- Your choice of mounting technique can radically alter the final appearance of the picture or photograph, as can be seen from this picture, which has been mounted in three different ways.

  A normal window mount
  A float
  A double mount

CUTTING A MOUNT

Select a suitable colour of mounting card. We are mounting a brightly coloured painting, which needs a quieter coloured mount so that the painting stands out. We later added a coloured frame, which tied the scheme together. In addition to the mounting card of your choice, you will need:

◊ Cutting board (see page 129)
◊ Scraps of card
◊ Sharp pencil and ruler
◊ Set square
◊ Mount cutter
◊ Craft knife or razor blade
◊ Backing board
◊ Masking tape
◊ Acid-free tape (optional)

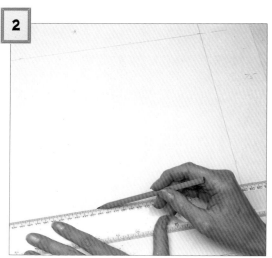

1 Measure the picture and decide on the area you want to show in the window of the mount. For this picture the window is going to be 33 x 23.5cm (13 x 9⅛in). The width of the mount at the top and both sides will be 7.5cm (3in) and the width at the bottom will be 9cm (3½in). Therefore, to calculate the total area of mount add the width of the window to twice the width of the side and add the depth of the window to the top and the bottom widths of the mount. In our example, that is 33 + 15cm (13 + 6in), which gives an overall width of 48cm (19in), and 23.5 + 7.5 + 9cm (9½ + 3 + 3½in), which gives an overall depth of 40cm (16in).

2 Lay the cutting board on a flat surface and place some scrap card on it. On the reverse side of the mounting card draw a rectangle to the outside dimensions of the mount – in our example this is 48 x 40cm (19 x 16in). Use a set square to make sure that the corners are exactly 90 degrees. Cut out the mount area.

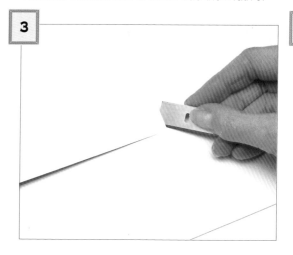

3 Again on the reverse side, draw the window opening. Measure in from the outside edge, in this case, 7.5cm (3in) from the top and sides, and 9cm (3½in) from the bottom. Cut the window. If the window does not fall out easily, use a sharp craft knife or razor blade to finish the corners. Make sure that they are clean and neatly cut.

4 Cut a piece of backing board the same size as the outside dimensions of the mount and lay the mount face down beside the backing board, with the long edges abutting. Use small pieces of masking tape to hold the top edges together. This hinges the mount and the backing board together.

5 Open out the mount and backing board and lay the picture on the backing board. Bring the mount over the picture and adjust the position of the picture. If your picture is not valuable, hold it in position under the edge of the mount with masking tape; a more valuable picture should be held with acid-free tape. Cut two pieces of tape and hold the picture in place at the top with these. Cut two further pieces of tape and cover the top ends of the tape to make sure that it is securely held.

USING THE MOUNT CUTTER

You should follow the instructions that come with your mount cutter, but the following guidelines apply to all makes.

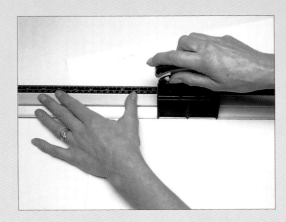

- Make sure that the blade is sharp and that it is set so that it just cuts through the mounting card and into the scrap card beneath.

- Lay the ruler so that the blade follows the pencil line. Insert the blade just beyond the corner and pull it towards you, finishing just beyond the corner nearest to you.

- Test to see if the cut is clean. Keeping the ruler in position, lift the edge of the card to check that the cut has gone right through. If it has not, slide the cutter down the line again.

Remember that, when you have completed each cut, you should move the scrap card so that the blade does not get stuck in the groove made by the first cut.

HANGING MATERIALS

You will need a range of rings and eyes to provide secure hangers for your finished frames. The specific items are listed with each project, but you are likely to need some or all of the following:

◊ D-rings
◊ Screw eyes
◊ Wire or cord
◊ Metal glass clips
◊ Plastic mirror clips
◊ Brown adhesive paper or masking tape

MAKING A CUTTING SURFACE

- Although you can buy special cutting mats in craft and art material shops, they are not cheap and they are, in any case, available in only a limited range of sizes. You can easily make your own, which will provide a suitable surface for cutting both the mounts and the glass and which can be almost any size you wish.
- To make a cutting surface measuring about 75 x 93cm (30 x 36in), which is large enough for most frames, cut a piece of hardboard and a piece of mounting card to the same size. Use an ordinary rubber-based adhesive to stick the mount to the shiny side of the hardboard, or, if you have one, use a staple gun to fix the two pieces together. The card will wear down eventually and need to be replaced, but this is not difficult.
- Always place a piece of scrap card between the mount you are cutting and the surface of your cutting board, and remember to move the waste card after each cut so that the blade does not stick in the groove and cause the cut to become ragged.

CUTTING GLASS

Glass cutting is much easier than you may think, and unless your frame is very large you should be able to cut glass to fit all your frames. You will need the following equipment:

◊ Glass cutter
◊ Wooden T-square or squaring ruler
◊ Pincers
◊ Felt-tipped pens

Buy a good glass cutter. The better quality the cutter, the easier your work will be. The best kind have a little built-in reservoir to hold white spirit or glass-cutting oil, which keeps the cutting head clean and running smoothly. If your cutter does not have this feature, you will need to dip the head into white spirit before each cut.

Picture frames take 2mm (⅟₁₆in) glass, which you can buy in small quantities from your glass merchant and which is much thinner and lighter than the glass used for windows. Buy a few off-cuts in the beginning so that you can practise your cutting technique.

A flat surface is absolutely essential. You can use a cutting mat or make a cutting surface as explained on page 129.

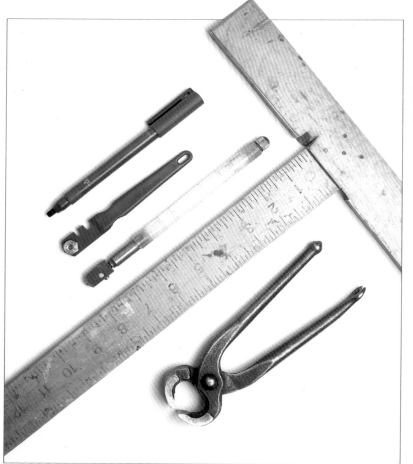

CUTTING GLASS TO SIZE

1 Lay a small piece of glass on the flat surface and hold your cutter between your first and second fingers, supporting it with your thumb so that it is almost upright. If you find this uncomfortable, you can hold the cutter between your thumb and first finger.

2 Practise scoring the glass. Do this a few times on different parts of some spare glass until you feel comfortable with the cutter and you can hear the satisfying sound that indicates that you have cleanly scored the glass every time. Throw away this piece of glass.

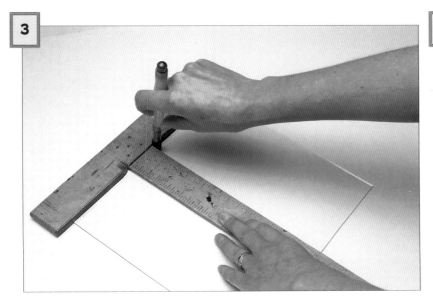

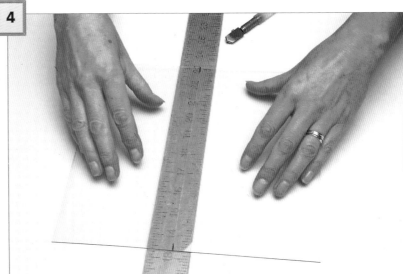

3 Put another piece of glass on your working surface. Lay the cross end of your T-square against the top of the glass so that the long piece is flat on the surface of the glass with the top edge butted up against the edge of the glass. Take your glass cutter and, pressing down firmly, pull it down one side of the T-square. Do not go over the scored line a second time or you will damage the cutter.

4 Carefully raise the glass at one side and slide the ruler under the cut, so that the edge of the ruler is exactly under the scored line.

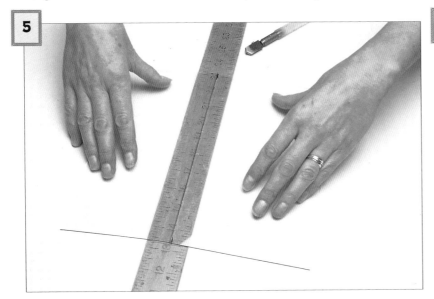

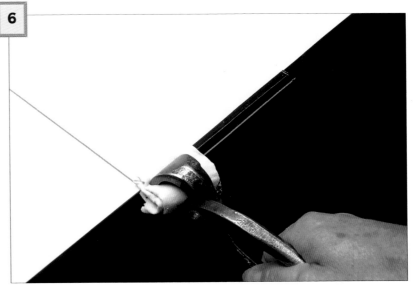

5 Place the fingertips of each hand on either side of the ruler and press down sharply. If your cut was good, the glass will break easily.

6 If the glass does not break smoothly or if you need to cut a small sliver from the edge, place the glass so that the edge of your work surface aligns with the scored line (which you may, for once, need to go over with your cutter for a second time). Put a piece of cloth in the jaws of your pliers or pincers, grip the edge of the glass and snap it off.

BASIC FRAME

This first frame is for a print of a colourful Mediterranean scene which looks good with white space around it. It will be framed to the edge of the paper without a mount. The moulding is fairly wide wood, which is easier to work with than narrow, flexible moulding – it is also easier to correct mistakes on wood.

You will need

◊ Moulding (see page 123 for estimating quantity)
◊ Mitre cutter and clamp
◊ Saw
◊ Plastic ruler and pencil
◊ Wood glue
◊ Drill and fine bit
◊ Panel pins
◊ Small hammer
◊ Nail punch
◊ 2mm (⅟₁₆in) glass
◊ T-square
◊ Felt-tipped pen
◊ Glass cutter
◊ 2mm (⅟₁₆in) hardboard
◊ Metal ruler
◊ Craft knife
◊ D-rings or screw eyes
◊ Masking tape
◊ Brown adhesive paper
◊ Wire or cord

1 Make the first mitre cut by sliding the moulding into the left side of the mitre cutter so that the screw clamp butts against the back of the frame. Protect the moulding with card or off-cuts of wood and screw the clamp firmly.

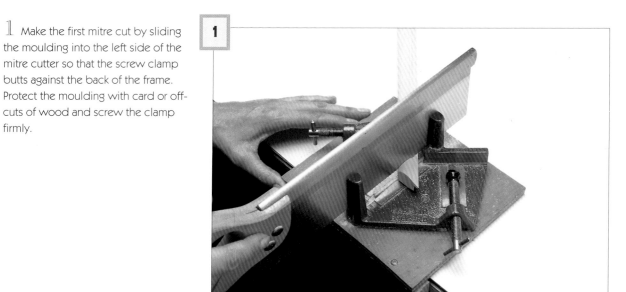

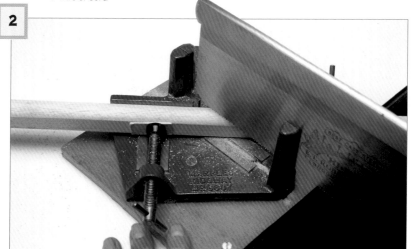

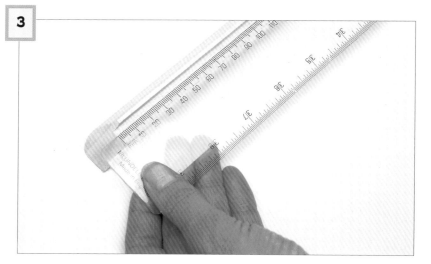

2 Gently push the nose of the saw into the slit that is nearest to you and slide it into the further slit. Without putting a lot of pressure on the wood, slide the saw backwards and forwards, using small, even strokes. Do not tilt the saw.

3 Unclamp the moulding and lay it on your working surface with the rebate side towards you. Working on the longest dimension first, use your ruler to measure from the inside of the corner you have just cut and mark the required length.

4 Slide the moulding into the right side of the mitre corner – that is, the opposite side from your first cut – and push the moulding along until your pencil mark is on the centre line of the mitre cutter.

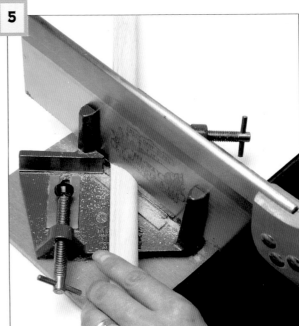

5 Clamp and cut it as the other side. Put the finished piece to one side.

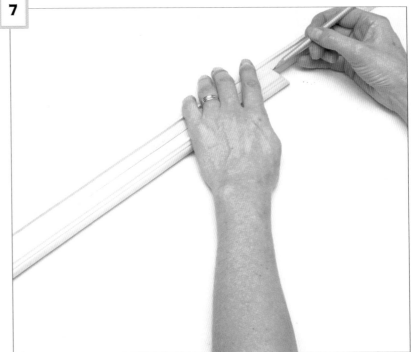

6 You now have to make a new 45-degree angle on the remaining piece of moulding by cutting off the waste. Slide the moulding into the left side of the clamp, screw it tightly in place and cut the new angle.

7 Measure the second long side. Place the first piece you cut so that it is back to back with the second piece. Carefully line up the corners and mark the length of the first piece on the back of the second piece. Slide the moulding into the right side of the clamp, line up your mark with the centre line of the clamp, tighten and cut.

8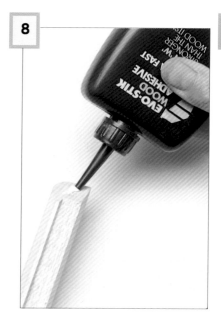

9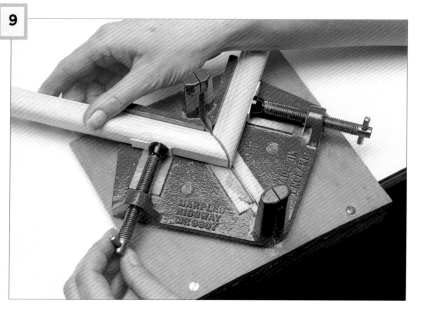

TIP

- If the corners you have cut do not fit well together, hold them tightly in the clamp, with the corners as close together as possible. Insert your saw and re-cut the corner. The two pieces should now fit neatly together. You might have to carry out the same procedure on the other corners because you will have altered the size very slightly.

8 Repeat steps 3–7 to make the two short sides. Then take a long piece and a short piece and put some wood glue on the corner angle of the long piece.

9 Place the two pieces, corner to corner, in the clamp, adjust and re-adjust until they fit neatly and tightly together and are firmly held.

10

11

10 Use a drill with a fine bit to make small holes for the panel pins. When you lay a panel pin across the corner it should be long enough to penetrate well into the other piece. A 2.5cm (1in) pin is usually long enough, but if you are using wide moulding you may need 5cm (2in) pins.

11 Hammer the pins in gently, using a punch to help drive the pins home. A punch is especially useful if the wood is hard. Repeat the steps for the opposite corner, making sure that the second long piece goes into the clamp on the same side as the first. You can now glue and pin the final corners to complete the frame. If you are going to paint your frame, this is the time to do so.

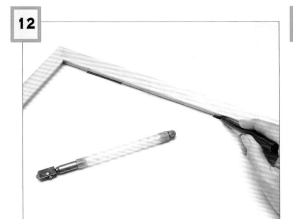

12 Cut the glass by transferring the dimensions of the picture to the glass with a felt-tipped pen, and lining your T-square against the marks before cutting on the inside of the marks by about 3mm (⅛in) to allow for the width of the head of your glass cutter. Alternatively, simply lay the frame on the glass at a corner so that the frame butts up to the edges of the glass. Use a felt-tipped pen to mark the edges that are sitting on the glass and cut as before.

13 Lay the piece of glass on the hardboard and draw around it so that it is exactly the same size as the cut glass.

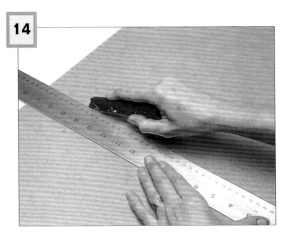

14 Lay a heavy metal ruler along the line and draw the blade of your craft knife down the line several times. Do not press too hard – you are not cutting right through the hardboard but scoring it. With the ruler held in the same position, sharply pull up one side of the hardboard. It should snap cleanly. If it does not, align the scored line with the edge of your working surface and snap it downwards.

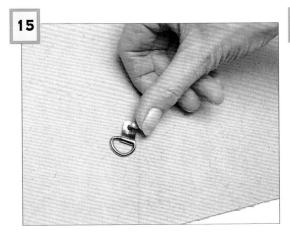

15 Mark positions for two D-rings on the hardboard – these should be about one-third of the way down and 5–6cm (2–2⅜in) in from the sides – and use a nail punch (or bradawl) and hammer to make the holes.

16 Place the D-rings in place and push through the rivets. Turn over the hardboard and, resting it on a flat surface, split open the rivets with a screwdriver and hammer them flat. Cover the rivets with small pieces of masking tape.

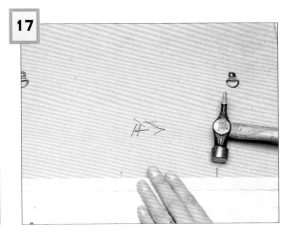

17 Sandwich the hardboard and glass together with the picture between them. Lay the components on your working surface and place the frame around them. Pick the whole piece up and turn it over. Hold the back in the frame by driving in a few small panel pins. Lay the pins on the hardboard and tap them carefully into the frame.

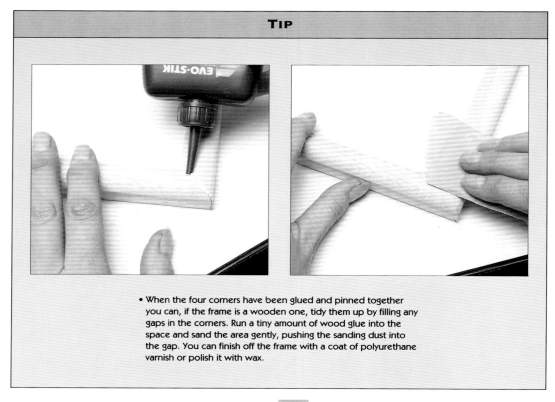

TIP

• When the four corners have been glued and pinned together you can, if the frame is a wooden one, tidy them up by filling any gaps in the corners. Run a tiny amount of wood glue into the space and sand the area gently, pushing the sanding dust into the gap. You can finish off the frame with a coat of polyurethane varnish or polish it with wax.

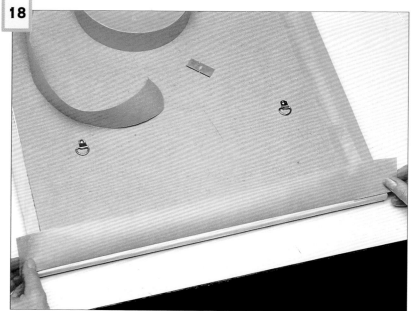

18 Use masking tape or brown gummed paper to cover the joins around the back, to help keep out insects and protect the picture from damp. A stamp roller is useful for moistening the gummed paper. Use a craft knife to trim off the ends of the tape or gummed paper.

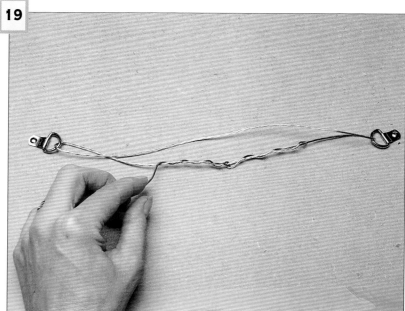

19 If you are using screw eyes rather than D-rings, insert them now, before attaching the wire or cord.

20 When it comes to painting the frame (see step 11) you can achieve great effects by matching one of the colours in the picture itself.

GLASS AND CLIP FRAME

This is a simple way of displaying small posters, postcards, children's drawings or photographs. It is best used with items that are not larger than about 60 x 60cm (24 x 24in) because the clips exert pressure on the glass, and if the area of glass is too large it is likely to crack. This project uses plastic glass clips and a wooden frame. The picture has been floated on black, to give it a definite edge, and the wooden frame has been painted black to match.

You will need
◊ Plastic ruler and pencil
◊ Mounting card
◊ Craft knife
◊ Adhesive tape or double-sided tape
◊ Length of 2.5 x 2.5cm (1 x 1in) wood moulding (see page 123) for estimating quantity
◊ Mitre cutter and clamp
◊ Saw
◊ Wood glue
◊ Drill and small bit
◊ Small hammer and nail punch
◊ 20mm (¾in) panel pins
◊ Wood filler
◊ Sandpaper and wet and dry papers
◊ Paint
◊ Glass
◊ T-square
◊ Felt-tipped pen
◊ Glass cutter
◊ Glass clips
◊ Hangers

1 Measure your print – ours was 35.5 x 28cm (14 x 11in) – and add 20mm (¾in) all round. Cut a piece of mounting card to this larger size.

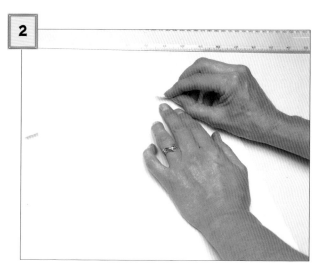

2 Use double-sided adhesive tape or make a hinge from ordinary adhesive tape to hold the picture in position on the mounting card. It is easier to move the picture if you make a mistake if it is held by a simple hinge rather than double-sided tape.

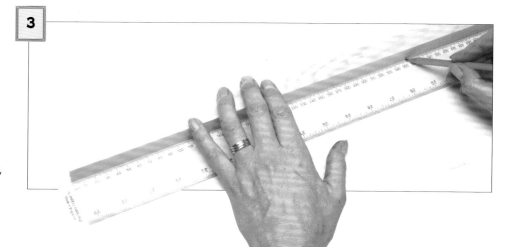

3 Cut the first angle on the frame, then measure along from the outside corner, using the long dimension first, and mark.

TIP
• If you are making a larger frame, use a piece of hardboard as a backing for the mounting card to give it extra strength.

4

5

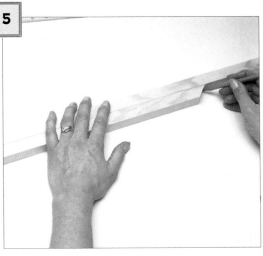

TIP

- This frame uses the same method as the main project, but the picture fits into the other side of the frame instead of being clipped onto the front of it.

4 Slide the timber into the clamp, align the mark with the central cutting line, screw the arms tight and saw. Because the timber has no rebate, you do not need to cut another angle – simply turning over the timber will give you the correct angle.

5 Use the first cut piece to measure the second long side, placing them back to back and marking the outside corners. Cut the two shorter sides in the same way.

6

7

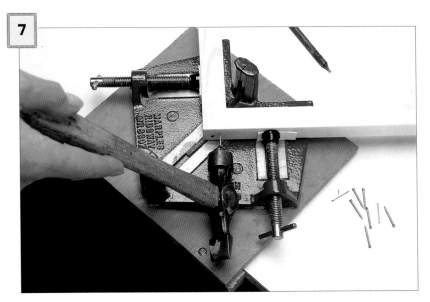

6 Apply some wood glue to one cut angle of a long side and place it in the clamp with a short side. Adjust and tighten when the angles sit neatly together.

7 Use a drill to make two small holes for the pins and drive them in, using a nail punch to drive them just below the level of the wood.

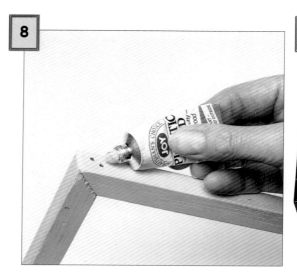

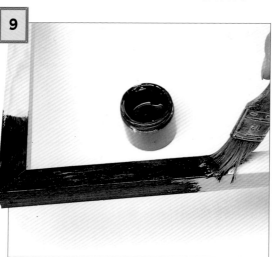

8 Fill the holes with wood filler, leave to dry and smooth with sandpaper.

9 Paint the frame to suit your picture. We used black to match the mounting card, but you could use a colour that harmonizes with the picture you are framing or one that will complement your furnishings. Leave to dry.

10 Use the finished frame as a guide to cut the glass. Lay the frame against a corner of the glass and mark the other two sides on the outside of the frame with a felt-tipped pen.

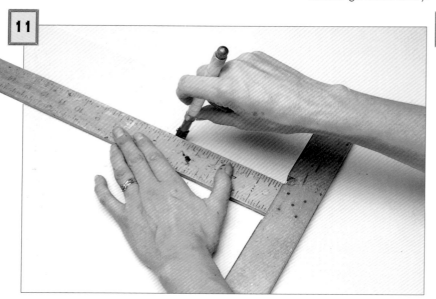

11 Use a wooden straight-edged ruler to cut the glass to size, then smooth the edges with wet and dry sandpaper, taking especial care at the corners. Clean the glass and sandwich the glass, the picture and the card. Lay them on the frame.

12 Use two glass clips on each side, making sure they are placed opposite each other. Mark the position of the holes in the clips all the way round and use the drill to make the holes. Screw the clips into position. The clips must be screwed sufficiently tightly to hold the glass securely but not so tightly that the glass cracks. Screw hangers in place on the back of the frame.

TIP

• The shops are full of frames made with metal clips and hardboard and they are so reasonably priced that you may not think it worthwhile to make your own, but they are a good way of using up the small pieces of glass and hardboard that are left over from larger projects. To make a frame with glass and metal clips, cut the hardboard to size, then cut the glass to exactly the same size. Smooth the edges of the glass. Fit D-rings to the hardboard, position the picture and slide on the metal clips, digging the metal legs into the back of the hardboard.

FABRIC AND PAPER FRAMES

Frames made in this way are ideal birthday and Christmas presents, and they are the perfect way of displaying all those school photographs that seem to accumulate.

You can use almost any paper you like – wrapping paper, hand-made paper or lightweight cotton. You might want to practise on some less expensive material before using hand-made paper, as we have done to make this double frame.

You will need
◊ Mounting card or equivalent
◊ Plastic ruler and pencil
◊ Mount cutter
◊ Polyester wadding
◊ Clear, all-purpose adhesive
◊ Sharp-pointed scissors
◊ Hand-made paper or fabric to cover frames
◊ Double-sided adhesive tape

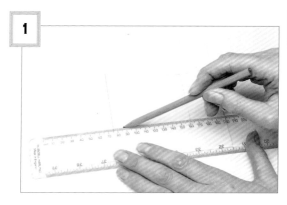

1 Cut four pieces of card. In our example the outside measurements of each are 16 x 14cm (6⅓ x 5⅛in). You will also need to cut a piece of card 16cm (6⅓in) long by 1 cm (about ⅛in) wide, which will form the spine of the frame.

2 In two of the larger rectangles of card cut a window; ours measured 8 x 6cm (3¼ x 2⅛in). (See page 129 for using a mount cutter.)

3 Cut two pieces of wadding to the same size as the window mounts and use a small amount of adhesive to glue them to the fronts of the mounts.

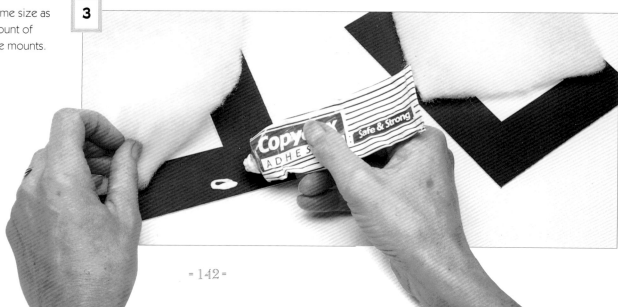

4

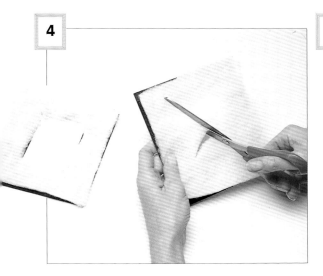

4 Use sharp scissors to snip a hole in the centre of the wadding, then trim away the excess to the edge of the window.

5

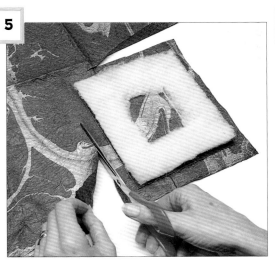

5 Cut one piece of hand-made paper for the back – ours measured 34 x 19cm (13½ x 7½in) – and two pieces for the front – ours measured 19 x 17cm (7½ x 6¾in).

6

6 Put the larger piece of paper on your working surface with the wrong side upwards. Lay the two backing cards on it so that there is 20mm (¾in) between them. Glue the thin strip of card into this space. Apply adhesive around the edges of the paper and carefully and neatly stick it over the card, working on the top and bottom edges first before turning in the sides. Pull the paper tightly over the edges so that it is taut all round. Trim the corners so that the paper lies neatly and flat.

7

7 Cut a strip of covering paper to cover the spine and glue it into position. Put aside until the adhesive is completely dry.

8

8 Take the two smaller pieces of paper and place them, wrong sides upwards, on the working surface. Lay the window mounts on this so that an even amount of paper shows all round. Glue down the paper all the way round, making sure that it is taut and that the corners are neat.

9

9 With the back of the mount towards you, use sharp scissors to make a hole in the centre of the mount. Make four cuts, just up to, but not right into, the corners.

10

11

10 Trim off the excess triangles of paper and glue and fold the inside edges, making sure that the front edges are neat and that there are no creases, especially in the corners. Trim off any excess paper or, if you have used fabric, any loose threads and frayed edges.

11 Use double-sided adhesive tape to stick the two front sections carefully to the back, leaving the top open so that you can slide in the photograph.

DOUBLE WOOD FRAME

This is the ideal frame for small pictures such as photographs or postcards. Because the fine inner frame is used in combination with a wider outer frame, the picture can be shown to advantage without having to use a mount.

You will need

◊ Narrow wood moulding (see page 123 for estimating quantity)
◊ Plastic ruler and pencil
◊ Mitre cutter and clamp
◊ Saw
◊ Craft knife
◊ Wood glue
◊ Drill and fine bit
◊ Panel pins
◊ Small hammer
◊ Wide wood moulding but with no rebate (see page 123 for estimating quantity)
◊ Nail punch
◊ White emulsion
◊ Acrylic paints
◊ 2mm (¹⁄₁₆in) glass
◊ T-square
◊ Felt-tipped pen
◊ Glass cutter
◊ 2mm (¹⁄₁₆in) hardboard
◊ Screw eyes
◊ Wire or card

1 Measure the photograph and assemble the frame from the narrow moulding as described in the Basic Frame (see page 132).

2 Use the completed inner frame to determine the dimensions of the outside frame. This is made from timber with no rebate. We used timber that was 30 x 5mm (1¼ x ¼in).

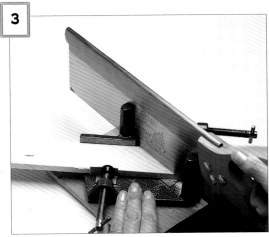

3 Make the first mitre cut, then make the two long sides and the short sides as described in the instructions for the Glass and Clip Frame (see page 138). Again this moulding has no rebate.

4 Glue and clamp the first corner together, then drill holes for the panel pins; we used 25mm (1in) pins, but you must use a size that will hold both pieces of wood securely. Use a nail punch to drive the pins in straight.

5 Paint the frames. Use contrasting colours for the frames, mixing acrylic paints with white emulsion until you find shades you like. Experiment on pieces of scrap wood before you paint the frame itself.

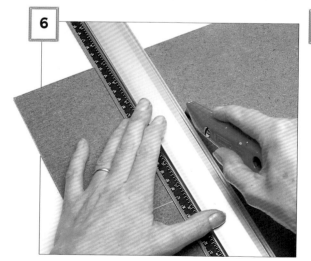

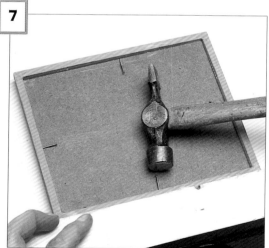

6 Cut the glass and a piece of hardboard to size, using the inner frame as a guide as to the dimensions. Fit the glass, picture, hardboard and inner frame together.

7 Hold the hardboard in place by driving some panel pins carefully into the edge of the inner frame.

8 Apply wood glue to the inside edge of the outer frame and push the inner frame through from the back. It should fit neatly. Insert the screw eyes and attach the wire so that you can hang your picture up.

BOX FRAME

This kind of frame is useful for holding three-dimensional objects such as a piece of embroidery or collectable items such as badges or medals. There are several ways of making box frames, but this is a simple and effective method. The size of the frame is determined by the backing board, which can be covered with coloured card or with polyester wadding and fabric. We have made the frame to display an arrangement of dried flowers mounted on card.

You will need

◊ Hardboard
◊ Plastic ruler and pencil
◊ Craft knife
◊ Polyester wadding
◊ Scissors
◊ Fabric
◊ Clear, all-purpose adhesive
◊ 2.5cm (1in) hockey wood moulding (see page 123 for estimating quantity)
◊ Mitre cutter and clamp
◊ Saw
◊ Wood glue
◊ Drill and fine bit
◊ Panel pins
◊ Small hammer
◊ 2mm (⅛in) glass
◊ Glass cutter
◊ T-square
◊ Card
◊ Masking tape or brown gummed paper
◊ Screw eyes
◊ Wire or cord

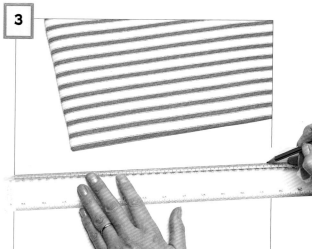

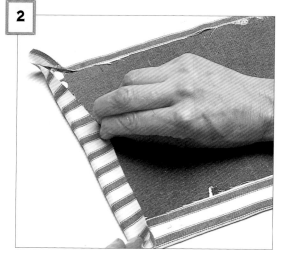

1 Cut a piece of hardboard to size – we used a piece that is 32.5 x 21.5cm (12½ x 8½in). Cover the hardboard with polyester wadding and cut a piece of fabric that is about 10mm (⅛in) larger all round than the hardboard.

2 Stretch the fabric over the wadding and glue it firmly to the back, making sure that the corners are neatly mitred.

3 Cut the first mitre in the moulding and, working on a long side first, measure the covered hardboard. Transfer this measurement to the outside edge of the moulding, measuring from one corner to the other.

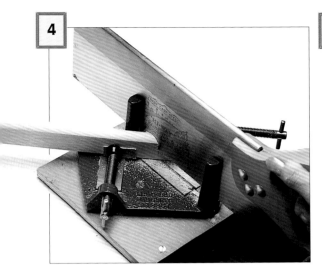

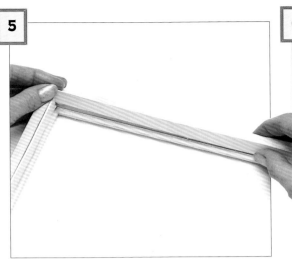

4 Slide the moulding into the mitre clamp and align the mark with the centre line of the vice. Cut the remaining three sides and assemble the frame as described in the instructions for the Basic Frame (see page 132). Once the frame is complete, cut a piece of glass to fit neatly inside the frame. Lay the frame face down on the table, clean the glass carefully and fit it into the frame.

5 Measure the depth of the side from the glass to the back of the frame – in our frame this was 20mm (about ¾in) – and cut four strips of thick card to this width and long enough to fit along the inside of the frame. Glue them in place, sticking the long pieces down first. These strips of card will hold the glass in position at the front of the box.

6 Attach the object or objects to the covered backing board. We used all-purpose adhesive to hold the card in place.

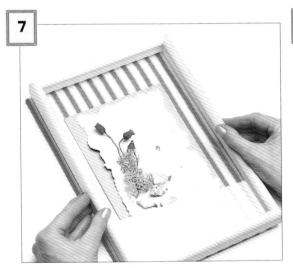

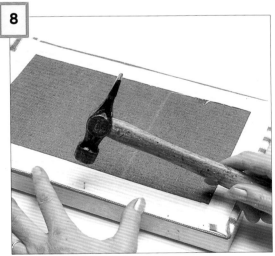

7 Place the frame over the backing board and carefully over the box.

8 Use small panel pins, tapped through the backing board into the frame, to hold the back in place. Cover the join with strips of masking tape or brown gummed paper.

9 With your hand drill, make holes, about one-third of the way down, on each side of the frame and insert the screw eyes. Attach wire or cord for hanging.

SHELL FRAME

If you have an old wooden frame that has seen better days, you can completely revitalize it by covering it with shells, feathers or even small bits of seaweed. Alternatively you can make your own frame, although you will need to use a fairly flat moulding or one that has only a gentle curve.

You will need
◊ Wooden frame
◊ White emulsion paint
◊ Acrylic paint
◊ Wire wool or a rag
◊ White candle (optional for wax resist)
◊ Screw eyes
◊ Mirror
◊ Panel pins and hammer
◊ Masking tape or gummed brown paper
◊ Strong adhesive
◊ Interior wall filler (optional for curved frame)
◊ Gold paint

1 If the frame is going to be painted, apply a coat of white emulsion and leave to dry.

2 Mix the acrylic paint, diluting it with a little emulsion to give a smooth, runny consistency. Experiment until you have a shade you like. Paint the frame and before the paint is completely dry use wire wool or a rag to drag some of the paint off.

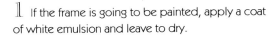

3 An alternative method is to use the end of a candle to draw patterns on the dried base coat.

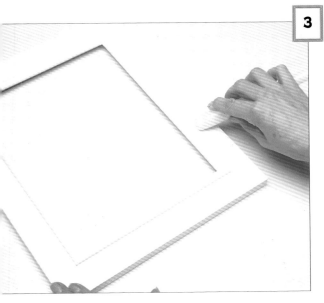

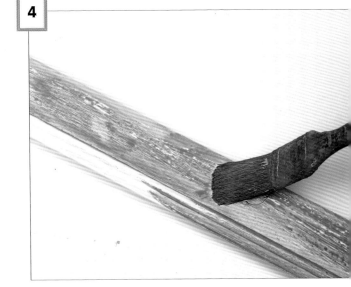

4 When you apply the acrylic paint, the wax will resist the paint and leave the white base coat showing through.

5

5 Screw the eyes into the back of the frame and, if you wish, insert the mirror, holding it in place with small panel pins. Cover the join with masking tape or gummed paper. Use a fairly strong adhesive to stick the shells and other ornaments into position. If the frame has a very uneven profile you may find it easier to mix a small amount of interior wall filler to press the shells into.

6 When you are happy with the final arrangement of the shells, add a touch of gold tube paint to create highlights on the shells, wiping off any excess before it dries.

6

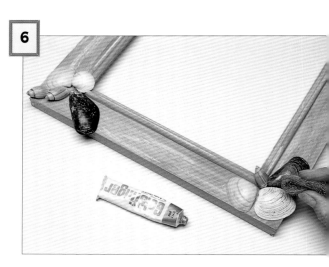

REVIVING AN OLD FRAME

You might come across an attractive old frame in a junk shop or on a second-hand stall, but, when you get it home you realise that not only is it in a worse state than you at first thought but it also will not fit the picture you intended to put in it. You can use your newly acquired skills to take the frame apart and re-make it with new glass so that it fits perfectly.

You will need

◊ Pliers
◊ Hammer
◊ Screwdriver
◊ Plastic ruler and pencil
◊ Mitre cutter and clamp
◊ Saw
◊ Craft knife
◊ Wood glue
◊ Drill and fine bit
◊ Panel pins
◊ Fine wire wool
◊ Emulsion paint
◊ Gold paint (in liquid, powder or tube form)
◊ 2mm (⅛in) glass
◊ Glass cutter
◊ T-square
◊ Masking tape or brown gummed paper
◊ Screw eyes
◊ Wire or cord

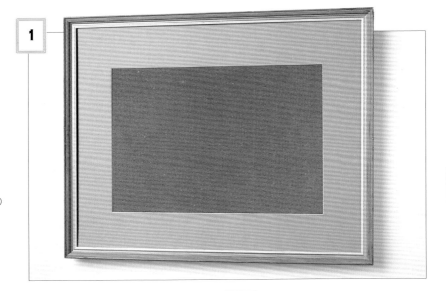

$\mathbb{1}$ First remove the backing and the glass from the old frame. Take care because the glass may be old and fragile. Stand the frame on a corner, hold the opposite corner and gently push down until the corners crack.

TIP

• If the frame is an old wooden one, always sand and stain it before applying a wax finish.
• Make a plain frame by applying two coats of a solid, dark paint.

$\mathbb{2}$ If pins have been used, push the sides apart and wiggle them apart. If the frame has been underpinned, use a screwdriver and hammer to drive the pins out.

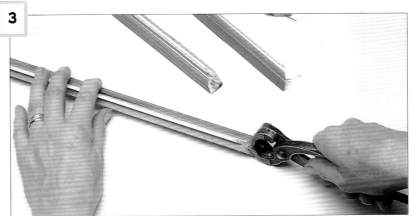

$\mathbb{3}$ Once the frame is in pieces, use your pliers to remove any remaining pins. Working on one of the long sides, cut a new mitred corner.

4

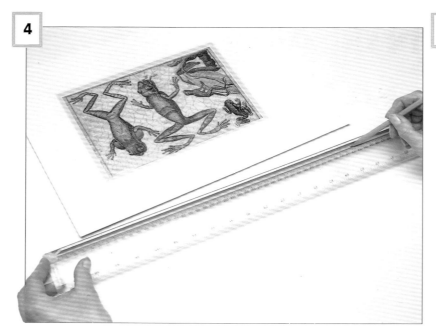

4 Measure the long side of the picture you want to frame and transfer the measurement to the inside of the newly cut side.

5

5 Slide the moulding into the mitre clamp and align the mark with the centre cutting line. Cut all the sides as for the Basic Frame (see page 132) and re-assemble the pieces.

6

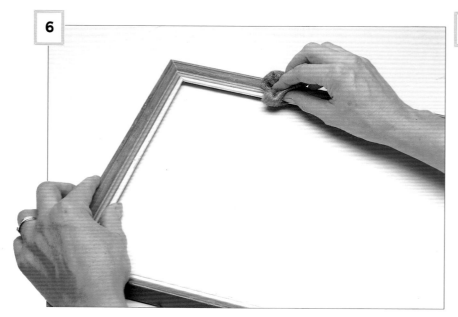

6 You can now decorate the frame, choosing a style that is in keeping with the picture that is going in it. We have used an old print of some frogs and want the frame to look suitably distressed and aged. To achieve this appearance, rub the frame all over with fine wire wool.

7

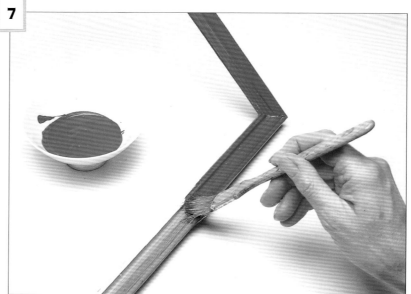

7 Apply a coat of dark brick-red emulsion all over the frame. Leave to dry. You may need to apply a second coat if the first did not cover the frame completely.

8

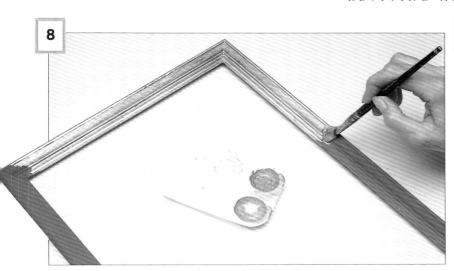

9

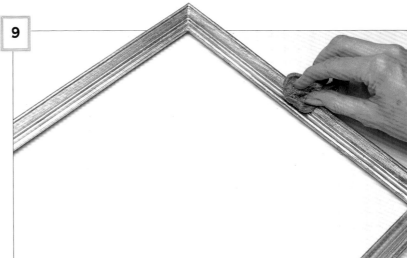

8 When the paint is dry, smooth it carefully with fine wire wool, then apply a coat of liquid gold leaf or another proprietary gold paint. Some gold powders need to be mixed with shellac or button polish, so always check the manufacturer's instructions.

9 When the gold paint is dry, rub it gently with fine wire wool to give a distressed look, with the red paint showing through in places. Insert the glass and finish off the frame as described in the instructions for the Basic Frame (see page 136).

PAPIER-MÂCHÉ FRAME

Making this frame for a mirror will allow you to combine your framing skills with the satisfying craft of papier-mâché. We have created a simple design, with fish swimming around the glass, although this is a technique that allows you to give your creative talents full rein.

You will need

◊ 1 x 1 cm (½ x ⅜in) plain wooden moulding (see page 123 for estimating quantity)
◊ Plastic ruler and pencil
◊ Mitre cutter and clamp
◊ Saw
◊ Craft knife
◊ Wood glue
◊ Drill and fine bit
◊ Panel pins
◊ Small hammer
◊ Tracing paper
◊ Mounting card or thick card
◊ Scraps of newspaper, torn into small pieces
◊ Masking tape
◊ Flour-and-water paste or wallpaper paste
◊ Masking tape or brown gummed paper
◊ Acrylic glue (optional)
◊ Clear, all-purpose adhesive
◊ White tissue paper
◊ Acrylic paint
◊ Polyurethane
◊ Screw eyes
◊ Wire or cord

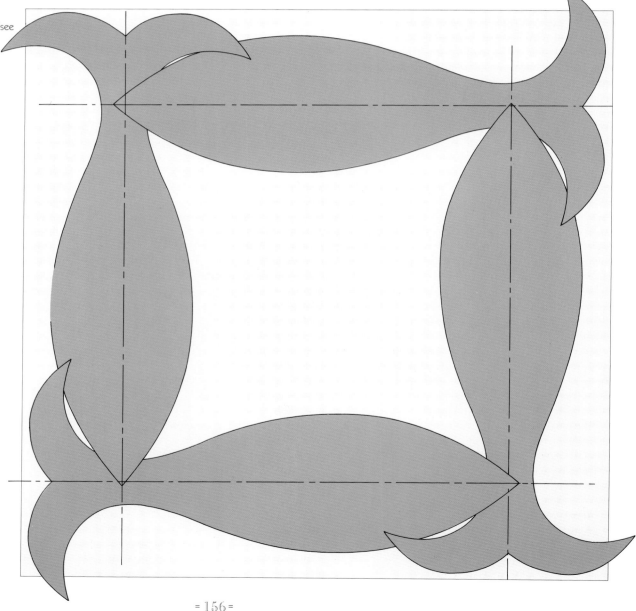

1 Use the wooden moulding to make a three-sided frame, following the instructions for the Basic Frame (see page 132). We have made a square frame, measuring 16.5 x 16.5cm (6½ x 6½in). Leave the opening at the top so that you can slip in the mirror.

2 Trace the fish design (or a motif of your choice) onto a spare piece of card. Use a craft knife to cut out four fish shapes.

3 Tear up some pieces of newspaper and scrunch them up loosely. Use tape to hold them onto the parts of the fish bodies that you want to be fuller and more rounded.

4 Mix the paste. If you use flour-and-water paste you can add a small amount of acrylic glue to make it stronger. Dip pieces of paper into the paste and begin to cover the fish bodies. Do not let the paper become saturated with paste, and if you find that the paper is too wet, lay some dry pieces over the shapes. When you are satisfied with the overall shapes, smooth the surface of each fish and leave them somewhere warm until they are absolutely dry.

5

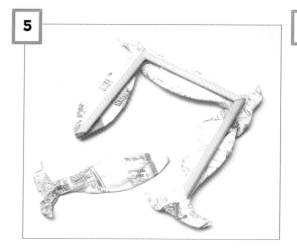

5 Take the frame and arrange the fish on it. When you are satisfied with the positions they are in, use a lot of adhesive to stick them, nose to tail, around the frame.

6

6 The fish at the top should be attached by its nose and tail. Place under a weight and leave until the adhesive is dry. Check that the mirror will slide into the frame, but do not leave it there yet. Add more layers of papier-mâché to the fish, using strips of paper across the back of the top fish to make sure it is firmly attached to its neighbours. Put back in a warm place to dry.

7

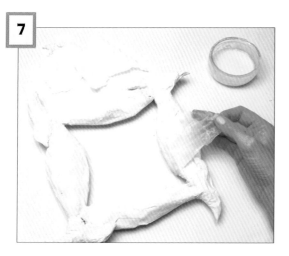

7 To finish the fish, cover them completely with two layers of white tissue paper. The colours of the paint will be much brighter and clearer if they are applied over a white base.

8

8 When the fish are dry, paint them in colours of your choice. Leave the paint to dry, then apply a coat of clear polyurethane.

9

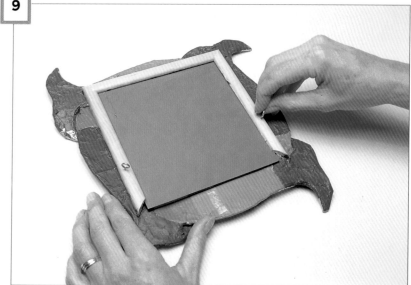

9 Insert the mirror and apply screw eyes on the sides to hang up the frame.

GLOSSARY

Acid Free: This is the term used to describe card, mountboard and tape that is made free from acid, and which ensures that the artwork you are framing does not become marked or damaged over a length of time.

Bevel: The sloping cut edge of a mount.

Bole: A clay applied over gesso as a base for goldleafing. Can also be used on its own.

Distressing: Making a gold leaf or painted frame look old by rubbing through to the base colour with wire wool.

Double mount: Two mounts one on top of the other. The window of the top mount is larger than that of the bottom mount.

Float: A piece of mountcard is cut approximately 1in or 2.5cm larger than the artwork. Centre the artwork onto the card and it floats with card showing all the way round.

Gesso: Chalk whiting and size which is used in layers to build up a base for gold leaf and other finishes.

Limed wood: Wood treated with a wash of white paint, lime paste or limed wax.

Mitre: A 45° angle used on moulding to make the corners of the frame.

Mitre box: A metal or wooden box used for cutting the 45° angle on the moulding.

Moulding: Specially turned wood with a rebate used for framing.

Mount or Mat: Card with a window in it that helps you hang and protect the artwork.

Rebate: The recess on the inside of a piece of moulding into which all the parts of the picture are fitted.

Ruling or mapping pen: A pen that has two parallel blunt nibs. When filled with watercolour or ink, it is used to draw wash lines on mounts.

Score: To mark a line on a piece of card or glass with a cutting tool to enable you to bend the card or sever the glass.

Wash: A layer of thinned paint, usually watercolour, used to acquire a translucent and delicate effect. Used in between wash lines, mainly for watercolours.

Window: The hole cut in a mount, through which you can see the painting.

Toleware

Special, yet simple, items to create while learning
the techniques of this decorative art

INTRODUCTION

Since its introduction in the early 18th century, painted tinware has been a popular – if not perhaps much publicized – craft. The name toleware originates from the French *la tole peinte* (painted tin) and it was the French, among other European manufacturers, who developed very sophisticated toleware or "japanning" to imitate the exquisite lacquerware being imported in the late 17th and early 18th centuries from Japan. Beautiful pieces were produced at this time, culminating in Chippendale and lace-edged trays, painted in elegant floral designs or decorated with gold leaf.

But it was the early settlers in the United States who became the first producers of household tinware. In 1740, the Patterson brothers of Berlin, Connecticut began importing sheet tin from England to make cooking utensils. This early tinware was undecorated – largely because the New England and Pennsylvanian settlers were Puritans and deeply opposed to ornamentation of any kind. It was not until the late 18th century that this US tinware was being japanned in the manner of the European ware. The early tin was elaborately decorated by skilled workmen, trained in the techniques used abroad.

These highly decorated items were bought by rich, moneyed families. Soon however, the rural tinsmiths began to produce a type of simple painted tin, intended for quick, cheap sale. Much of this 19th century ware was marketed through stores, although more of it was sold by pedlars, at first by foot and later by cart as these travelling salesmen made ever longer reaching journeys.

The country tinsmiths decorated their tin with brushstroke painting which all apprentice decorators learnt. The painted household objects were various: trays, cookie boxes, pitchers, canisters, coffee pots and trinket boxes. The American housewife was quick to seize upon these bright new items to cheer her home after years of dull tin and pewter.

Today, we can recapture the pleasure of those early artists and the housewives who bought their wares by creating colourful and personal accessories to grace our own homes.

BASIC EQUIPMENT AND MATERIALS

PAINTS

Water-based acrylic paints and primers have been used for all the projects contained in this book because of their ease of application, quick-drying properties, absence of toxic substances, and also because brushes and containers can easily be cleaned with mild detergent and water.

Until recently it was felt preferable to use oil-based products on tinware because of the non-absorbency of the surface and because painted surfaces on tin tend to chip more easily. However, the phasing out of oil- or solvent-based products has brought water-based versions to the fore, and advances in paint manufacturing mean that acrylic primers and paints are now available for painting toleware successfully.

PRIMERS

There are two types of primer, one for galvanized or zinc-plated tin, and one for non-ferrous metals, (brass and copper, etc). The majority of tin items fall into the galvanized category.

BASECOATS

Acrylic paints in large containers can be bought from art shops and suppliers. **Emulsion paints**, which can be used as basecoats for wooden items are not suitable for painting on to tinware. These paints adhere to surfaces by sinking into them, which they cannot do with metal.

Oil-based basecoats can be used but they must be applied on top of an oil-based primer. Brushes should be cleaned in turpentine or white spirit. However, oil-based paint and water-based paint do not sit happily together, so if you wish to paint your design in acrylics you will need to paint a coat of shellac or sanding sealer over the dry basecoat. Once this, in turn, is dry you can paint your design in acrylics.

Enamel paints can be used on metal and give a glossy, lacquer-like finish which is similar to "japanned" articles. These paints are oil-based, so once again a coat of shellac or sanding sealer will be needed to isolate the basecoat from your acrylic designs.

Finally, cellulose metal paints and **car spray paints** can be used. They are compatible with acrylics and the design can be painted directly on to these finishes.

DESIGN PAINTS

Acrylics can be purchased in tubes or jars – the latter being preferable for brushstroke work as they are more fluid. There is a huge variety of colours from which to choose or they can be mixed. They can be thinned with water to a looser consistency when needed, as in liner or script work. Brushes are washed in soapy water to clean them.

OTHER MATERIALS

RUST INHIBITOR

A proprietary "paint" that contains chemicals to seal in and prevent further rusting. It is available from hardware or DIY stores. You will need this if you are preparing old, rusty tinware.

SHELLAC, SANDING SEALER AND WHITE POLISH

These products seal and protect. They are available from specialist suppliers. They are solvent-based, quick-drying, and are compatible with both oil-based and water-based preparations. Wash brushes in methylated spirit.

METHYLATED SPIRIT

Widely available, methylated spirit has many uses. Apart from cleaning brushes, it can remove acrylic and water-based paints from surfaces – either where paint has been spilt accidentally or where the intention is to remove paint as an antiquing or distressing device.

GOLD LEAF

Gold leaf can be real gold (very expensive), or Dutch metal leaf which is more economical and has been used for the projects in this book. It is available as loose leaf or transfer leaf. The transfer leaf is the easiest to handle as it is on a backing paper. Try not to touch the metal leaf more than you need to because it can be marked very easily. Unlike real gold leaf, Dutch metal leaf will tarnish and needs to be varnished or lacquered to prevent this.

BRONZE POWDERS

Bronze powders are fine metallic powders made from copper, silver, aluminium or alloys. They too need to be protected with varnish or lacquer.

GOLD SIZE

Gold size is used in gilding to adhere the metal leaf to the surface and is available in many different drying times ranging from 30 minutes to 24 hours. 3-hour gold size has been used on the gilded projects in this book.

VARNISHES

Oil-based and water-based varnishes are available and both can be used over your projects whether the design work is in oils or acrylics. The only time you must be sure to use oil-based varnish is with crackle varnishing.

Oil-based varnishes take a long time to dry, 24 hours or longer, and can "yellow" your colours because of the linseed oil content. Water-based varnishes dry very quickly which means that you can apply several coats in a day, if you wish. As they contain no oil, they will not yellow with age.

You can also buy special **crackle-varnish** kits. These contain one oil-based varnish, which is applied first, then a water-based varnish, which is coated on top of the nearly dry oil-based varnish. The result is an aged, distressed appearance to the item being decorated.

BRUSHES AND APPLICATORS

OTHER EQUIPMENT

WIRE BRUSH

Useful for brushing off flaking rust on old tin items in readiness for washing and applying a rust inhibitor.

SANDPAPER

The coarser grades of sandpaper are needed to sand down enamel-painted items before priming. The finer grades of sandpaper can be used between coats of varnish.

Chalk is useful when positioning your design on larger objects.

PAPERS

Tracing paper is used for tracing designs and patterns. To transfer the designs you will need tracing-down paper. This wax-free carbon-paper comes in a variety of colours, (white, yellow, blue, black), and can be removed with an eraser. It is used in conjunction with tracing paper to transfer the design on to the item you are decorating. Trace-down should not be confused with ordinary carbon-paper. New varieties coming on to the market include papers whose traces disappear when painted over.

MASKING TAPE

Used for either holding the tracing and transfer papers when applying a design, or for isolating adjoining areas when painting, the masking tape you use needs to be "low-tack". If the adhesive on the tape is too sticky it may pull off the paint when removed.

Brushes cover a huge range in design, type and price. For decorative painting they fall into two types: base-coating or varnishing brushes and design brushes.

VARNISH BRUSHES

Varnish brushes are flat and can be bought in a variety of sizes. The 2cm (1in) and 4cm (1⅛in) sizes are most useful for small items and can be used for primers, basecoats and varnishes. Inexpensive ½cm (½ in) decorators' brushes are good enough for applying spirit-based products, like shellac, because the product will ruin good brushes.

DESIGN BRUSHES

Design brushes come under the heading of artists' brushes. Most of the projects in this book have been completed using "round" brushes, sizes 2 and 4. A liner or script brush is useful for fine lines or tendrils and a flat brush or angled shader can be used for heavier borders. Synthetic brushes are quite satisfactory for use with acrylics, do not be tempted to buy the expensive sable brushes.

SPONGE

A natural sponge is preferable as it will give a greater variation in pattern than a synthetic sponge. Squeeze out in water before using and never leave it soaking in harsh solvents.

STYLUS

A stylus is a multi-purpose tool. In toleware it is used when tracing designs on to objects, and it can be used for adding dots of paint to the design.

TECHNIQUES

PRIMING

The items you will find or purchase for decorating will fall into one of three categories; new tinware, old tinware or enamelled tinware, (this last type includes previously painted tinware).

The first step for any of the above will be a good wash and scrub. If the tinware is old it is probably dusty and dirty. If it is new galvanized tin it will probably have a protective oily coating which will need removing before painting. Once the item has been washed it will need drying thoroughly in case any water is in the seams. If left, this will cause rust

to break out which would eventually break through your design work. A small item could be put in the oven at a low temperature for a while. If this is not possible, stand the item in a warm place in the house for a day or two. If the item is enamelled, or has been previously painted, give it a wash to remove any dirt or grime.

Once the new metal is clean, the item will be ready for priming. If old metal, the next task is to examine the item for any rust patches or spots. If there are any, remove any loose rust by brushing with a wire brush or very coarse sandpaper. Then

treat with rust inhibitor. Once this has dried, the item will be ready for priming. If the item is enamelled or painted, give it a sand down with coarse sandpaper to form a key to which the paint can adhere.

Once the above steps have been carried out, the primer can then be applied. Check that you have the correct primer for the type of metal you are painting. Once the primer is dry, you can carry on with your base-coating. Metal often needs two basecoats; give the first coat plenty of time to dry before applying the second.

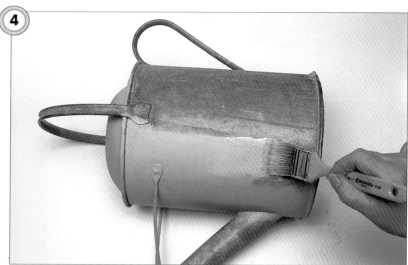

BRUSH STROKES

As mentioned in the Introduction, decorative and folk art painting are based on brushstrokes, the most common being the comma and "S" strokes. The technique for these strokes may take a little time to learn but it is well worth the time spent practising.

Comma

Using a round brush, try the comma stroke first. Hold the brush perpendicular to the paper. Gently put the whole length of the brush down on to the paper, then apply a little pressure so that the brush hairs flare out forming the rounded head of the comma. Pull the brush slowly back towards you releasing the pressure on the brush and letting the hairs return to a point. Keep pulling back towards you and lifting the brush until you come to a fine point. Stop and then lift off.

'S' stroke

The "S" stroke is like a long pulled-out letter 'S', with the beginning and end strokes heading in the same direction. Begin on the tip of the brush. Pull the brush towards you, gradually increasing pressure. Change direction, still increasing pressure, until you are halfway through the "S". Start to decrease pressure while still pulling back towards you. Change direction back to the original, and carry on lifting pressure until you are back on the tip of the brush. Stop, then lift off.

The amount of paint you need on the brush will come naturally after a while: a good rule of thumb is that the paint should reach about halfway up the hairs. Paint should be the consistency of cream, so you may need to add a little water.

The liner or script brush is used for plant tendrils and fine lines. Water the paint down to an ink-like consistency and always hold the brush in an upright position.

Stylus Dots

The stylus, or the end of the brush, can be used to put dots in the painting, (for example, flower centres). If you want the dots to be consistent, you will need to dip the stylus or brush handle in the paint each time. If you keep going with the same paint load, the dots will diminish in size.

GILDING

Some simple techniques have been used in two of the projects in this book. Full instructions have been given in each section, see pages 177 and 185.

CRACKLE GLAZE

This finish is frequently confused with crackle varnish. Crackle glaze is applied between two layers of paint. The basecoat is applied and, when dry, the crackle glaze is applied where wanted. This too is allowed to dry and then the top coat is put on. The glaze will immediately start "working" and cracking the paint. The crazing will go on for some time, so it is best to leave the item until the reaction stops, overnight is safest. With this finish, the basecoat and topcoat need to be contrasting colours in order that the coat underneath will show through when the cracking appears.

CRACKLE VARNISH

Crackle varnish works when two layers of special varnish are applied at the end of painting. Following the completion of the design work, the first oil-based coat of varnish is applied. This is left until nearly dry and then the second water-based coat is applied. This is left until dry and then heat is applied – a hairdryer works well – and the top coat of the varnish will crack. It is often difficult to see the web of cracks until the antiquing is applied, and this is done next. Mix a little Raw Umber oil paint with a drop of white spirit and, using a soft cloth, rub it all over the crackle varnish surface. Then take a piece of kitchen paper towel and wipe off the excess oil paint. The antiquing will stop in the varnish cracks and you will be able to see the crazed effect. Finish off with a coat of oil-based varnish; this coat cannot be water-based.

Always practise these effects on scrap items before applying them to your finished object.

VARNISHING

The cardinal rule of varnishing is to remember to apply the varnish sparingly. Several fine coats are better than one heavy one. It is preferable to varnish in daytime, and it should be carried out in a dry, dust-free environment. Work on a small section at a time, overlapping each section slightly. If you wish to, you can sand down after each coat of varnish with a very fine sandpaper. Always varnish your projects when completed to protect your precious work from damage and deterioration.

WATERING CAN

A second-hand discovery, a little tender loving care, and one of my favourite designs made this watering can both useful and decorative. The background foliage is simply sponged on. Don't be daunted by painting all the flowers: with a little practise, they'll flow happily from your brush.

You will need
◊ Watering can (primed and painted with dark green basecoat)
◊ Tracing paper
◊ Transfer paper
◊ Masking tape
◊ Stylus
◊ Sponge
◊ Kitchen paper towel
◊ Nos. 2 and 4 round artists' brushes
◊ No. 5/0 script artists' brush
◊ Palette or plate for paint
◊ Acrylic paints in Fawn, Antique White, Raw Umber, Hooker's Green, Ocean Green, Leaf Green and Yellow Oxide
◊ Varnish
◊ Varnish brush

1 Trace the daisy design (see page 197) on to
tracing paper and attach to the side of the watering can using masking tape. Slide transfer paper underneath the tracing paper. Trace only the dotted line on to the can.

2 Take the sponge and dampen it. To create a background of foliage for the flowers you will need to fill in the space below the traced-on dotted line with the three shades of green. First, sponge on the darkest green at the bottom of the design to a height of about 4 cm (1½ in). Blot excess paint on to kitchen paper as you work.

3 The mid-green is sponged on next and the lightest green is applied last, letting this colour run up to the dotted line. Take care not to leave a line between each colour; merge them to make the foliage look natural.

4 When the paint is dry, replace the traced design, hold in place with masking tape and slide the transfer paper underneath. Now trace down the whole of the design, using the stylus, and repeat for the smaller design on the top of the can.

5 Using the Fawn paint, and a No. 4 brush, base-coat in the daisy petals.

6 Take the Raw Umber and the No. 2 brush and base-coat in the centres of the daisies.

7 Now finish the daisy petals with the Antique White applied with the No. 4 brush.

8 Complete the centres of the daisies by adding highlights. Use Yellow Oxide and the No. 2 brush and pat in some colour on the part of the Raw Umber centres where the light would catch them.

9 Finish off the centres with a few random small, white dots applied with the stylus.

10 Use the very palest green to paint in the tendrils, stalks and sepals.

SET OF PITCHERS

A favourite design of mine, and one which is based on an early 19th century French pattern. The design is modified for the different sizes of the pitchers and is painted over a basecoat, devised specially to create an old, aged appearance.

You will need
◊ Set of pitchers (primed, ready for basecoats)
◊ Basecoats in Deep Orange and Brown Umber
◊ Brush to apply basecoats
◊ Tracing paper
◊ Transfer paper
◊ Masking tape
◊ Stylus
◊ No. 5/0 script artists' brush
◊ Nos. 2 and 4 round artists' brushes
◊ No. 4 flat brush
◊ Palette or plate for paint
◊ Acrylic paints in Burnt Umber, Leaf Green, Antique Gold, Bonnie Blue, Persimmon, Antique White and Hooker's Green
◊ Varnish
◊ Varnish brush

> **TIP**
>
> • Do not skimp with preparation: apply two basecoats to the metal before decoration, allowing the first coat adequate time to dry before applying the second.

1 Before beginning the design, paint the pitchers with a Deep Orange basecoat and then apply a Brown Umber wash (50:50 paint:water) over the top. Leave to dry.

2 Trace the designs (on page 198) on to tracing paper and, selecting the appropriate design for the size of your pitcher, attach it to the side with masking tape. Slide the transfer paper underneath the tracing paper and transfer the design with the stylus.

3 Using the script brush, paint in the stalks in Burnt Umber.

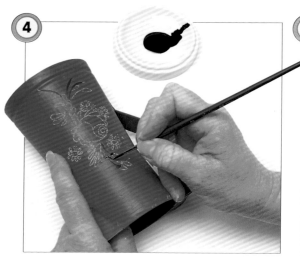

4 Thoroughly rinse the script brush, and paint in the rosebud stalks with Hooker's Green.

5 Paint in the leaves using the Leaf Green and the No. 2 brush.

6 Rinse the No. 2 brush and paint in the petals on the pinwheel daisies with Bonnie Blue.

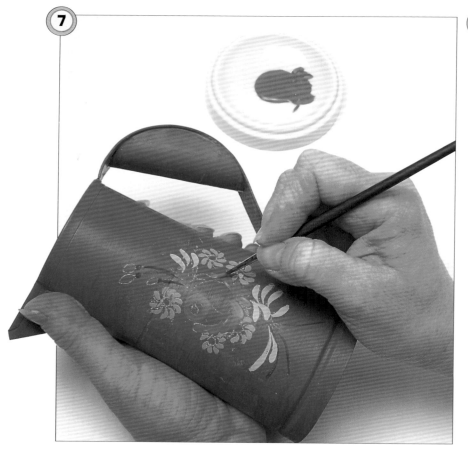

7 Using the No. 4 brush, and the Persimmon, paint in the base petals of the rose, the heart of the rose, and the rosebuds.

8 Take the Burnt Umber and apply with the No. 2 brush to paint in the centre of the rose and the centres of the pinwheel daisies.

9 Put some Persimmon paint in your palette and add some white to create a paler red. Use this colour and the No. 4 brush to paint in the bowl of the rose.

10 Complete the design by adding highlights to the daisy centres, the rose and the rosebuds, using Antique White and the No. 2 brush.

11 These pitchers are offset by a burnished-style golden rim. Use the No. 4 flat brush and the Antique Gold to paint the top and bottom of the pitcher, and to rim the edges of the handle. When the paint is completely dry, apply a coat of varnish.

WATER FOUNTAIN

This novel fountain is designed for washing soiled and muddy hands in the garden or outhouse. I pictured it in an old country-style garden, so decided to give it a crackled-painted effect for an aged and well-worn look. The trailing, overgrown ivy complements the garden theme.

You will need

◊ Water fountain (primed and painted with pink basecoat)
◊ Chalk
◊ Crackle glaze
◊ Brush to apply glaze
◊ Contrasting topcoat – we have used cream
◊ Brush for applying the topcoat
◊ Tracing paper
◊ Transfer paper
◊ Stylus
◊ No. 5/0 script artists' brush
◊ Nos. 2 and 4 artists' brushes
◊ Palette or plate for paint
◊ Acrylic paints in Hooker's Green, Ocean Green, Salem Green, Leaf Green, Antique White, Fawn and Raw Umber
◊ Varnish
◊ Varnish brush

1 Choose the areas where you want the paint to crackle and outline them with chalk. Apply crackle-glaze to these areas. Leave to dry.

2 Apply the top, contrasting, coat of cream-coloured paint to the whole fountain. When going over the crackle-glazed areas, paint lightly and use only one or two strokes. If overworked, the crackle-glaze will not craze correctly.

TIP

• Some of the solvents recommended for cleaning brushes used for oil-based paints or varnishes are expensive. It would be more economical to use a cheap brush and discard after use.

3 Leave the container to dry, preferably overnight. The crackle glaze will start to work immediately, cracking the paint, and you will find this will continue for some time.

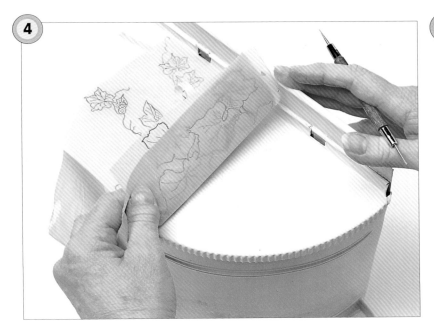

4 Trace the trailing ivy design (see page 199) on to the tracing paper. Attach these to the container with masking tape and, sliding the transfer paper under the tracing paper, transfer the designs with the stylus. At this point, transfer only the outline of the leaves and not the veins.

5 Using the No. 4 brush, paint in the leaves using the Hooker's Green for the leaves marked A on the design; Ocean Green for the leaves marked B, Salem Green for the leaves marked C and Leaf Green for the underleaf areas marked D. Leave to dry.

6 Replace the traced designs, attach with masking tape and slide the transfer paper under the tracing paper. Transfer the veins on to the leaves. Using the script brush, paint in the veins using Leaf Green.

7 To complete the design, paint the roots in Raw Umber, and the tendrils in Hooker's Green, once again using the script brush. When dry, apply a coat of varnish.

GILDED TRAY

This project gives you the opportunity to try your hand at using gold leaf. The combination of black and gold provides such a rich and opulent finish. Here, I have used a Russian technique with an early American pattern.

You will need

◊ Tray (primed and painted black)
◊ Transfer Dutch metal leaf
◊ Gold size
◊ Brush to apply size
◊ Cotton
◊ Shellac or sanding sealer
◊ Brush to apply shellac
◊ Tracing paper
◊ Transfer paper
◊ Stylus
◊ Masking tape
◊ Nos. 2 and 4 round artists' brushes
◊ No. 5/0 script artists' brush
◊ Palette or plate for paint
◊ Acrylic paints in Black, Turquoise and Yellow Oxide
◊ White polish
◊ Brush to apply polish
◊ Soft cloth

1 Apply a coat of gold size to the centre of the tray where the gold leaf is to be laid. Follow the picture here as a guide.

2 Test for tack with your knuckle; it should have the same stickiness as adhesive tape.

TIP

• Unlike real gold leaf, Dutch metal leaf is less expensive, but it will tarnish and a coat of shellac will be required to prevent this.

3 Take a sheet of transfer Dutch metal leaf and, holding it by the backing paper, lay it carefully onto the tray.

4 Before removing the backing paper, rub your fingers over the metal leaf to make sure it is stuck down and that there are no bubbles. Then remove the backing paper. When applying the next piece, overlap the first piece by about ½ cm (¼ in).

5 Repeat steps 1 and 2 when going round the edges of the tray, but cut the metal leaf into small strips, overlapping the pieces as you apply them. Leave overnight.

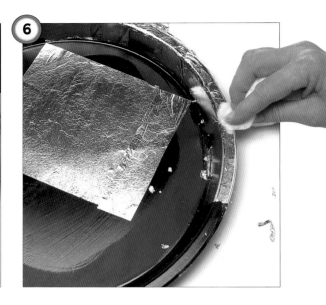

6 Next day, take a piece of cotton and gently rub over the tray, removing any loose leaf. Paint with a coat of shellac or sanding sealer.

7 Trace the design on page 200 on to tracing paper and attach to the tray with masking tape. Slide the transfer paper underneath and trace down the design with the stylus.

8 Paint in the background of the design with black paint using the No. 4 brush.

9 Paint in any fine lines with the script brush.

10 Using the No. 2 brush, paint in the detail on the large flowers. Now take the Script brush and paint the tendrils in Turquoise. Use the Turquoise also to edge the lower leaves on the border of the tray.

11 Using the No. 2 brush, finish with a little Yellow Oxide to the edges of the buds. Give the tray an application of white polish and buff with a soft cloth.

NAPKIN HOLDER

This deep blue napkin holder has been picked out with a pretty white lacy design – the perfect complement to a table laid with fine linen or damask. The technique of painting lace, perfected by the Australian decorative artists, is one of my favourite creative ideas.

You will need

◊ Napkin holder (primed and painted in dark
  blue basecoat)
◊ Tracing paper
◊ Transfer paper
◊ Stylus
◊ Masking tape
◊ Palette or plate for paint
◊ No. 2 round artists' brush
◊ Acrylic paint in Antique White
◊ Varnish
◊ Varnish brush

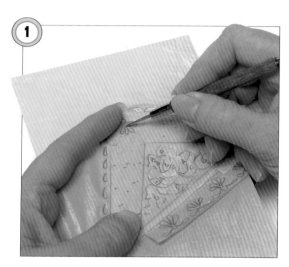

1 Trace the lacy design on page 200 on to a piece of tracing paper. Transfer on to the napkin holder with the transfer paper.

2 Mix the Antique White with some water to give a thin wash. Apply this to the front of the holder.

TIP

• Do not overload the brush with paint. A good rule of thumb is that the paint should reach halfway up the hairs.

3 With the No. 2 brush and the Antique White, apply another wash over the rose and the areas marked B.

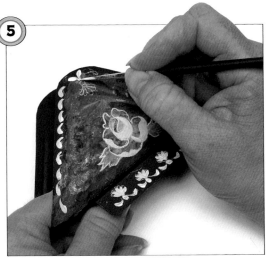

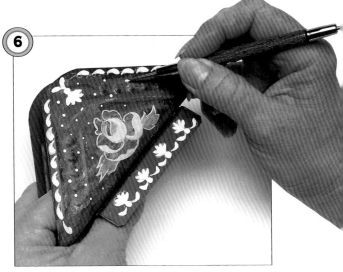

4 Paint in a final wash over the parts marked C. Leave to dry.

5 Discard the wash and return to using the Antique White paint undiluted. Paint in the commas around the edge with a No. 2 brush. This creates a lacy trim to the napkin holder.

6 Finally, randomly drop in some dots of white with the stylus. This completes the lacy impression of the design. When the piece is completely dry, coat it with varnish.

TIN TRUNK

Antiqued with crackle varnish, this quaint little storage trunk has been decorated with a Swedish-inspired cream and blue design. The colours work so well because the various shades of blue harmonize beautifully together.

You will need
◊ Trunk (primed)
◊ Basecoats in cream and blue
◊ Brush to apply basecoats
◊ Old toothbrush
◊ Paper towel
◊ Tracing paper
◊ Transfer paper
◊ Masking tape
◊ Stylus
◊ No. 5/0 script artists' brush
◊ No. 4 round artists' brush
◊ Palette or plate for paint
◊ Acrylic paints in Adriatic Blue, Bonnie Blue, Blue Wisp and Cape Cod Blue
◊ Two-part crackle varnish
◊ Brushes to apply crackle varnish
◊ Tube of raw umber oil paint
◊ White spirits
◊ Soft cloth
◊ Oil-based varnish
◊ Varnish brush

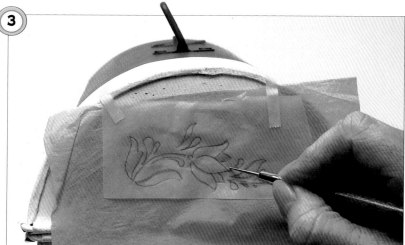

1 Measure about halfway up the sides of the trunk and mark with chalk or pencil. Paint in contrasting colours, as shown here.

2 Using the darker colour and an old toothbrush, spatter the top, lighter half of the trunk. Spatter by dipping the toothbrush in some watered-down paint, dabbing off the excess on some paper towel and then running your finger along the brush. Practise before using on the piece you are painting.

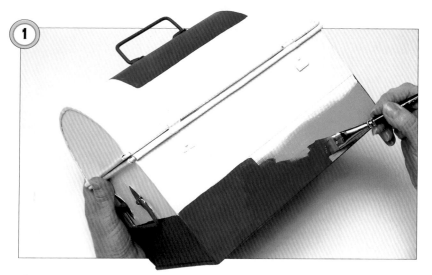

3 Trace off the design shown on page 198 on to tracing paper and attach it to the trunk. Slide the transfer paper underneath and transfer the design on to the front and sides.

4 Paint in the smallest leaves and the stalks in Adriatic Blue, using the No. 4 brush for the leaves and the script brush for the stalks.

5 Paint in the larger leaves in Bonnie Blue.

6 Paint the tulips with Blue Wisp.

7 Paint the commas on to the tulips using Cape Cod Blue.

8 Paint the trunk with the first coat of the crackle varnish and leave until the varnish is nearly dry.

9 Test to see if the varnish is ready for the second coat to go on: press it lightly with your fingers. It should feel almost dry but with a slight stickiness. Apply the second coat and allow to dry, preferably overnight. Apply heat with a hairdryer; a web of cracks will appear but will be difficult to see until the Raw Umber is applied.

10 Mix some Raw Umber oil paint with a drop of white spirits and rub on to the trunk. Take a piece of paper towel and rub off the excess. Varnish with oil-based varnish.

TIP

• If the crackle varnish does not turn out as you hoped, remove the top, water-based coat by washing it off. You can then start again with the first coat of varnish without damaging the underlying painting.

BOX OF FRUITS

A simple technique which makes use of bronze powders. The wonderful lustre of these metallic powders lifts any design from the ordinary to the special. I have based the motif on an early New England pattern.

You will need

◊ Round tin (primed and then painted in black paint)
◊ Tracing paper
◊ Transfer paper
◊ Masking tape
◊ Stylus
◊ Gold size
◊ Small, old brush to apply the size
◊ White spirits
◊ Bronze powders in gold, bronze and antique bronze
◊ No. 4 round and No. 4 flat artists' brushes
◊ Any large, soft brush
◊ Cotton
◊ Palette or plate for paint
◊ Acrylic paints in Salem Green, English Yew Green, Adobe Red, Straw, Leaf Green, Plum and Antique Rose
◊ Varnish
◊ Varnish brush

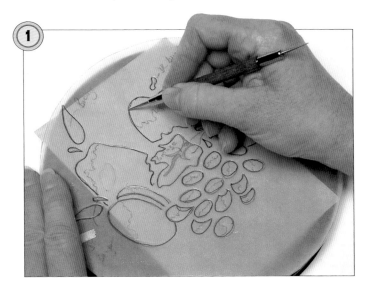

1 Trace the fruit on page 200 on to tracing paper and attach this to the side and lid of the tin with masking tape. Slide transfer paper underneath and transfer the design on to the tin using the stylus.

2 Paint the gold size sparingly into the smaller areas of the fruit marked off by the dotted lines. Leave for 5 minutes to "set". While you are waiting, clean the brush in white spirits.

3 Take the large, soft brush and dust bronze powder across the sized areas of the cherries on the side of the tin. Leave for about an hour and then dampen some cotton and wipe off the excess powder.

④ Now turn to the lid. Apply size as in Step 2. Using the large, soft brush, dust the antique bronze powder on the leaves and stalks. Do the same with the gold powder on the fruit. Leave for an hour and then dampen some cotton and wipe off the excess powder.

⑤ Using the No. 4 round brush, paint in the first washes of colour (50 per cent water, 50 per cent paint) on the fruit; pat the colour in roughly to make a textured finish. When dry, give a second coat, in the same way as you did the first.

⑥ Paint in the leaves and stalks on the border in normal, undiluted colours using Salem Green, English Yew Green and Leaf Green.

⑦ Take the No. 4 flat brush and paint a border around the lid with the Adobe Red. Varnish the tin when it is completely dry.

UMBRELLA STAND

A florist's vase gave me the idea for an umbrella stand. An immensely practical yet decorative item for any lobby area. The decorative bands are adapted from a design used on an antique New England tray.

You will need

◊ Container (primed and painted with khaki green basecoat)
◊ Tracing paper
◊ Transfer paper
◊ Masking tape
◊ Stylus
◊ Chalk and ruler
◊ Nos. 2 and 4 round artists' brushes
◊ No. 5/0 script artists' brush
◊ Palette or plate for paint
◊ Acrylic paints in Adobe Red, Straw, Leaf Green, Salem Green, Cayenne, Putty, Burnt Umber and Antique Gold
◊ Varnish
◊ Varnish brush

1 To position the band and keep it level, first measure with a ruler along the container to the required place and chalk in a line.

2 Trace the design (see page 198) on to tracing paper and then attach it to the container with masking tape, using the chalk line as your guide. Slide the transfer paper under the tracing paper and transfer the design with the stylus. At this point do not trace the details on the leaves or roses.

3 Using the No. 4 brush and the Putty acrylic, paint in the beige-colour commas.

4 Now take the script brush and the Cayenne paint to describe the border lines.

5 Paint in the leaves, using Leaf Green and a No. 4 brush.

6 Thoroughly rinse the No. 4 brush and, using the Adobe Red, paint in the daisies.

7 Complete the daisies by patting in the centres using the No. 2 brush and the Antique Gold.

8 The old yellow roses are base-coated in the Straw paint. Use a No. 4 brush.

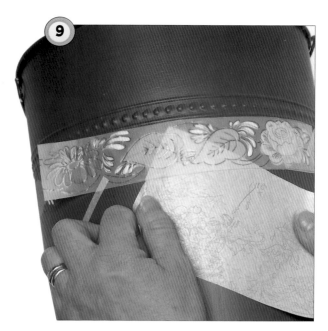

9 Take your traced design once more and reposition it over the painted areas. Slide the transfer paper underneath the design and transfer the details on to the leaves and the roses.

10 Finally, using the script brush, paint in the veins on the leaves with Salem Green and the details on the rose using Burnt Umber. When the container is completely dry, apply at least one coat of varnish.

LADLE

A nest of bluebirds in the bowl of the ladle, together with more birds and hearts decorating the handle, make this a simple but effective design for beginners to tackle. Finish the ladle with a flourish of colourful ribbons and hang it in the kitchen or family dining area.

You will need

◊ Ladle (primed and painted with cream-coloured basecoat)
◊ Tracing paper
◊ Transfer paper
◊ Masking tape
◊ Stylus
◊ Nos. 2 and 4 round artists' brushes
◊ Palette or plate for paint
◊ Acrylic paints in Antique White, Cerulean Blue, Bold Red, Yellow Oxide and Black
◊ Varnish
◊ Varnish brush

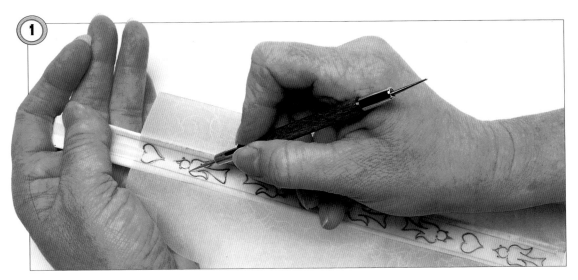

1 Transfer the three parts of the design (see page 200) on to tracing paper. Place the first part of the tracing on to the handle of the ladle using masking tape to hold it in position. Insert the transfer paper under the tracing paper and, using the stylus, copy the design on to the handle.

TIP

• Some skill is required with the paintbrush. Practise the brush strokes on a scrap of paper before you begin.

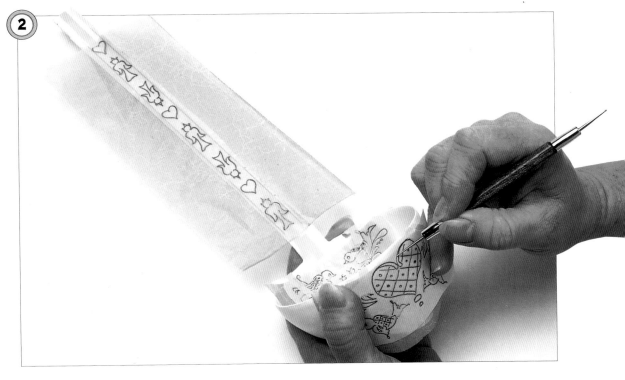

2 Transfer the other two parts of the design to the inside and outside of the bowl of the ladle, again using masking tape to hold the tracing in place and carefully sliding the transfer paper underneath the tracing paper.

3 Work on the handle using a No. 4 brush, and paint in the bluebirds in Cerulean Blue and the little hearts in Bold Red.

4 On the bowl, paint in the bluebirds in Cerulean Blue and the heart, nest and leaves in Bold Red.

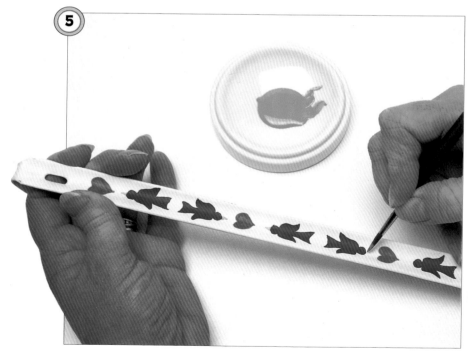

5 Acrylic paints dry very quickly, so you can now paint in the beaks of the bluebirds on both the handle and the bowl using a No. 2 brush and Yellow Oxide.

6 Mix a little Antique White with Cerulean Blue to make a pale blue and, using the No. 2 brush, paint in the lines on the wings of the bluebirds on the inside and the outside of the bowl.

7 Using the handle of the No. 2 brush, and the Bold Red paint, put in the dots on the heart and the nest.

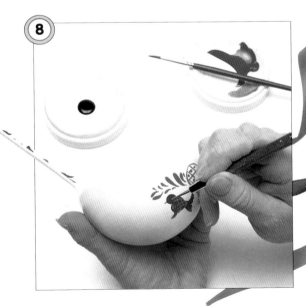

8 To complete the design, take the stylus and, using the pale blue, put in the dots on the bluebirds' wings. Clean the stylus, then with the black paint, dot in the eyes on all the bluebirds. Make sure the design is completely dry before applying a coat of varnish. Red ribbons add an attractive flourish.

FLAT IRON

Rescued from an old junk shop, this rusting flat iron was washed and scrubbed with a wire brush before being painted with rust inhibitor and then primed. The design is based on old-English, traditional barge painting, a naive style of strong brush strokes that can look most effective.

You will need
◊ Flat iron (primed and painted with black basecoat)
◊ Tracing paper
◊ Transfer paper
◊ Masking tape
◊ Stylus
◊ Nos. 2 and 4 round artists' brushes
◊ No. 6 flat artists' brush
◊ Palette or plate for paint
◊ Acrylic paints in Bright Green, Holly Green, Bright Red, Crimson, Antique White and Butter Yellow
◊ Varnish
◊ Varnish brush

1

1 Using Holly Green and the flat brush, paint the handle as indicated. Paint a green band on the base of the iron with the same brush.

2

2 Trace the three parts of the design for the handle, base and foot of the iron (see page 200) on to tracing paper. Using masking tape to hold the design in place, slide the transfer paper underneath the tracing paper. Trace the design on to the foot of the iron but do not trace any dotted lines at this stage.

3

3 Trace the leaves and daisies on to the handle and the scalloped border on to the base using the same method as described in step 2.

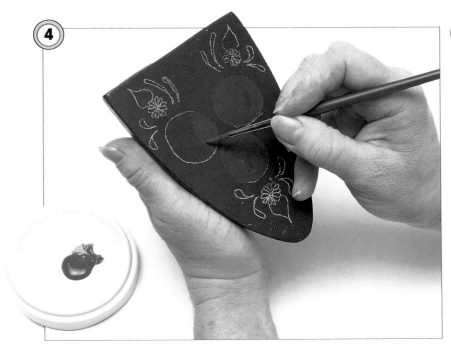

4 Turn the iron on its end and basecoat the roses using Crimson and a No. 4 brush. Leave to dry.

5 Replace the tracing and transfer papers to the foot of the iron and trace in the dotted lines on to the roses.

6 Using Bright Red and a No. 4 brush, paint in the rose petals with comma strokes. This will form the petals of the flower.

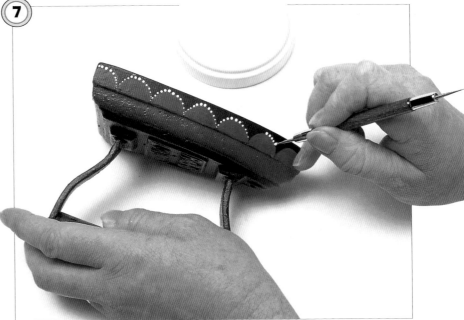

7 Paint the lower scalloped border on the base of the iron in Bright Red and, using the stylus, finish with an edging of white dots.

8 Work on the handle and foot of the iron, painting in green leaves with a No. 4 brush and Bright Green. Use a No. 2 brush, Antique White, and the comma stroke to paint in the daisies. Leave to dry.

9 For the decorative detail, take the Butter Yellow and apply with a No. 4 brush to add the comma strokes. Then use the No. 2 brush and the same yellow to put in the stamens on the roses. Use the stylus to add the centres of the daisies to the handle and the foot. Varnish when completely dry.

TEMPLATES

TIP

- These templates may be reduced or enlarged to suit the tinware item of your choice. Use a photocopier to increase or decrease the template by your chosen percentage. To increase these templates to the size used in this book, enlarge them by 64% (or from A4 to A3).

Watering Can

Umbrella Stand

Tin Trunk

Set of Pitchers

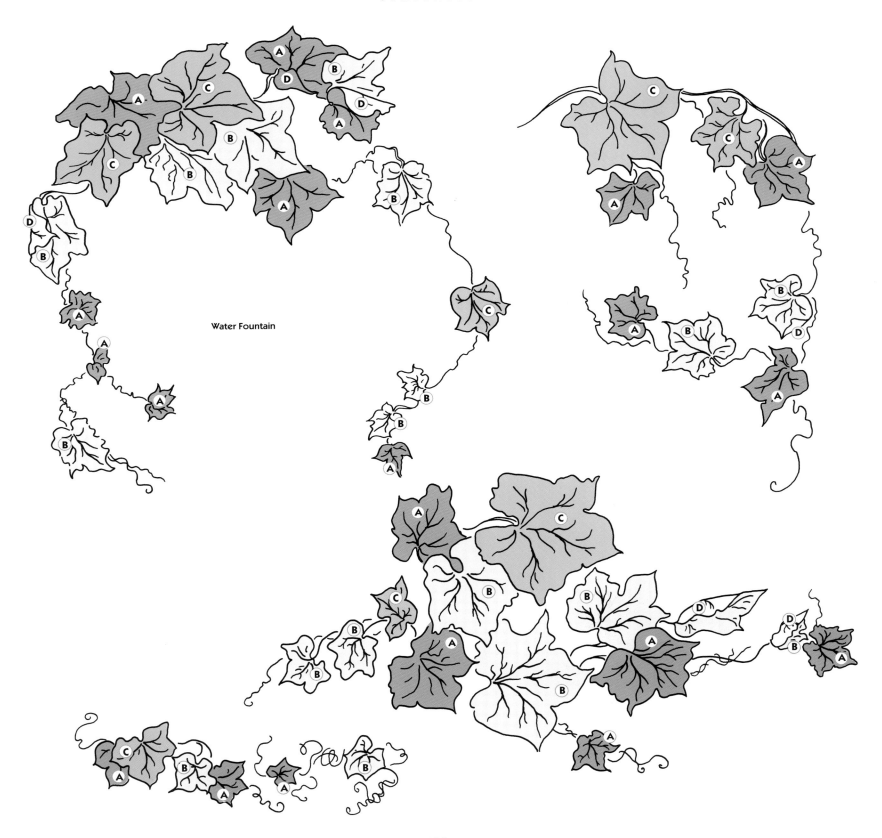

Water Fountain

Gilded Tray

Ladle

Box of Fruits

Flat Iron

Napkin Holder

Bead work

Create unusual and attractive jewellery using
an endlessly fascinating variety of beads

INTRODUCTION

There are those who believe that beads can become an obsession - if so, it is one I can happily recommend.
I have worked with beads on a full-time basis for nearly twenty years, and the pleasure I derive from their diversity and their history has increased over the years.

There are few crafts that offer such scope for creativity yet that require so few specialist tools
and that do not need a special workshop. All you need are a table, good light, a few tools and some carefully selected beads and findings, and with these you can design and make really exciting pieces of jewellery.
You can create something that will attract compliments every time it is worn – or even a piece that will become a family heirloom.

The projects are divided loosely between earrings, necklaces and bracelets, and within each overall group
the projects become progressively more difficult. You do not, however, need to begin at the beginning
and work through them. If you refer to the techniques section and the instructions for each piece you should be able to make any of them.

The projects use a wide range of techniques and materials in order to extend your skills and offer you opportunities to use your own creative talents. Even if the beads specified for each project are not available
from your local supplier, you should be able to use other, similar kinds. All the findings listed for each projec'
should be available in bead and most craft shops or by mail order.

Sizes and quantities are difficult to specify. If you are 1.6m (5ft 3in) tall and your friend is 1.7m (5ft 10in) tall,
you will not both want to wear the same length of necklace. The quantities specified will allow you to
lengthen the projects a little if necessary or to discard some of the smaller beads, if they become dropped or damaged, which will inevitably happen.

The important aspect of these projects is that you should use them to gain an understanding of the basic techniques and to learn how to use the different materials and then quickly begin to apply and adapt them to projects of your own.

If you do become obsessed with beads and want to know more about them, you will find several other
books that outline their history and that show some of the potential. You might also want to join a
local bead society so that you can share your ideas and experiences with fellow enthusiasts.
But that is for later.

Start with the projects and ideas here and remember, whatever happens, enjoy the beads you use.

MATERIALS AND TECHNIQUES

Before you start to make bead jewellery you need to learn a little about the beads that you can use. You also need to know about the tools, the findings – that is, the necklace fasteners and so on – and the different threads that are available. There is not a lot to learn, but understanding the basics will not only mean that your finished pieces look more professional but will also give you more scope for creativity.

BEADS

Beads are now easier to find and come in a wider range of materials than ever before. Most towns have a craft or haberdashery shop that sells beads, and some larger towns may even have specialist bead shops. You can also obtain a wide variety of beads by mail order, so you should easily be able to make the projects described in this book. Remember, too, that you can also use beads from old or broken necklaces, and, of course, one of the great advantages of bead jewellery is that if you are bored or dissatisfied with a piece, you can simply take it to pieces and use the components to make something quite different.

There are not many technical names for beads, but you should make a note of rocailles and bugles. Both are made of glass: rocailles are small and round, and they range in size from 11/0 (the tiniest) to 6/0 (the largest); bugles are small and tubular. They can usually be bought, by weight, in packets. Although they are often used in bead weaving, loom work and embroidery, they are useful in other designs. Most beads are sold by size, which is quoted in millimetres and which refers to the diameters, not the circumference, of the bead.

When you start to use beads you don't need to know much more about beads than whether you like the shape and colour, but as you become fascinated by them you will want to learn the names of the different kinds and understand the different materials. You will discover a world of Japanese lamp beads, Indian kiln glass beads, Ghanaian powder glass beads and many, many more. This book can introduce you to only a few of the dozens of kinds that are available.

When you buy beads in a shop, always check them for damage. Many beads are made quite roughly, so take care that the ones you are buying are perfect. Make sure that the holes are good and can be easily threaded and, of course, that the colours go well together.

FILE

SHARP SCISSORS

WIRE CUTTERS

ROUND-NOSED PLIERS

FLAT-NOSED PLIERS

TOOLS

You can do a lot with beads with only a few tools. The most essential tool is a pair of round-nosed pliers which you will use, among other things, for making loops for earrings. You need pliers with fairly short, fine points so that you can get close to your work. When you come to make necklaces and use crimps and calottes, you will need some flat-nosed pliers. Sprung round-nosed pliers are also available, and these are excellent for both earring and necklace making. Hold the pliers as shown in the photograph. If you work with beads a lot you should try out different kinds of pliers so that you know which kind you feel most comfortable with. In the projects round-nosed pliers have been specified when they are essential; otherwise the choice is yours.

You will need a pair of sharp scissors for most of the projects, and when you start to work with wire, you will need some wire cutters. The sprung wire (see page 207) responds better to heavier wire cutters, but you will be able to cut most wires with quite a light tool. When you work more extensively with wire – the Lapis and Silver Necklace on page 232, for example – you will need a file and a hammer. The file should be fine, and the hammer can be light. As you start to do knotting and beadwork you will need a selection of needles, and you will find a pair of fine-pointed, curved tweezers useful but not essential.

Finally, if you take up loom work you will need a loom. Although the metal looms are not as expensive as the wooden ones, they are not as easy to use. If you become enthusiastic about this technique it will be worth buying a wooden loom.

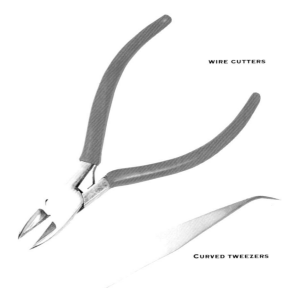

WIRE CUTTERS

CURVED TWEEZERS

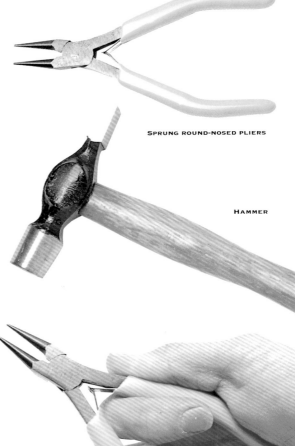

SPRUNG ROUND-NOSED PLIERS

HAMMER

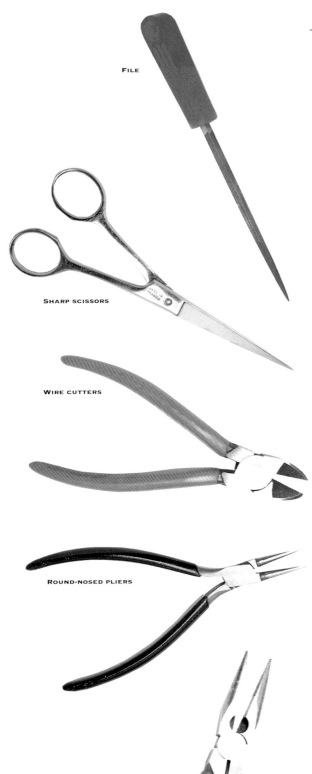

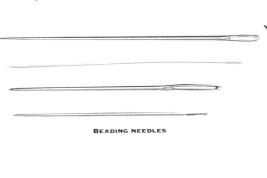

BEADING NEEDLES

HOLD THE PLIERS LIKE THIS

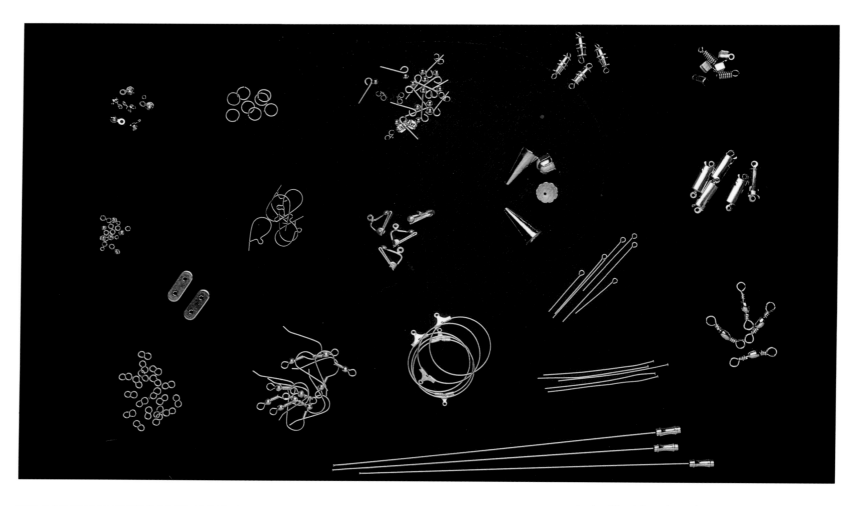

FINDINGS AND THREADS

This is an area in which you need to know some technical terms. All the findings mentioned here are available from many good craft stores, from specialist bead suppliers, and by mail order.

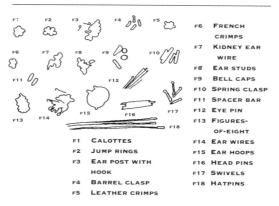

F1	CALOTTES
F2	JUMP RINGS
F3	EAR POST WITH HOOK
F4	BARREL CLASP
F5	LEATHER CRIMPS
F6	FRENCH CRIMPS
F7	KIDNEY EAR WIRE
F8	EAR STUDS
F9	BELL CAPS
F10	SPRING CLASP
F11	SPACER BAR
F12	EYE PIN
F13	FIGURES-OF-EIGHT
F14	EAR WIRES
F15	EAR HOOPS
F16	HEAD PINS
F17	SWIVELS
F18	HATPINS

MAKING EARRINGS

To make straight drop earrings, you will need to put the beads onto an eye pin or a head pin. Eye pins are more versatile than head pins because you can hang other beads from the loops and make longer earrings by adding two together. They are used with their own loop at the bottom of the earring to give a neat finish. If you have large, heavy beads, you can thread them onto 0.8mm or 1.2mm wire or you can use hat pin wires, but you need to clip the ends from the hat pin wires before you use them.

Hoop earrings can be made with 0.8mm wire, as shown on page 208, or from bought hoop findings.

If your ears are not pierced, you will need to use screws or clips, and it is now possible to obtain combined screw/clip findings. All of these are fitted in the same way that we have shown ear wires being fitted. For pierced ears, you will need ear wires, and most of the earrings in the projects in this book have been made with hook or French ear wires. You can, however, also use a post with hook findings, and these are held in place with scrolls or butterflies. Another possibility is kidney wires. You will know from the earrings you have bought and worn in the past which kind of fastening you find most comfortable.

Always buy nickel-free ear wires to avoid allergic reactions. The wires used in the projects shown here are available in sterling silver, and it is well worth the additional expense. Some people can only wear gold, and you can still follow the instructions by simply using gold-colored eye pins, balls and so on, and by buying a few pairs of gold ear wires. You will soon be so adept at making your own jewelry that you will quickly be able to swap the wires from earring to earring.

MAKING NECKLACES AND BRACELETS

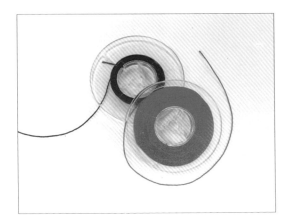

POLYESTER THREAD

When you make a necklace or bracelet you need to know about the different threads and findings that are available.

Simple necklaces and bracelets can be threaded on nylon monofilament, which is available from craft and bead shops and also from fishing equipment shops (you will need to ask for line with a breaking strain of about 6.75kg (15lb). This is best finished with French crimps because it doesn't knot well. Nylon line often shrinks eventually, which makes the necklace or bracelet rather rigid, so it is a good idea to leave about 5mm (¼in) between the last beads and the French crimps.

Tiger tail is nylon-covered steel cable, and it is, as you might expect, ideal for heavy beads. It does not

hang well with light beads, although it is suitable for short necklaces and bracelets. Use it with French crimps and take care that it does not kink as you work.

When you want a necklace that will hang beautifully or when you want to incorporate knotting (see page 225), use either polyester thread or silk thread. These can be finished with French crimps, calottes or knots. There are also some nylon threads on the market, but polyester or silk thread should meet most of your needs. Some colours of polyester thread are available in a waxed form, so you do not always need to use a needle. If you do decide to use this kind of thread with heavy beads, allow the threaded piece to hang for a few days before you finish it because the thread will stretch a little.

Silk thread is strong but delicate, and when you buy it on a card you will find a fine needle attached. The projects using silk thread have been planned to allow you to make the best possible use of your needles.

A fine, strong polyester thread is used with a beading loom.

You will also need a variety of fasteners, depending on the kind of thread you use, if you are sensitive to metals, buy clasps made of sterling silver or gold. The spring clasp, which is used in many of the projects in this book, is efficient and strong. More classic designs might call for screw clasps or bolt rings, which are used with jump rings. Multi-strand necklaces need cones or bell caps.

There are lots of other findings: little figures-of-eight for hanging; spacer bars with two, three or

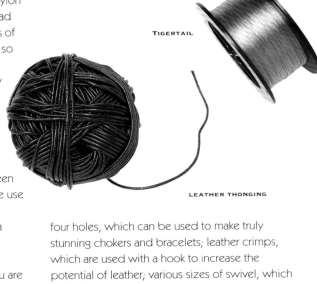

NYLON MONOFILAMENT

TIGERTAIL

LEATHER THONGING

four holes, which can be used to make truly stunning chokers and bracelets; leather crimps, which are used with a hook to increase the potential of leather; various sizes of swivel, which are fun for earrings or chains; and hatpins, which are self-explanatory, but you may have to ask for the clutch on the end separately.

There are also several thicknesses of silver wire, which will be available from the best suppliers. Leather thonging can be bought on a roll or by the metre (yard). Finally, sprung wire is a new idea, which can be bought by weight.

SILK THREAD

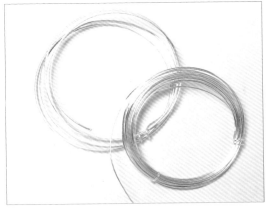

SILVER WIRES

SPRUNG WIRES

HOOP EARRINGS

You will need

◊ 0.8mm wire
◊ Black tubing (optional)
◊ 4 small glass beads
◊ 2 large glass beads
◊ 8 x 3mm silver plated balls
◊ 2 jump rings
◊ 2 ear wires

Other equipment

◊ Round former
◊ Wire cutters
◊ Round-nosed pliers

1 Form a loop around a round object, choosing a suitable size for the finished loop. We used a marker pen. Wind the wire around the former. Carefully slide the wire off the former and cut the loop so that the ends overlap by about 8mm (⅜in).

2 Roll one end of the wire around your pliers. Gently turn the loop so that it is at right angles to the hoop.

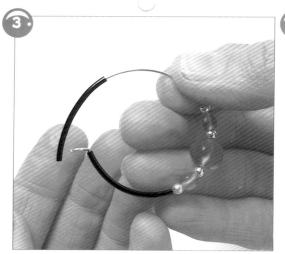

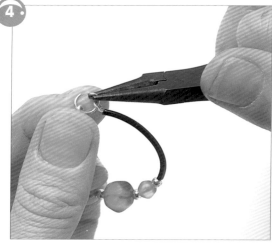

3 If you are using tubing cut it into four pieces to fit on either side of the beads; you will have to adjust the length of the tube to fit the size of the beads and the hoop. Thread on the beads. Add the second piece of tube and form another loop (see step 2).

4 Open a jump ring, slide it through the loop and close it.

5 Open the loop on an ear wire, hook it into the jump ring and close the loop.

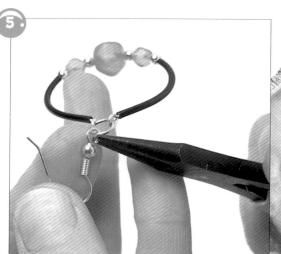

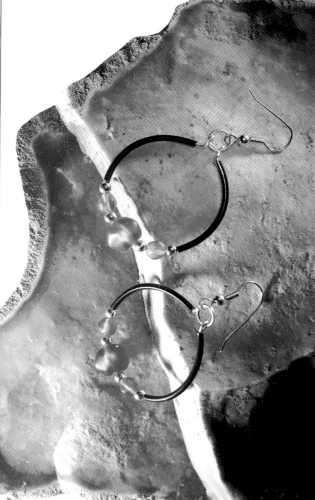

STRAIGHT EARRINGS

You will need
◊ 2 x 50mm (2in) eyepins
◊ 2 round Peruvian beads
◊ 2 Peruvian tube beads
◊ 6 x 3mm silver plate balls
◊ 2 ear wires

Other equipment
◊ Round-nosed pliers

1 Thread the beads on the eyepins, leaving a gap of about 8mm (⅜in) at the top of the pin. Rest the eyepin on your third finger and hold the beads firmly in place with your thumb and first finger. Hold the top of the eyepin with your pliers, which should be close to the beads, and bend the eyepin towards you at an angle of 45 degrees.

2 Begin to make a loop by moving the pliers to the top of the eyepin and rolling the wire of the eyepin away from you, around the top of the pliers. If you do not complete the loop in a single movement, take out the pliers, reposition them and roll the wire again.

3 Take one of the ear wires and open the loop sideways.

4 Put the ear wire through the loop of your earring and close it again.

TIPS

• Remember that your first few loops are almost certain to be untidy, so have some spare eyepins and wire cutters to hand so that you can cut the loop off the drop and try again with a new pin.
• Always open the loops on eyepins or ear wires sideways.
• If the metal of an eyepin or ear wire feels weak, reject it and use another one.

BASIC TECHNIQUES

KNOTTING

If you are using precious or fragile beads you should put a knot between each bead to protect them – if a knotted necklace breaks, you will lose only one bead. When you rethread an old knotted necklace, you will probably have to replace the knots so that your necklace does not become too short. You will need an additional 50 per cent more thread than the length of the finished necklace to make the knots. The Jasper Necklace on page 225 uses knots.

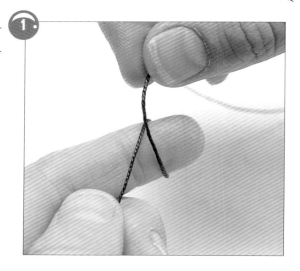

1 Start to make the knot around your finger.

2 Make it a double knot and pull the thread through both loops.

3 Before you tighten the knot, place the needle in the knot so that you can control it.

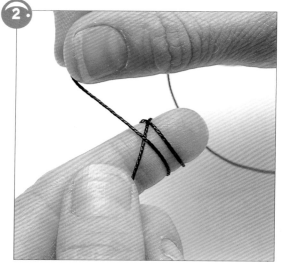

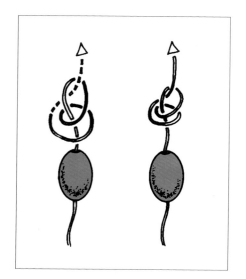

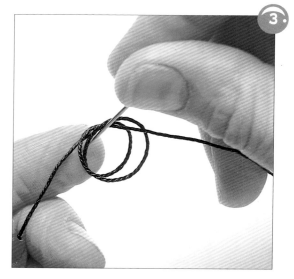

FROSTED NECKLACE

You will need
◊ Nylon monofilament or tiger tail
◊ 4 French crimps
◊ 1 fastener
◊ 8 x 18mm frosted pink beads
◊ 7 x 18mm frosted green beads
◊ 10 x 18mm frosted blue cones
◊ 6 x 15mm frosted blue cones
◊ 16 x 3mm silver plated balls

Other equipment
◊ Scissors
◊ Round- or flat-nosed pliers

4 Thread on the beads in your chosen pattern.

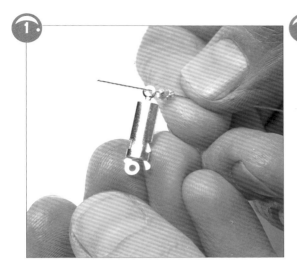

1 Cut a length of line about 55cm (21⅛in) long. Put two French crimps at one end of the line and thread through one end of the fastener.

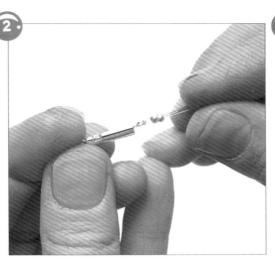

2 Bring the line back through the crimps and make a neat loop, which should be small and tidy but not too tight against the fastener.

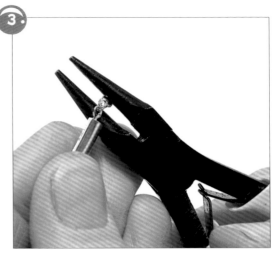

3 Squeeze the crimps with your pliers, making sure that they are tight but not so tight that they damage the line.

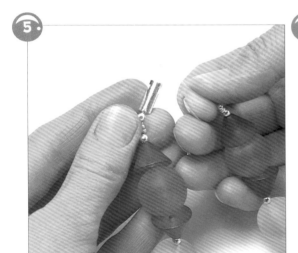

5 When you reach the other end, thread on the other two crimps. Thread the line through the fastener and loop it back through the crimps.

6 Squeeze the crimps firmly with your pliers and trim any loose ends with the scissors.

STARS AND MOONS

This delicate necklace and earring set uses crimps and gives an opportunity to practise your basic earring-making techniques and to do a little wirework.

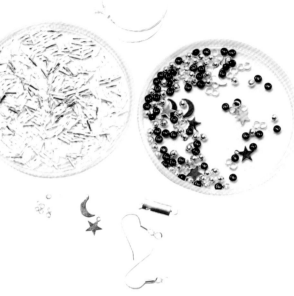

You will need

◊ 2 x 38mm (1½in) eyepins
◊ 4 x 25mm (1in) eyepins
◊ 7 stars
◊ 6 moons
◊ 30 small black glass beads
◊ 50 x 3mm silver plated balls
◊ 2 earring hoops of 0.8mm silver plated wire and jump rings or hoop findings
◊ 2 ear wires
◊ 70 silver plated 6mm Heishi tubing
◊ French crimps
◊ Fastener
◊ 7 figure-of-eight findings
◊ Tiger tail

Other equipment

◊ Round- or flat-nosed pliers
◊ Wire cutters
◊ Scissors

TIP

• Have some spare eyepins close to hand in case you overwork the metal as you open and close the loops. You will be able to feel with your pliers if the metal becomes weak.

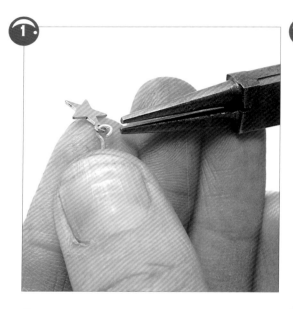

1 Beginning with the earrings, use your pliers to open the loops in the eyepins sideways. Put on the stars and moons, arranging them on the three eyepins as you wish. Carefully close the loops.

2 Thread the silver balls and black beads on the eyepins and roll the top by bending the top 8mm (⅜in) of the pin towards you to an angle of about 45 degrees. Move your pliers to the top and roll the wire around your pliers, away from you. If the loop is not quite closed, use your pliers to adjust it until there is no gap.

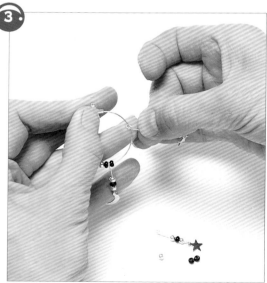

3 If you are using a ready-made hoop finding check that one side is firmly closed and open the other side, which will slide out from the hanger at the top of the hoop. Thread the beads and eyepins on to the hoop, beginning with a silver ball and a black bead. Remember that the loops in the tops of the eyepins should face in the same direction and there should be a black bead between each one.

4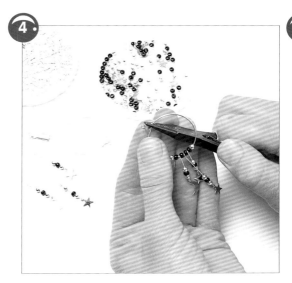

4 Slide the end of the hoop back into the hanger and use your pliers to press the metal of the hanger together to trap the end of the hoop. You will need to press quite hard to secure the hoop firmly.

5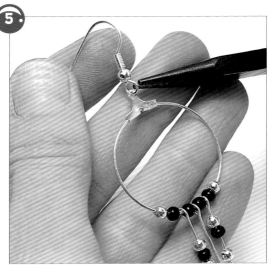

5 Use your pliers to open the loop on the ear wire sideways. Insert it in the top of the hanger and close the ear wire, making sure that the point of the ear wire and rough side of the hanger face in the same direction.

6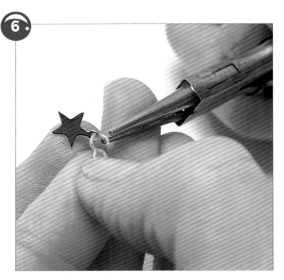

6 Begin the necklace by attaching the moon and stars to the figure-of-eight findings so that they hang flat. Open one loop of the figure-of-eight sideways, put on a moon or a star and close the loop again with pliers.

7 Cut a piece of tiger tail to the length you want your necklace, adding an extra 2cm (about ¾in) at each end for the crimping. Put two crimps on one end of the tiger tail, taking care not to kink the tiger tail as you work. Thread the tiger tail through the fastener and back through the crimps. Squeeze the crimps tightly with the base of round-nosed pliers or with the tip of flat-nosed pliers. Begin to thread on the silver tubing and work to the centre of the design. Thread on the stars and moons on their findings. When you have finished the central pattern, finish off with silver tubing to match the first half.

8 Check that the pattern is symmetrical, then put on two more crimps and thread the tiger tail through the other end of the fastener. Take the tiger tail back through the crimps, check the spacing to make sure that the beads are not too tight but that there are no gaps. Squeeze the crimps and trim off the loose ends.

7

8

TIP

- If you cannot obtain hoop findings, make a hoop as shown in the techniques section (page 208).

VENETIAN-STYLE GLASS NECKLACE

This dramatic necklace and glamorous matching hatpin are made from lovely Indian beads, which are made in the same way as old Venetian beads, and Thai silver beads. These are simple pieces to make but will give you some ideas for designs of your own.

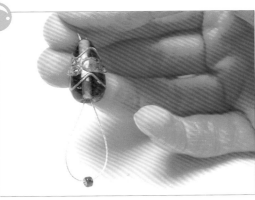

You will need

◊ Tiger tail
◊ 40 tiny blue beads size 7/0
◊ 12 ornate drop beads
◊ 8 ornate round beads
◊ 4 small Thai silver beads
◊ 1 large Thai silver bead
◊ 50 x 5mm blue glass beads
◊ 50 x 6mm turquoise beads
◊ French crimps
◊ Fastener
◊ Hatpin with clutch

Other equipment

◊ Scissors
◊ Round- or flat-nosed pliers
◊ Clear, all-purpose adhesive

TIP

• Cut a good length of tiger tail but take care that it does not kink as you work.

1 Cut a length of tiger tail, allowing an extra 3cm (1¼in) at each end. Thread on a tiny blue bead and slide it to the centre of the tiger tail. With both ends together, thread on a drop bead. Still using two threads together, thread the hanging group of beads, ending with the large Thai silver bead.

2 Separate the two threads and work on one side at a time. Thread on a tiny blue bead and continue as follows: turquoise round bead, tiny blue bead, ornate drop, 5mm blue, turquoise round bead, 5mm blue, ornate round, 5mm blue, turquoise round bead, 5mm blue bead, ornate drop (upside down), tiny blue bead, turquoise round bead, tiny blue bead, small Thai silver bead.

3 This pattern is used one and a half times on each side of the necklace. Take care to push the beads down towards the centre as you thread them on. Make sure that both sides are symmetrical.

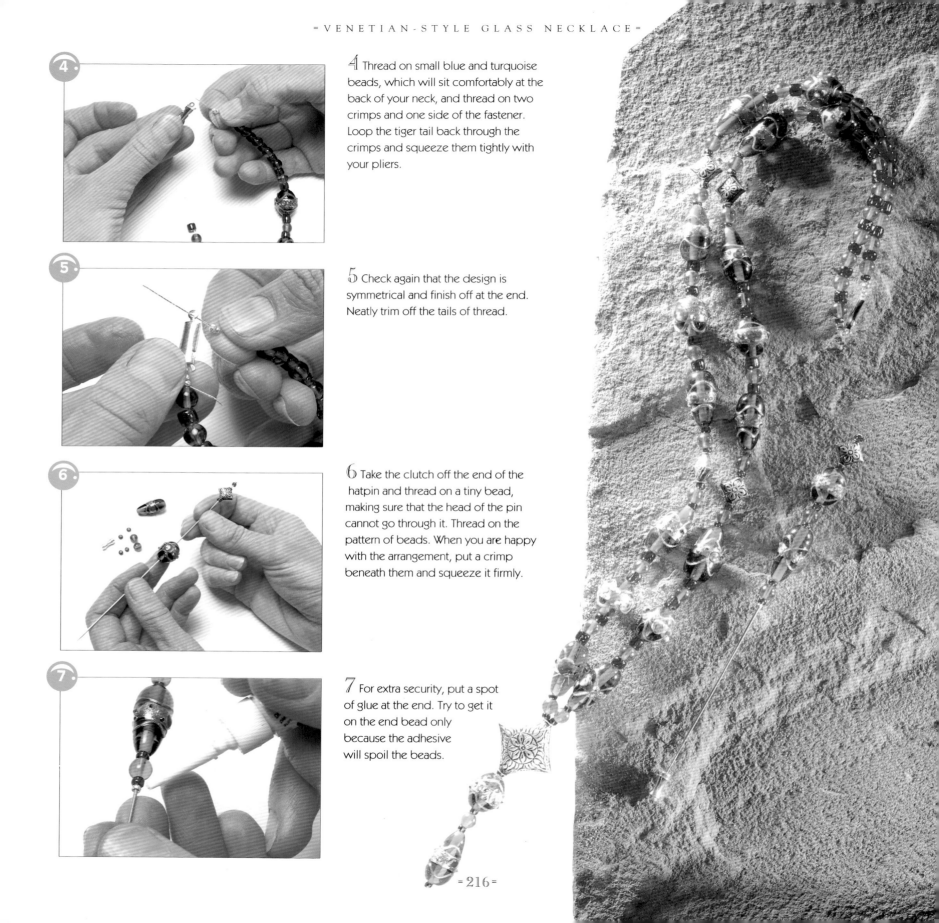

4 Thread on small blue and turquoise beads, which will sit comfortably at the back of your neck, and thread on two crimps and one side of the fastener. Loop the tiger tail back through the crimps and squeeze them tightly with your pliers.

5 Check again that the design is symmetrical and finish off at the end. Neatly trim off the tails of thread.

6 Take the clutch off the end of the hatpin and thread on a tiny bead, making sure that the head of the pin cannot go through it. Thread on the pattern of beads. When you are happy with the arrangement, put a crimp beneath them and squeeze it firmly.

7 For extra security, put a spot of glue at the end. Try to get it on the end bead only because the adhesive will spoil the beads.

A CHAIN OF FISHES

Ceramic fish and painted fish beads from Peru swim along on a chain of swivels. Simple earring-making techniques have been built up to make this chain and matching earrings.

1 Start with a fish bead, an eyepin and some tiny beads and balls. Thread on the main bead with the small beads on either side. Roll the top of the eyepin by bending the wire towards you until it is at an angle of 45 degrees. Move the pliers to the top and roll the wire around the pliers to make a neat loop.

2 Carefully open the loop to the side, insert a swivel and close the loop.

You will need
◊ 6 fish beads
◊ 25 x 50mm (2in) eyepins
◊ 70 tiny grey beads, size 8/0
◊ 70 x 3mm silver plated balls
◊ 17 x 18mm (¾in) swivels
◊ 8 striped ceramic beads
◊ 4 ceramic fish
◊ 2 ear wires
◊ Fastener or extra swivel

Other equipment
◊ Round-nosed pliers

> **TIP**
>
> • If any of the eyepins feel weak, reject them and use a new one.

3 Add another eyepin to the swivel by opening the bottom loop of the eyepin and hooking it through the swivel. Close the loop neatly.

4 Thread a striped bead onto the eyepin with some small beads on either side and roll the top.

5 Continue to build up the chain in the same way, working alternately at each side of the first fish bead to make sure the design is symmetrical.

6 The chain is long enough to go over your head, but if you want to use a fastener, add it instead to one of the swivels between one of the fish bead and striped bead sections. Hook it between two loops in the same way as the other pieces.

7 Make the earrings in the same way as the chain, using a painted fish bead and a swivel. Open the loops of the ear wires and hang the swivels from them. Close the ear wires neatly.

CHINA BLUE NECKLACE

———◦———

This project demonstrates how very simple techniques can produce very sumptuous results. By threading a variety of Chinese porcelain beads and different glass beads and by using basic crimping techniques, you can make a really stunning necklace.

You will need

◊ Black or blue polyester thread
◊ 10 round Chinese beads
◊ 1 triangle bead
◊ 10 oblong Chinese beads
◊ 16 enamelled bead caps
◊ 8 x 8mm round beads
◊ 80 blue glass beads
◊ 100 green frosted beads
◊ 200 small black beads
◊ 20 French crimps
◊ 2 cones
◊ Fastener

Other equipment

◊ Scissors
◊ Round- or flat-nosed pliers

TIP

• Stand in front of a mirror and hold the strands in front of you so that you can check your choice of beads in the reflection.

1 Cut four lengths of thread, each about 50cm (20in) long, and lay them out. Thread beads on to each one at the same time, working to achieve a pleasing balance among the different strands. Aim to have the smaller beads towards the outside of the pattern and leave about 8cm (3¼in) of thread at each side of all the threads. The enamelled bead caps should be threaded either side of the plain 8mm round beads to give the extra richness.

2 When you are happy with the pattern of the strands, hold each strand carefully at each end to check that it hangs well. Take this opportunity to reposition any beads that do not look right. At this stage you should still have some of each of the beads left.

3 Make a small loop at one end of a strand, slide a crimp on it and squeeze the crimp with your pliers. Move the beads towards this end, make a loop, add a crimp at the other end and squeeze the crimp. Repeat with the other strands and trim off all loose ends.

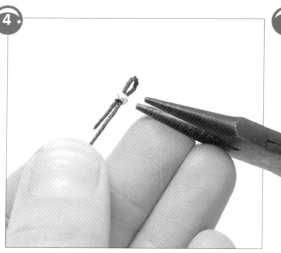

4 Cut two more lengths of thread, each about 20cm (8in) long, and make a loop at one end of each.

5 Take the short pieces of thread through the loops at the end of the beaded strands. Pass the threads back into their own end loops.

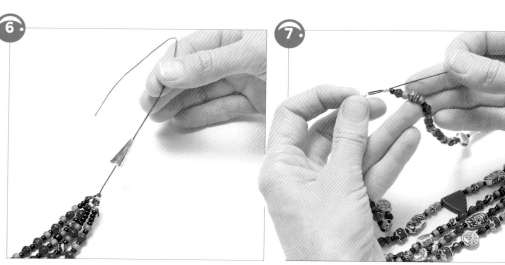

6 Thread a cone onto each short piece so that the ends of the beaded strands are neatly hidden.

7 Thread beads onto the two short ends; you can make these symmetrical or work a slightly random pattern. When you are happy with the length of the necklace, put two crimps on one end of one of the threads and take the end through a loop in the fastener and then back through the crimps.

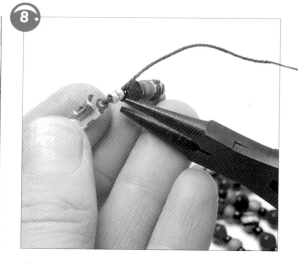

8 Squeeze the crimps with your pliers and check that they are tight. Repeat this at the other side with the other end of the fastener before trimming off all loose ends.

CLAY AND TILE BEAD NECKLACE

This necklace is more complicated to make, but if you work through the steps carefully,
you will make a lovely thick cluster of rope and tassels.

1 Cut four lengths of thread, each about 80cm (32in) long, and thread 10 white tiles and 11 small brown beads alternately on the centre of each. Thread two of these into each side of the clay ring so that four lengths emerge from both sides.

2 Put these four threads through a large clay bead on either side of the central ring.

3 Working on one side, thread on five white tiles and six small brown beads alternately on each of the threads and put all four threads through a clay disc.

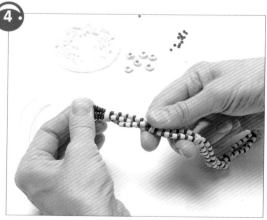

4 Work four more sections and push all the beads back towards the central ring. Pick up five small brown beads on each thread and push them back.

You will need
◊ White polyester thread
◊ 300 white tile beads
◊ 400 tiny brown beads
◊ 1 clay ring
◊ 2 large round clay beads
◊ 10 clay discs
◊ French crimps
◊ Wire
◊ 2 bell caps
◊ Fastener

Other equipment
◊ Glue
◊ Round- or flat-nosed pliers
◊ Wire cutters
◊ Clear, all-purpose adhesive

5 Make a small, neat loop at the end of each thread and put a crimp on it. When the loops are neat and even on each thread, squeeze the crimps.

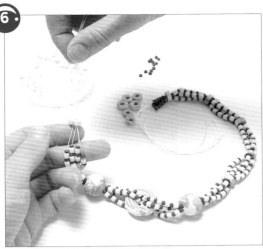

6 Repeat the pattern on the other side, making the patterns symmetrical and pushing the beads back towards the centre before crimping the loops at the ends of each thread.

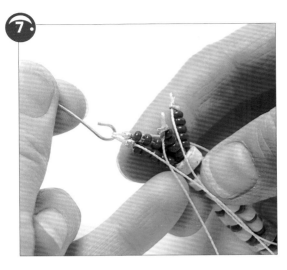

7 Use wire cutters to cut a small length of wire. Roll the wire around the round-nosed pliers to make a loop. Put the loops on the ends of the threads through this and close it neatly.

8 Trim all the ends of thread.

9 Put the bell cap on the wire. Clip the wire, leaving just sufficient to make a neat loop.

10 Make the loop with your pliers, open it sideways to hook on the fastener and close the loop neatly. Repeat to match at the other side.

11 Cut three pieces of thread, each about 18cm (7in) long, and make a firm knot at one end of each length, adding a spot of adhesive to the knot. Leave the glue to dry and thread on some small brown beads and white tile beads. You can make the threads the same or slightly different lengths if you prefer.

12 As each short length is half-threaded, work it through the clay ring, then add the beads to the other end of the thread.

13 Make a knot at the loose end of each length, placing a needle in the knot so that you can slide it back towards the beads. Make sure the beads are close together but not so tight that they are rigid. When you are happy with the knot, put a spot of adhesive on the knot, avoiding the beads if possible, and trim the ends of the tassels.

JASPER NECKLACE

These chunky semi-precious beads are knotted onto thick thread to create an ethnic look.
Making this necklace will allow you to master the knotting technique that can be used with
different kinds of beads to give different effects.

1 Cut a length of thread that is almost double the length that you want the necklace to be. You need extra thread to knot between the beads, plus some extra for knotting near the fastener. Make a single knot about 10cm (4in) from one end and place your needle through it. Tighten the knot but leave the needle in place.

2 Put the fastener on, tying it with a single knot about 2cm (¾in) from the first knot.

3 Make a series of neat single knots to fill the gap between the two original knots. Make a loop around the main thread, bring the short end through and tighten it.

You will need
◊ Polyester thread, silk or similar thread
◊ About 20 20mm jasper beads
◊ Fastener

Other equipment
◊ Scissors
◊ Needle
◊ Clear, all-purpose adhesive
◊ Curved, fine-pointed tweezers (optional)

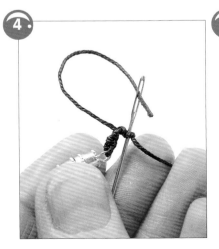

4 When you reach the first knot and needle, thread the short end through the needle and draw it through the original knot. This will make the end secure.

5 Thread on the first bead. If you can, push the short end through it to neaten the end. If you cannot, trim the short end and put a spot of adhesive on the short end to hold it. Wait until the adhesive is dry before pushing the bead against the knot.

6 Make a double knot after the bead when it is in place and put the point of a needle into the knot. Use the needle to guide the knot, pulling the thread gently and carefully so that the knot lies close to the bead. Pull the thread as you remove the needle so that the knot continues to tighten against the bead.

7 Keep on adding beads, making a double knot between each one. You are certain to make some knots that do not lie as neatly against the beads as you would like, but you can unpick the knots with fine tweezers, although you must take care not to damage the thread.

8 When the necklace is the correct length, make a simple knot close to the last bead and leave a needle through it. Take the end of the thread through the fastener, again leaving a gap of about 2cm (¾in). Make single knots next to the fastener to match the first side.

9 Take the short end through the needle and draw it through the knot that is next to the last bead. When the knots are neat and tight, take the short end of thread through the last bead if you can. Alternatively, cut it neatly and add a spot of adhesive, taking care not to get glue on the beads.

AFRICAN CHOKER

This choker uses powder glass beads from Ghana and old Czech beads, which were made mainly for the African market. The project involves a macramé technique, which is an attractive and useful way to use threads to finish necklaces and chokers.

1 Cut the thread in five lengths, four about 1m (3ft 3in) long and one 50cm (20in) long. Use the four longer threads to make the central patterns.

You will need
◊ 31 powder glass beads
◊ 120 brown Czech beads
◊ 2 four-hole spacer bars
◊ 4.5m (15ft) black polyester thread

Other equipment
◊ Scissors
◊ Needle
◊ Clear, all-purpose adhesive

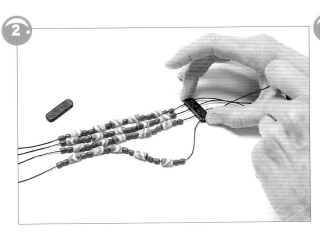

2 Thread a spacer bar on each side, then continue to pick up the beads on the four threads in pattern.

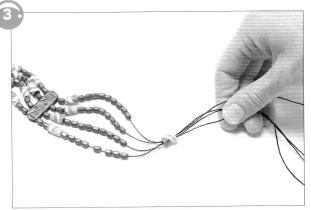

3 Use all the beads but one, which is used as a fastener, and finish off by working the four threads through a powder glass bead at each end. Loosely knot one side and trim the ends level but do not cut them short.

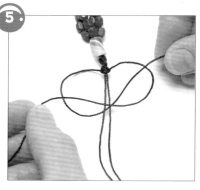

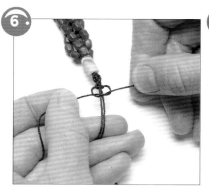

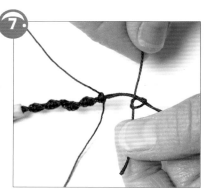

4 Make a macramé braid with the lengths of thread by keeping two threads straight in the centre and by bringing the left-hand thread under these centre threads and over the right-hand thread.

5 Take the right-hand thread over the centre threads and under the original left-hand thread.

6 Pull the ends evenly from both sides and, at the same time, pull down the centre threads to create a firm, even braid. Continue to braid the threads in this way until the choker is about 3cm (1¼in) shorter than the length you want.

7 Attach the short length of thread cut in step 1 to the centre threads.

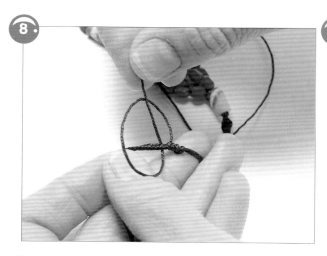

8 Use the thread to bind the centre threads to form a button loop. Take the thread over the centre threads, bring it back through its own loop and pull tightly. Continue until you have bound 2cm (¾in) of the centre threads.

9 Form the bound length into a loop and arrange all the loose ends so that they lie towards the choker. There should be a gap between the button loop and the macramé work. Return to the macramé threads and continue to work over all the loose ends by the original braiding method (steps 4, 5 and 6). Pull the threads tight as you work towards the button loop to keep the braid even and secure.

10 Check that the powder glass bead will go sideways through the loop, and pull the braid tight. Trim all loose ends close to the braid.

11 Thread the macramé ends on a needle and weave them into the braid to finish securely.

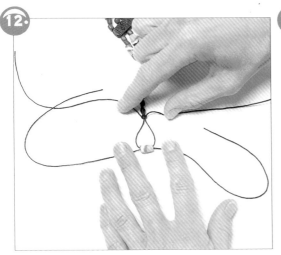

12 Undo the loose knot at the other end and push all the beads towards the other end before you start to make a braid. Use the macramé technique with the four lengths of thread, stopping about 2cm (¾in) from the finished length. Pick up the powder glass bead by threading the two central threads through the bead from opposite sides.

13 Turn these ends back towards the choker and continue with the macramé technique working firmly over these ends. When you reach the powder glass bead, pull the threads tightly together.

14 Finish off in the same way as at the other end, trimming the loose ends neatly and running the working threads back through the braid with a needle.

SPECIAL BEADS AND LEATHER

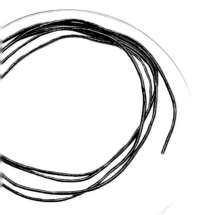

This is a good way of using "collectable" beads – some beads you might have picked up when you were on holiday abroad, for example, or from an antique shop or bead fair. If you cannot find beads exactly like the ones listed here, look out for something similar.

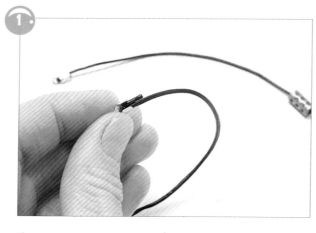

1 Arrange the beads on a length of thonging. Fold one end, and put the leather in a leather crimp. If you are using fairly thick leather, you will not need to fold it.

2 Use pliers to press down one side of the crimp. Then press down the other side over the first so that the leather is held firmly in the crimp.

3 If you cannot buy a hook for the crimps, make one by cutting about 3cm (1¼in) of wire.

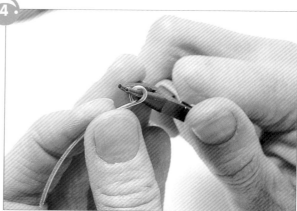

4 Hold the end of the wire with your pliers and use your thumb and first finger to roll the wire into a small loop.

You will need
◊ 1 Pumtek bead from Mizoram
◊ 2 Venetian millefiori beads
◊ 2 old Turkish beads
◊ 2 brass beads from Mali
◊ 6 Indian matt glass beads
◊ Leather thonging
◊ Leather crimps
◊ 1.2mm silver plated wire

Other equipment
◊ Round-nosed pliers
◊ Wire cutters
◊ File

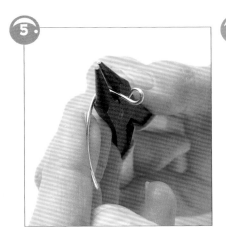

5 Use the curve in the wire and bend it around the wider part of the pliers.

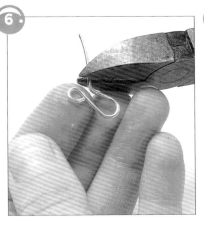

6 When you have made a neat hook, bend the point a little and clip the remaining wire with wire cutters.

7 File the end smooth.

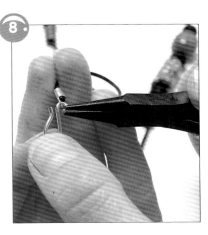

8 Open the loop on the hook sideways and insert one of the leather crimps. Close the loop. The hook will go through the leather crimp on the other end when you wear the necklace.

LAPIS AND SILVER NECKLACE

This is a stylized, somewhat abstract piece, which will develop your wire working skills and encourage you to use more tools.

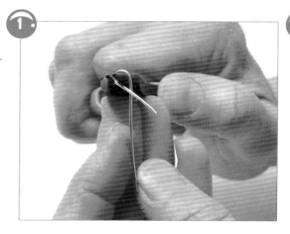

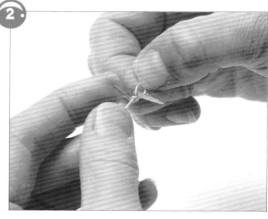

You will need

◊ 6 coral glass beads
◊ 6 black glass beads
◊ 6 old silver beads
◊ 1 antique spotted bead
◊ 1 large lapis bead
◊ 4 lapis shapes
◊ 0.8mm silver plated wire
◊ 1.2mm silver plated wire
◊ Leather thonging
◊ Leather crimps

Other equipment

◊ Round-nosed pliers
◊ Wire cutters
◊ File
◊ Hammer

1 Wire the lapis shapes so that they will hang from the necklace. Some of the shapes that are available have holes running from top to bottom, and if you have this kind, cut a piece of 0.8mm wire and make a loop with a long end.

2 Use your fingers to wrap this end around the bottom of the loop.

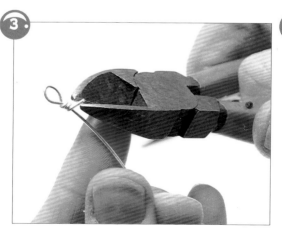

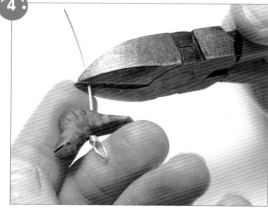

3 Make some neat coils beneath the loop, clip the end of the wire and use pliers to flatten the end of the wire under the bottom of the coils.

4 Pick up the lapis, trim the wire and use pliers to make a neat loop under the shape to hold it securely.

TIP

• Practise bending the wire and try hammering pieces on different surfaces before you start work on this project.

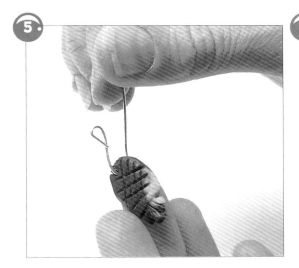

5 If the lapis shapes you have are those with a hole running from side to side, make a loop in the wire and thread it through the shape, curving the wire as you do so. Leave a gap between the loop and the lapis shape.

6 Use your finger and thumb to bend the wire firmly around the base of the loop a few times. Clip off the end of the wire and use pliers to flatten it under the coils.

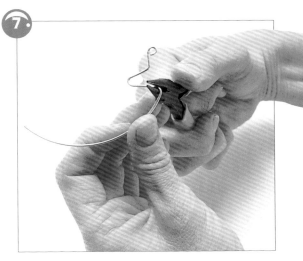

7 Make the abstract wire pieces from pieces of thicker gauge wire about 20cm (8in) long. Roll the bottom end of the wire then form it into interesting shapes by curving it from side to side against your pliers.

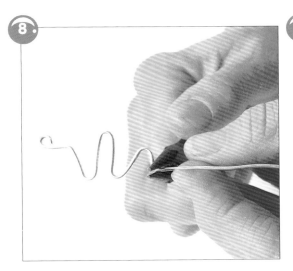

8 Continue to work until you are happy with the zigzag shape. You will need three of these shapes in all, but they need not be identical.

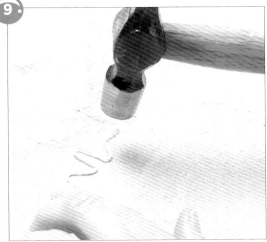

9 To make the necklace even more interesting, you can hammer the silver wire flat. This roughens the surface and allows you to glimpse the brass beneath the silver plating.

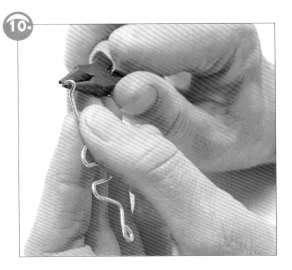

10 Roll the tops of the finished zigzag shapes so that they can be threaded.

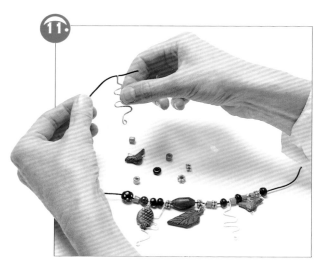

11 Thread the pieces onto the leather. These pieces look most effective if the arrangement is asymmetric.

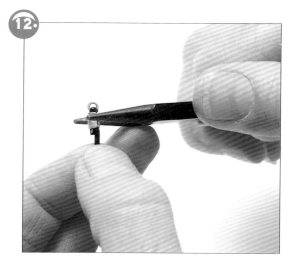

12 Put leather crimps on the ends and make a hook to fasten the necklace as described in steps 3–8 of the previous project.

LOOM-MADE BRACELET

This is an easy project to work on a beading loom. When you have mastered this bracelet you will be ready to try some more ambitious pieces.

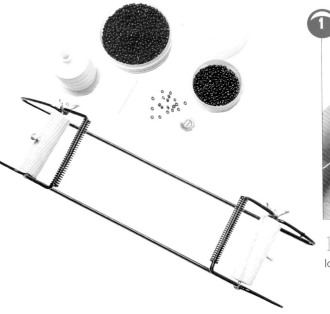

You will need
◊ 160 white rocailles, size 8/0
◊ 60 black rocailles, size 8/0
◊ 30 blue rocailles, size 8/0
◊ White polyester loom thread
◊ Button

Other equipment
◊ Loom
◊ Scissors

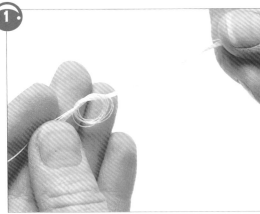

1 Cut seven warp threads, each 80cm (about 32in) long, and knot them together at one end.

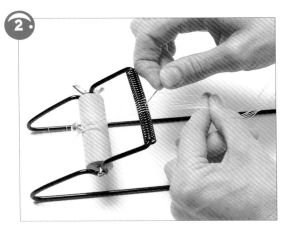

2 Tighten the bars on the loom, then hook the warp threads on one end of it and bring them over the bar. Use a needle to separate the threads until they lie side by side in the grooves of the loom.

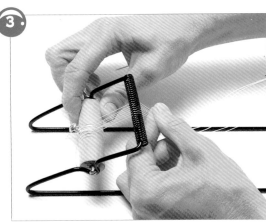

3 Turn the roller a few times to make sure that the warp threads are taut.

4 Take the threads down the loom and separate them over the opposite grooves at the other end. Secure the warp threads around this roller, keeping the threads as taut as you can.

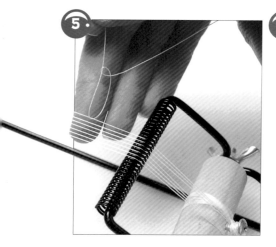

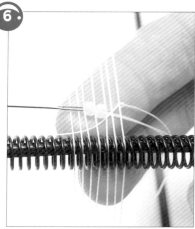

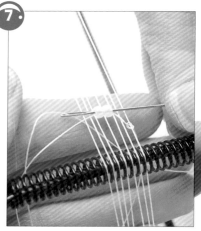

5 Cut a beading thread about 1.5m (5ft) long and tie it to an outside warp thread. Thread it on a needle.

6 Keeping the beading thread below the warp threads, position two rocailles in the centre two spaces. Bring up your needle before the two outside warp threads.

7 Thread the needle back through the two rocailles, working over the warp threads. Repeat this step with two beads four more times and then take the beading thread down between the first and second warp threads. Use four rocailles for two rows.

8 Start to work over the full width of the warp threads so that six rocailles fit into the spaces. Work the pattern with black and blue rocailles.

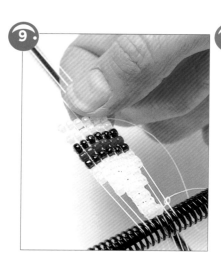

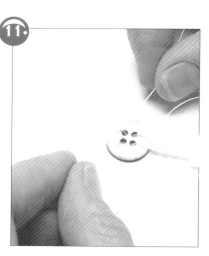

9 As you work along the loom, keep moving the rocailles back against the previous row to keep the work firm.

10 When you have completed the pattern and reduced the number of rocailles at the other end of the bracelet, loosen the rollers at both ends and take the bracelet off the loom.

11 Put the button on one end by threading four of the warp threads through the buttonholes, knotting them neatly behind and working the warp threads back into the bracelet.

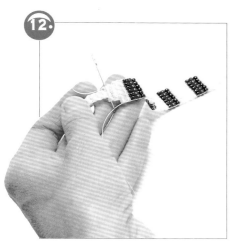

12 Work the other warp threads at this end back into the rocailles and trim them neatly once they are securely finished off.

13 At the other end, use a needle to thread about eight additional rocailles (depending on the size of the button) onto each of the centre two warp threads.

14 Work each thread back down the opposite row of rocailles to form a loop with the two threads running through it in opposite directions. Tighten the threads and use a needle to weave the ends back into the bracelet. Finish this end by weaving the warp threads back into the bracelet and trimming off the loose ends once they are securely finished off.

SPRUNG WIRE BRACELET

This and the following project illustrate two different ideas for bracelets.

Sprung wire is easy to use, but you do need strong hands.

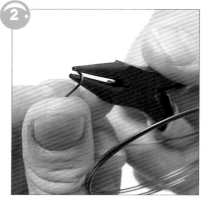

1 You can sometimes buy cut lengths of sprung wire or you can cut the necessary amount from a longer roll. You will need to press hard to do this.

2 Use pliers to roll a loop at one end. This is quite hard to do, and you should keep moving your wire and making little turns while you hold the wire with your other hand.

3 Thread on the beads. The pattern can be random, but distribute the larger beads evenly among the smaller ones. You will need to unroll the wire from time to time so that the beads can slide down.

You will need
◊ 3 loops of sprung wire, approximately 60cm (24in)
◊ 6 small Peruvian beads
◊ 33 frosted green beads
◊ 15 turquoise and green round glass beads
◊ 65 tiny black glass beads

Other equipment
◊ Wire cutters
◊ Strong round-nosed pliers

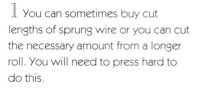

4 Leave about 1cm (⅜in) at the end of the wire and roll the end with your pliers.

Stencilling

Use this versatile craft to decorate a whole range of objects
from a simple gift tag to reviving an old piece of furniture

Introduction

Welcome to the joys of stencilling!

Stencilling will take you on a simple, step-by-step guided tour of 11 imaginative projects, and by the time you reach the end of this section you will have experienced the wonderful and creative world of stencilling and all it offers.

A stencil is simply a design shape cut out of a piece of wax card, thin metal or plastic film. When paint is applied through the cut-out, the shape is reproduced on the surface below.

Stencilling is not a modern craft. It has been used for centuries as a means of decorating fabrics, books, pottery and of course, the home itself. Early examples can still be seen in homes and museums all over the world, especially in the USA. When expensive European wallpapers were imported to the USA in the 19th century, most people could not afford to buy them. The designs provided stencil artists with new inspiration, and the art of stencilling meant that the effects of the wallpaper could be imitated at a fraction of the cost of the real thing.

Eventually, mass-production meant that even the expensive wallpapers were within the reach of most people, and stencilling lost its popularity. However, in recent years, as people have looked for new ways to bring individuality to their homes, stencilling has come back into fashion.

The projects in this book explore the versatility of the craft. They range from a very simple yet effective gift tag, through more complicated items to the challenge of designing your own stencil. The projects have been planned to allow you to develop your knowledge and skills of stencilling in a gradual way, so that when you have mastered one technique you will have the confidence to move on to more creative, demanding things. Each project includes extra ideas to inspire you and helpful tips to enable you to produce professional-looking stencils.

The materials you will need can usually be found at your local art shop or do-it-yourself store, and you can also buy a wide variety of ready-made stencils. If you want to make your own stencils, see Designer's Delight (see page 270), which covers designing and cutting. A selection of our designs can be found in the pattern library at the back of the book.

So, let's go! All you have to do is gather your tools and materials together, follow the projects in this book, and you can take part in the revival of this appealing and rewarding craft.

Happy stencilling!

Jamie Sapsford and Betsy Skinner
The Bermuda Collection

Materials and Equipment

PAINTING KIT
You will need some or all of these materials:

Ready-made Stencils
There is a wide choice available, but do consider the size, shape and intricacy of a design when you are deciding what would be most appropriate for a particular project.

Stencil Brushes
Thick bristled brushes are used to apply paint through the stencil, and they are available in a variety of sizes. A good range to start would be sizes 4, 8, 12 and 16.

Low-tack Masking Tape
You must make sure that the stencil lies flat in place for painting, and low-tack tape reduces the risk of damaging your work surface, such as a wall. Spray adhesive is an alternative for fixing your stencil temporarily in place.

Stencil Paints
Artist's acrylics can be applied to most surfaces. Fabric paints should be used for fabrics, and special paints are available for use on ceramics and glass. Use fast-drying paints to avoid smudging problems during layering. Water-based paints are easier to clean up.

Bowls
Old, small china bowls are useful for mixing colours, and they are easy to clean.

Paper Kitchen Towel
This is essential for general cleaning up and for removing excess paint from your brush.

Scrap Paper
Have plenty of scrap paper handy so that you can practise.

Ruler
Always have a ruler for measuring and placing your stencils.

RIGHT
Painting materials.

Scissors

Apart from trimming some of the papery projects, you will need a pair of scissors for dozens of other uses.

Pencil, Sharpener and Rubber Eraser

Finally, make sure your pencil is sharp so that you always cut along a clean line.

> After every project, clean up when you have finished and wash out your brushes and stencils made of polyester with soap and warm water.

CUTTING KIT

Polyester Drafting Film

This is excellent material for making your own stencils. The frosted transparent film is easy to draw on and perfect for lining up extra layers. It is also hard wearing and can be used repeatedly. Thick, waxed paper is an alternative.

Cutting Knife

You will need a scalpel knife with extra blades to cut your own stencil designs because a very sharp blade is necessary. A blade set at an angle is ideal for cutting arcs and circles.

Cutting Mat

A "self-healing" mat, obtainable from most artist's materials suppliers, is best for cutting out your stencil designs because it will not disintegrate or blunt your blade as quickly as a cutting board would.

Tracing Paper and Graph Paper

You will find that both of these items are extremely useful for copying and reproducing balanced designs.

Now that you have all the materials and equipment you will need, let's start with the first project.

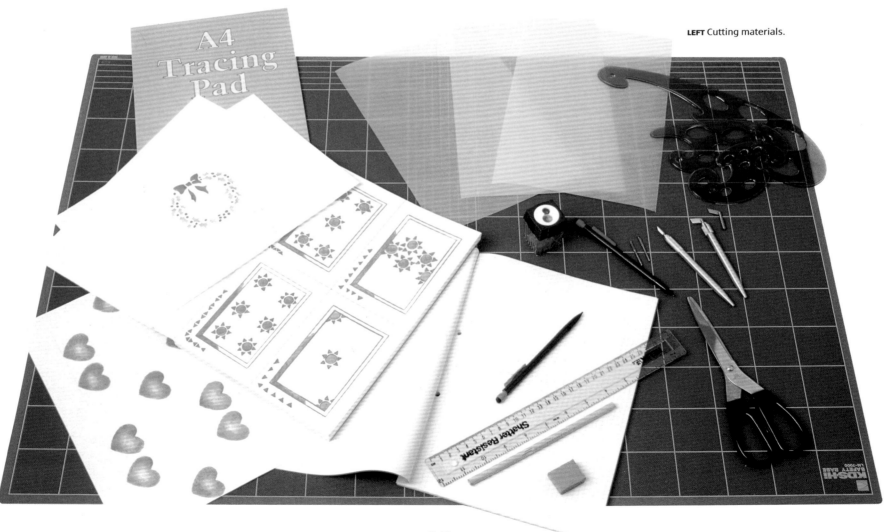

LEFT Cutting materials.

Fun Gift Tag

This is a great project to introduce you to the art of stencilling because it is simple yet effective. Enhance your gifts with a specially stencilled gift tag and delight everyone.

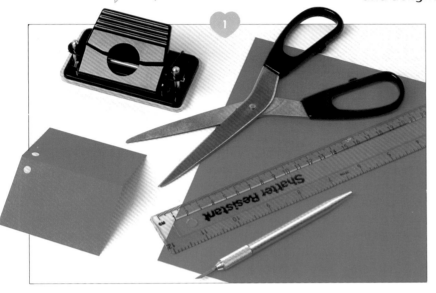

You will need
◊ Painting kit with acrylics
◊ Pad of coloured paper
◊ Hole punch
◊ Curling ribbon

1 We have chosen to stencil a white heart on red paper. Choose an appropriate stencil and paper colour. Measure and cut your paper to approximately 3 × 4in/7.5 × 10cm, and fold it in half along the 2in/5cm line. Decide whether your tag will be horizontal or vertical and punch a hole in the top left-hand corner, leaving enough room for your design.

2 For our practice session we chose to stencil a red heart onto white scrap paper. Put a small amount of paint into a bowl. Dip the bristles of a medium sized brush into the paint and rub off any excess paint on kitchen towel. Your brush should be very dry.

3 Place your stencil design over your scrap paper and hold it with one hand. Hold your stencil brush upright and press it through the stencil cut-out, moving it in a circular motion around the inside edge of the stencil. Continue to build up the colour by moving the brush around the edges. You can do this quite quickly. Try approximately 10 turns but do not let the colour build up in the middle of the cut-out.

4 Practise, practise, practise! If your brush is too wet with paint it may result in a flat, filled-in stencil shape that bleeds around the edges; see the top heart. The brush really does need to be very dry — drier than you would imagine — although the very faint heart has taken this

to the extreme. The heart at the bottom of the photograph, with the shaded edges and light area in the middle, is perfect.

5 Once you are confident with your practice session you can apply exactly the same principle to your pre-cut tag. Use a clean, dry brush. Choose your paint colour and put a little into a clean, dry bowl. Dip the brush in the paint and wipe off the excess. Position the stencil over the tag, hold both firmly in place and build up the colour in a circular motion around the edge of the cut-out.

HANDY HINTS
When you are cutting out your tag, placing your cutting knife along the edge of a ruler offers a more accurate line than cutting with scissors. Use a metal ruler and hold the ruler and paper firmly in place, taking care to keep your fingers out of the way!

Finally, twirl a good length of ribbon and feed it through the hole. Just look at the wonderful gift tags you can easily make yourself. If you want to impress your friends by stencilling the wrapping paper to match too, read on!

All Wrapped Up

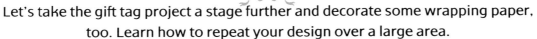

Let's take the gift tag project a stage further and decorate some wrapping paper, too. Learn how to repeat your design over a large area.

You will need
◊ Painting kit with acrylics
◊ 1 large sheet of coloured paper

1 We chose to use the same tag stencil as the previous project to make some matching wrapping paper. First, plot some evenly spaced points on a few sheets of scrap paper. Now try some different design layouts.

2 Put some paint in a clean bowl. Dip a clean brush in the paint and wipe off the excess on some kitchen towel. Position your stencil where you want to start on the scrap paper and hold both down firmly. Move your upright brush in a circular motion around the inside edges of the stencil.

3 There are endless ways of building up your own layouts with any stencil. Move the stencil along the grid to see. Try stencilling several different layouts before you decide which you prefer.

4 Sometimes simplest is best. This design is easy to plot, and you don't have to remember to skip any gaps.

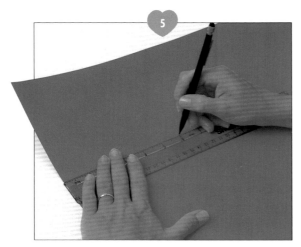

6 Position the stencil on the grid. Trace the points of the paper grid on to the stencil using a pencil or permanent ink. This will make it easy for you to position the stencil every time by simply matching the dots so that your alignment will always be perfect.

7 Now stencil your wrapping paper. Get a fresh bowl, brush, paint, and kitchen towel. Place your stencil on the paper and match up the alignment points of the stencil and paper. Hold the stencil and paper firmly and begin.

8 Continue stencilling the whole sheet, remembering to line up the stencil points and paper grid. Compare the stencilled images with each other so that they are roughly the same intensity, but don't try to match them perfectly because their differences add to the appeal of this craft.

The finished wrapping paper with its own matching tag from the first project. A beautiful job, well done!

5 Having chosen your layout, plot the same grid on the real paper. Use very light pencil dots — dark enough for you to be able to use them as a guide to line up your stencil, but not so dark that they detract from your creative efforts.

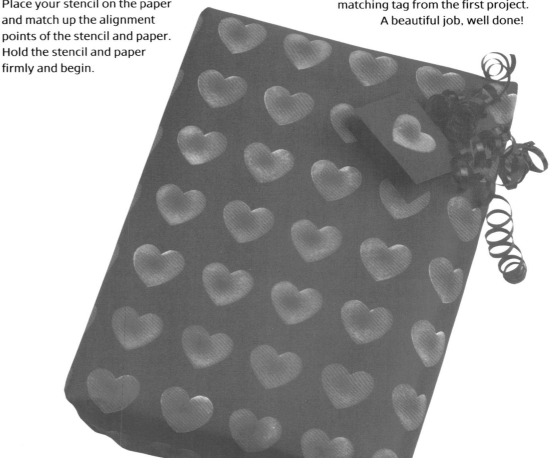

HANDY HINTS

◊ Do not worry if your stencil images do not fit perfectly within the edges of the paper — when you wrap your gift you may end up cutting off some of the design.

Great Greetings Cards

You can make greetings cards to suit any occasion, but we chose a Christmas card. This project shows you how to use two colours in your design as well as being able to produce several cards at once.

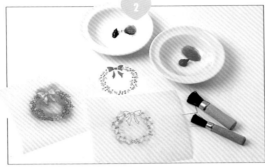

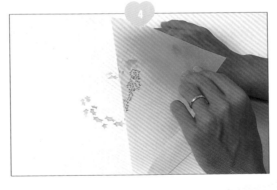

You will need
◊ Painting kit with acrylics
◊ Set of matching cards and envelopes

1 Have at least five plain cards with matching envelopes ready. Make sure that your chosen stencil design is a suitable size for your cards.

2 A two-part stencil gives you an opportunity to use two colours within different parts of the design. Our wreath stencil has separated the green leaves from the red bow and berries. Have ready two bowls, two brushes, two different colours, some kitchen towel and pieces of scrap paper.

3 Try out your first stencil on scrap paper. On a good two-part stencil the first image is cut out and the second image, intact, is drawn in with dotted lines. These dotted lines indicate the rest of the design and are invaluable when you come to line up your second image correctly. Move your brush confidently around the cut-out several times in one direction.

4 Hold the first stencil in place and lift off one corner to peek at your efforts so far. If the image is not strong enough replace the stencil and continue to build up the colour.

5 Now take your second bowl, brush, colour and stencil. Lay the second stencil over the first image. The wreath now shows the bow and berries cut out. The leaves are intact and shown as dotted lines, allowing easy alignment. Stencil your second image.

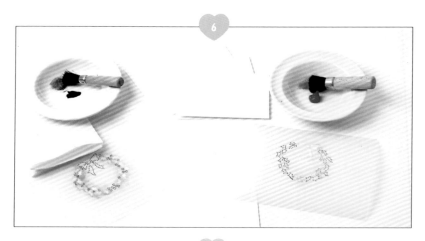

6 Once you are happy with your practice efforts, have everything to hand to stencil your set of five matching cards.

7 Place your stencil in the appropriate position on the card and hold both firmly. Stencil all five cards in succession with your first image and first colour. Remember to peek at your progress.

8 Carefully position your second image, using the dotted lines for alignment. Hold it down securely to stop it moving.

9 Stencil all five cards with the second image in the second colour. Remember to move your brush in a circular motion in one direction.

You could add a detail of the design to the envelopes for a wonderful finishing touch. Congratulations! You have just completed a production line of hand-decorated cards.

HANDY HINTS
◊ Always use a clean, dry brush for each colour.
◊ Transparent stencils make it easy to line up two or more colours.
◊ You may find a ruler helpful if you cannot easily position your stencil by eye.
◊ When you have very small cut-outs do not try to stencil the edges of each one. You will achieve effective results by simply moving the brush over the cut-outs repeatedly but in only one direction.

Magical Mirror

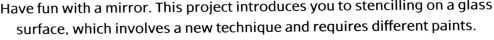

Have fun with a mirror. This project introduces you to stencilling on a glass surface, which involves a new technique and requires different paints.

You will need
◊ Painting kit with ceramic paints
◊ Mirror to decorate
◊ Practice mirror

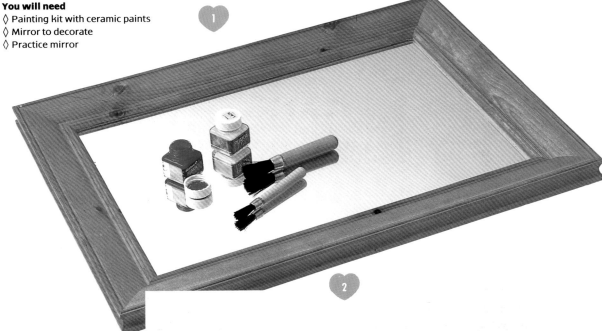

1 Consider the size and shape of your mirror and choose a stencil design accordingly.

2 Practise some design layouts on scrap paper. Note, too, that our shell design has been given some red shading to give it more definition. You will see how to achieve both a highlighting technique (light paint on dark) and a shading technique (dark on light) later on in this project.

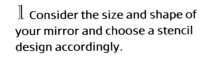

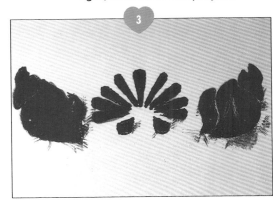

3 Practise your stencilling technique on a spare mirror. Glass is not absorbent, so take care not to use too much paint, or it will smudge.

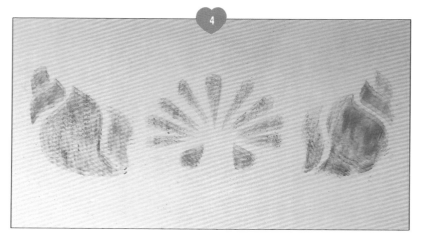

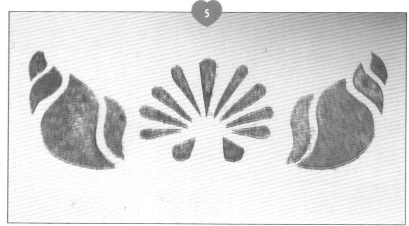

4 Do not use too little paint either. Here the outline of the image is barely distinguishable.

5 This is what you need to aim for. The combination of the properties of this type of paint and this slippery surface means you will need to use more paint and allow it to build up.

6 Now practise stencilling with your first colour.

7 Choose a lighter second colour for the highlighting technique. Hold the brush upright and use an up-and-down motion to stipple your brush into the middle of the cut-out. For the real mirror we use the shading technique.

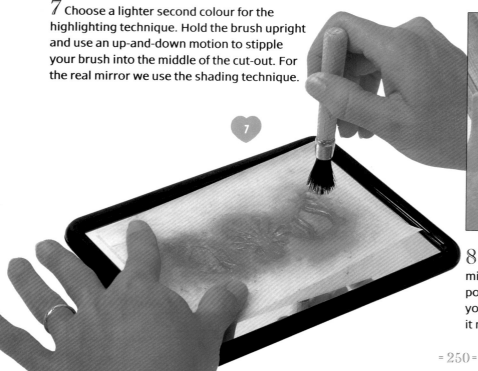

8 When you are ready to move on to the real mirror offer up your stencil to judge the best position. Use your sketches for inspiration. Fix your stencil in place with masking tape to stop it moving about on the slippery surface.

9 Continue your layout with the first colour.

10 For the shaded technique use a darker colour and stipple the edges of the cut-outs with an up and down motion.

A plain mirror has been transformed into a highly individual and decorative piece.

HANDY HINTS
◊ If you need to section off part of your design use masking tape as shown on pages 267—269, or simply hold some spare pieces of paper in place.
◊ Check the drying times of your ceramic paint on the manufacturer's instructions.

Merry Mugs

Stencilled mugs will brighten any kitchen and they also make great gifts. In this project we made a set of three.

You will need
◊ Painting kit with ceramic paints
◊ 3 matching mugs in a plain colour

1 Decide on a design that will suit the shape and size of your mugs. We chose stars.

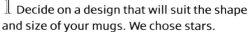

2 Experiment with colours on a scrap piece of coloured paper. Silver and gold are ideal for stars, and they work well on a blue background.

3 Holding your stencil with masking tape on the curved surface will make stencilling easier.

4 Stencil your first image in the usual way. You may need to stipple the edges to deepen the colour on this dark, non-absorbent surface.

7 As a finishing touch, spatter some silver paint over the mugs. Put more paint on your brush, then pull back the bristles so that they are a little way from the mug and let them flick onto the mug so that small flecks of paint are deposited on the mugs — and everywhere else too! Before you do this, protect anything you do not wish to spatter, including the insides of the mug.

8 Finish off the other mugs also using the spattering technique. It works especially well with the star stencil design, giving the impression of distant galaxies!

Here is your new set of mugs. Treat a friend or yourself!

5 Continue to apply the first image to all three mugs. By the time you have stencilled the third mug, the first mug should be dry enough for you to apply the next image.

6 We have chosen smaller silver stars for the next image. Use a freer and less regimented approach here and build up the small stars into an attractive pattern.

HANDY HINTS
Personalize a mug with a stencilled name to make the perfect gift.

Pots of Gardener's Delight

Stenciling is a wonderful way of transforming plain terracotta flowerpots into a gardener's dream.

You will need
◊ Painting kit with ceramic paints
◊ Any number and size of terracotta pots

1 Select your stencil design according to the size and shape of the pots. You might like to coordinate the colors of the stencil with the plants that are to go into them.

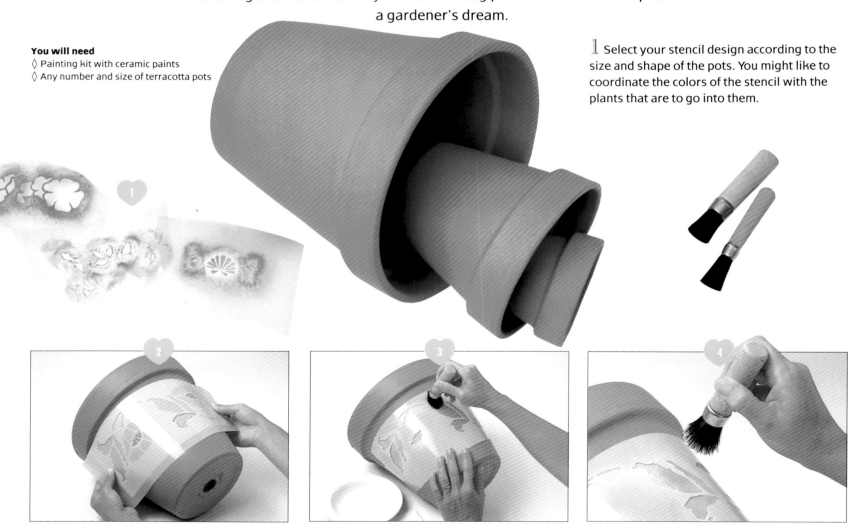

2 Calculate the position of the image by trying out the stencil on the pot. You may need to stretch or squeeze in a repeat pattern.

3 Use masking tape to secure the stencil to the pot, then stencil on your first color.

4 Stipple the design to add depth before moving the stencil along to continue the first color.

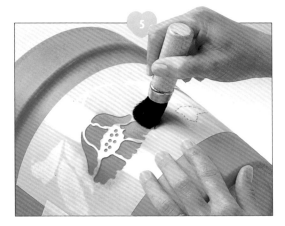

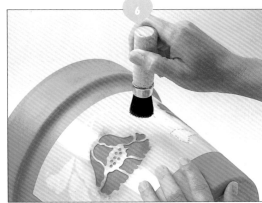

7 The finished design on a large pot shows the effect achieved by the stippling technique.

8 Just look at what you can do. Rather than continuing the design around this pot, we felt that it would work better as a central feature.

A selection of different sized pots and designs.

5 Align your second stencil and apply your second colour.

6 Use the stippling technique again to deepen the edges of the design. Move the stencil around the pot to complete your design.

HANDY HINTS
◊ You may find your stencil more manageable if you trim it to follow the curve of the pot.
◊ This porous surface may require more paint than usual to build up the colour.

Friendly Floor Covering

Let's move your stencilling talents to the floor. A scatter rug can be decorated to suit any room, and this is a good introduction to working on a larger scale. Remember to apply a varnish to protect the design against inevitable foot traffic.

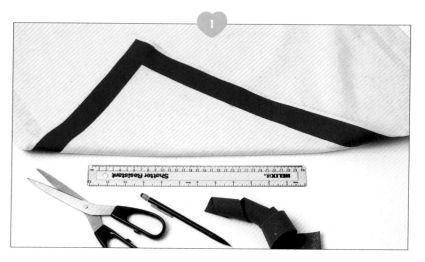

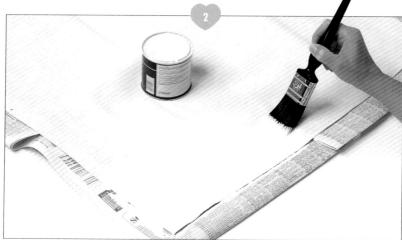

You will need
◊ Painting kit with acrylic paints
◊ Decorator's heavy twill dust sheet or canvas
◊ Iron-on hemming tape or sewing machine
◊ Small tin of matt emulsion paint
◊ Small tin of varnish
◊ Decorator's paint brush

1 Measure and cut your fabric to a manageable size – ours is 2 × 3ft/60 × 90cm. Fold down and seal your edges with hemming tape or use a sewing machine to turn down a hem.

2 Apply a coat of matt emulsion paint to the rug to seal the fabric. Leave to dry. Wash out your brush.

3 Choose a stencil and sketch some possible layouts on scrap paper, remembering to allow for a border line. There are so many ways you can build up designs with your stencil.

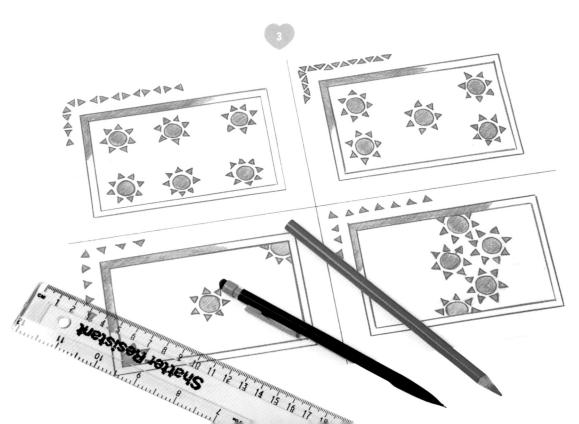

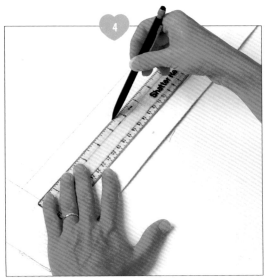

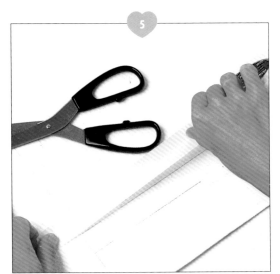

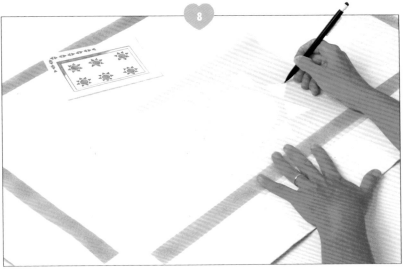

4 Once the paint is dry, measure and mark the border line on your rug. We have marked our pencil lines approximately 2½in/7cm and 4in/10cm from the edge.

5 Apply the masking tape to the pencil lines, leaving a 1½in/3cm gap between.

6 Allow the masking tape to overlap at the corners to create an interesting break in the border.

7 Use a large brush to stencil the 1¼in/3cm gap all around the rug.

8 Remove the masking tape to reveal your border. Refer to your sketches for inspiration and offer up your stencil design to calculate the best spacing. Mark key points.

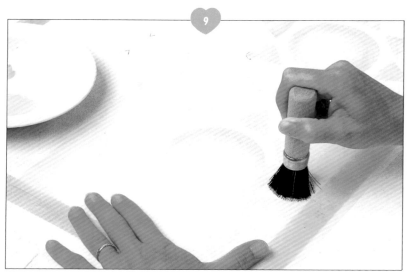

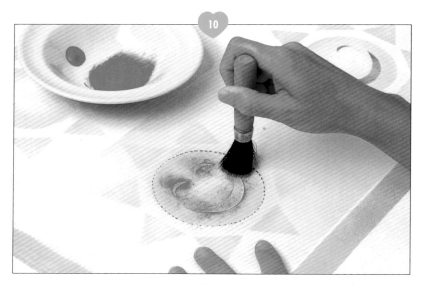

9 Use your key points to place the stencil and apply your first image over the whole rug. Hold or tape your stencil in place.

10 Line up and apply the second image and continue over the whole rug.

11 On the other side of your border line build up another border with a detail from the stencil. We cut two triangles as a separate stencil for ease of application.

12 Once all the yellow triangles are complete, flip over the stencil and place some upside-down triangles in the design using another colour.

13 Apply at least two coats of varnish to the whole rug.

A truly friendly floor covering to brighten any room!

HANDY HINTS
◊ Choose a background emulsion colour that will suit the room in which you will place the rug.
◊ When you apply the emulsion and varnish, place some newspaper under the rug to protect your work surface.

Child's Cheerful Chair

This is your first attempt at decorating a piece of furniture. A plain child's stool can be made to look extra special with a stencilled seat and is certain to be a hit!

You will need
◊ Painting kit with acrylics
◊ A new, wooden child's stool, untreated (i.e. not varnished or waxed)
◊ Pair of compasses
◊ Fine-grade sandpaper
◊ Tin of polishing wax

1 Select an appropriate stencil design and a suitable colour scheme. Give the stool a light rub down with fine sandpaper.

2 We decided to stencil our floral design in a circular layout. Start by drawing your circle with the compass on rough paper. Placing an edge of your image on the pencil mark and following the line of the circle will enable you to calculate how close the repeats should be to complete the circle.

3 Apply your first colour. Because you are being creative with this approach, you will be unable to rely on your stencil for the exact spacing of the images, so line them up by eye as well.

4 Apply your second colour, following the line of the circle. Again you will need to line up the stencil by eye as you work around the circumference.

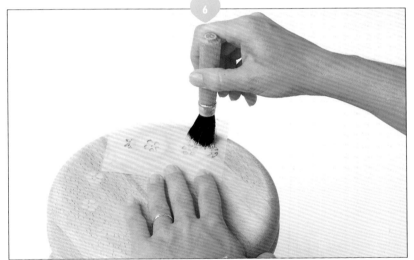

5 Use your compass to mark a light circle on the seat of the stool. Allow enough room between the line and the edge of the stool for your design.

6 Roughly calculate the position of the design and apply your first colour, following the line of the circle.

7 When you have completed the circle with the first colour apply your second image and second colour.

8 Add any finishing touches to suit the piece.

9 Seal your design by applying a coat of wax polish. Buff it up to obtain a deep lustre.

This chair will cheer up any child's day!

HANDY HINTS
◊ When you are working out how to place your design, it may be helpful to mark key points. You must continue to check the placement as you work.
◊ Remember that these small designs need a lot of paint to build up the colour.

A New Lease of Life

You can give any old piece of furniture a new lease of life by adding a stencilled decoration. Resurrect something from your attic and bring it back into your home. We have given an old school desk a pretty, rustic feel.

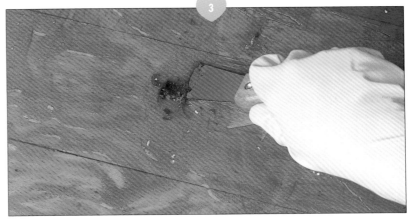

You will need
◊ Painting kit with acrylics
◊ Paint and varnish stripper
◊ Fine-grade sandpaper
◊ Small tin of emulsion paint
◊ Old piece of furniture
◊ Small tin of varnish

1 Almost any old piece of furniture can be used as long as it is in good repair and is well prepared. You will need to remove old paint and varnish.

2 Consider your stencil design and colour scheme and gather the materials you will need.

3 The old varnish on this desk must be removed. Apply the varnish remover and scrape it off. Take care with these materials;

always follow the manufacturer's instructions and wear protective clothing.

4 When it is dry, rub down the surface with fine sandpaper to give a smooth, clean surface. Dust off with a brush or cloth.

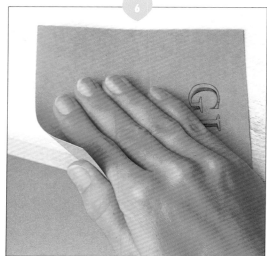

5 Apply a coat of slightly thinned emulsion paint in your chosen background colour. Allow to dry.

6 Rub down the emulsion coat with fine sandpaper to highlight the grain.

7 The combination of the beech wood grain and emulsion give the desired rustic effect.

8 We have chosen a border design for the desk lid. Measure and mark a light guideline so that you can position the stencil correctly.

9 Make sure that the stencil is applied in the correct place and fix it with masking tape.

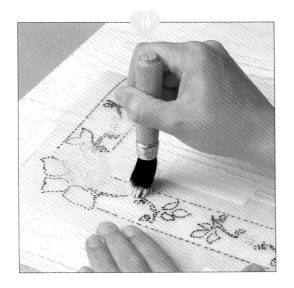

10 Apply the first colour over the whole area.

11 Line up your second stencil and apply all of the second colour.

12 Continue with a third colour.

13 A close-up of the completed design reveals that the yellow and green are a little bright for the overall rustic feel of the desk.

14 We stencilled the edges of the design with a little burnt sienna to tone down and add depth to the flowers and leaves.

HANDY HINTS

◊ If your piece of furniture needs only a good clean, use sugar soap.

◊ When you apply the coat of emulsion, paint your strokes in the same direction as the grain.

◊ To give an even more rustic look, lightly sand over your finished design.

15 The result is an "older" and much more interesting design.

16 Add some finishing touches to suit the piece.

17 Seal in the effect and design with two coats of varnish.

A total transformation – the desk is worthy of pride of place!

Finishing Touches

Stencilling on a wall can bring a room to life. A design above a picture or a plain window can provide the perfect finishing touch, and this project provides an opportunity to coordinate colours with the rest of the room.

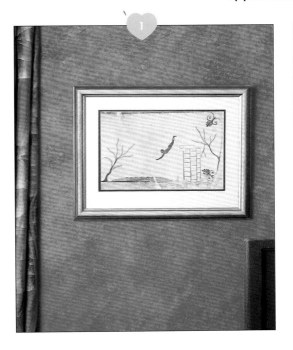

You will need
◊ Painting kit with acrylics
◊ Clean, dry wall
◊ Tape measure
◊ Step ladder

1 The space above this picture is the perfect place for a ribbon stencil.

2 With the picture in place, measure and mark the centre point above it.

3 Centre the stencil above the picture, making certain it is straight, and mark the key points.

4 Remove the picture. Line up your stencil on the key points and fix it in place on the wall with masking tape.

5 We have chosen iridescent gold for this project to complement the gold highlights in the picture frame. Stencil in the usual way.

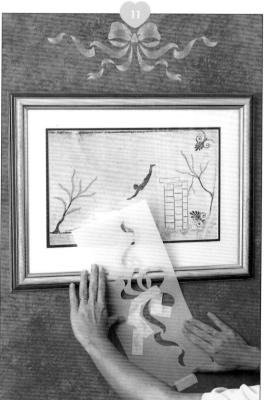

6 A peek at our efforts shows that we need to build up this transparent medium on such a dark background.

7 Heavy stippling is required on key edges of the design.

8 Now that's more like it!

9 Hang your picture back up and admire your handiwork. Does it need anything else?

10 Add a finishing touch by selecting a bit of the design. Tape off the specific areas you want to use.

11 Measure and mark the centre and key points again. Stencil as before.

The stencil has provided an elegant finishing touch for this study.

HANDY HINTS
When you tape off part of your stencil, be sure to add tape to both sides so that the sticky side of the tape does not damage your earlier work.

Designer's Delight

The aim of this project is to design, cut and apply your own border stencil. Your inspiration should come from your own surroundings. We have chosen some lobelia flowers and used them to create a glorious border for a living room.

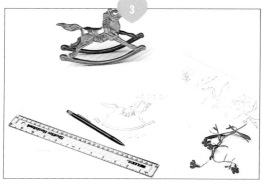

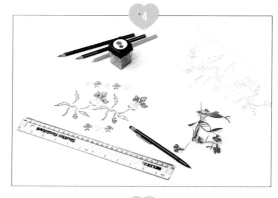

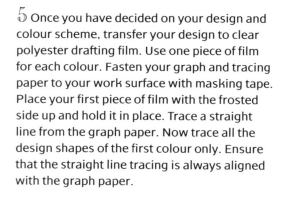

You will need
◊ Cutting kit
◊ Painting kit with acrylics
◊ Appropriate wall space to decorate
◊ Reference material
◊ Coloured pencils
◊ Permanent felt-tip pen

1 Look around for inspiration for a design for your own border stencil.

2 Choose simple objects and practise simplifying the shapes. Look at your chosen object and break it down into sections.

3 Trace the design you like best and hold it in place over graph paper with masking tape. The graph paper will be invaluable in building a straight border. Choose a simple shape from your design to build the outside border.

4 Experiment with different ways of developing your design and also with colours, bearing in mind the room in which you will be stencilling. Make sure that your design is straight by using masking tape to attach your tracing paper to graph paper.

5 Once you have decided on your design and colour scheme, transfer your design to clear polyester drafting film. Use one piece of film for each colour. Fasten your graph and tracing paper to your work surface with masking tape. Place your first piece of film with the frosted side up and hold it in place. Trace a straight line from the graph paper. Now trace all the design shapes of the first colour only. Ensure that the straight line tracing is always aligned with the graph paper.

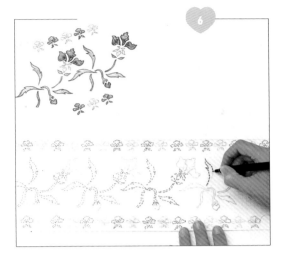

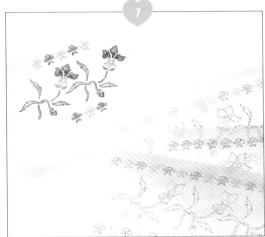

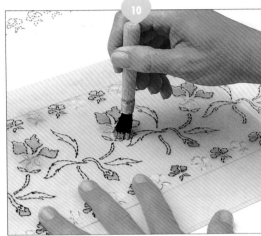

9 Continue in the same way with all three pieces of film. Each piece should have its own shapes cut out to correspond to your planned colour design.

10 Now you can do a trial run with your new stencil on a piece of rough paper. Stencil your first colour, align and stencil your second image and continue with your third.

11 Now you are ready to move to your chosen wall.

6 When you have traced all the shapes for your first colour on to the first piece of film, trace the rest of your design in dotted lines with a permanent felt-tip pen. These dotted lines are essential if you are to align the stencil accurately.

7 On the second piece of film trace all the second colour shapes in a continuous line. Then trace the rest of the design in dotted lines. Continue in the same way for your third colour image.

8 Now you can begin cutting your own stencil, but practise on a spare piece of film first. Use your cutting mat and a sharp blade. Turn the stencil when you come to a corner rather than trying to turn your blade. Cut out the shapes of the continuous line from each piece of film. Do not cut any dotted lines.

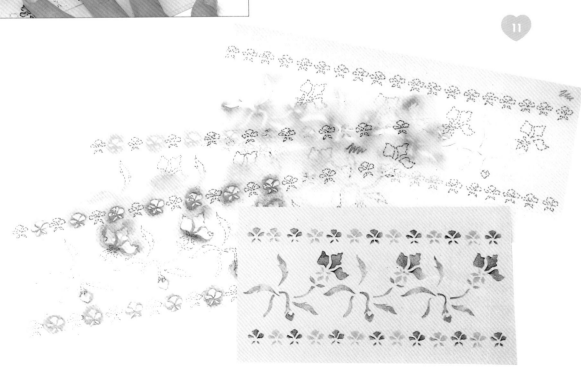

12 This pretty room needs a little something to finish it off.

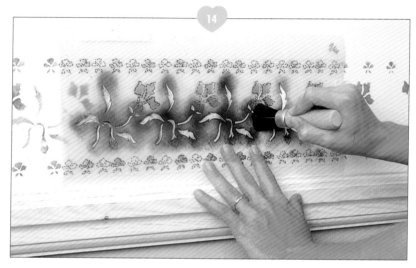

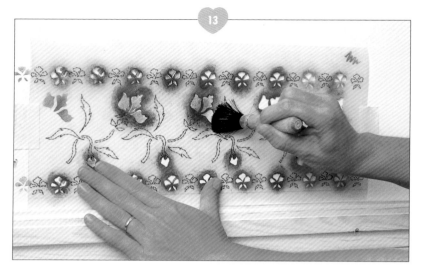

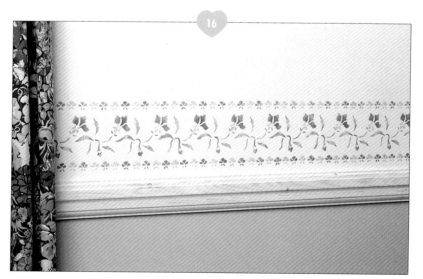

13 Start your first stencil in a relatively inconspicuous place because you will become more confident as you proceed and your technique will improve. This way your best efforts are most visible. After using your first stencil once, move it along and position the repeat by laying your first cut-out over the last image.

14 Once you have completed all of the chosen area with the first colour, proceed with the second colour. Your dotted lines will make alignment simple.

15 Complete the design with the third colour.

16 Put your room back together

Congratulations! A work of
art and a cause for celebration.

HANDY HINTS
◊ The more of your repeat you
can fit on to your stencil, the
more images you will be able
to colour in one go.
Remember, though, that the
cutting time will be increased.
◊ When you align your repeat
by laying a cut-out over a
stencilled image, as in Step 13,
do not worry if alignment is
not exact. You have cut this by
hand, so it is bound to be a
little different.
◊ Do not use more than three
colours.
◊ If your design cuts or tears, it
can be easily mended; apply
tape on both sides of the tear
and trim the excess tape with a
blade.

Pattern Library

◊ Magical Mirror

◊ Pots of Gardener's Delight
(Use the shell template from Magical
Mirrors for the small pot) Add pollen
dots by hand

◊ Pots of Gardener's Delight

◊ Gift Tag *and* All Wrapped Up

◊ Gift Tags *and* Merry Mugs

◊ Designer's Delight

◊ A New Lease of Life

◊ Great Greetings Cards

◊ Gift Tag

◊ Finishing Touches

◊ Child's Cheerful Chair

◊ Friendly Floor Covering

Batik

This beautiful craft, based on one simple principle, enables you to produce stunning pictures, cushions, bags and fabric

INTRODUCTION

◇

Batik is an ancient method of applying coloured designs to fabric. It is called a "resist" method because traditionally hot wax is used to penetrate the cloth to prevent or "resist" the dye spreading to areas so protected. Rice paste or mud is sometimes used instead of wax. Designs may be of one colour or of many colours, depending on the number of times the resists are applied and the fabric is dipped into baths of different dyes. Modern, simple-to-use dyes allow the technique of "pool" batik to be practised. In this process wax is applied to surround complete areas of fabric and to prevent the dye spreading from one area to another, which means that colours can be used next to each other to give results that would be more difficult to achieve by the traditional immersion method.

The precise origins of batik are disputed. There is early evidence of batik in the form of garments depicted in Indian wall paintings; linen cloth dating to the 5th century has been excavated in Egypt; in Japan batik was made into silk screens from the 8th century, the work probably being carried out by Chinese artists; and in Java 13th-century temples show figures possibly wearing batik cloth. It is more certain that as early as AD 581 batik was being produced in China and probably being exported to Japan, central Asia, the Middle East and India via the Silk Route.

Wherever it originated, however, the batik method was adopted more enthusiastically in Indonesia, especially Java, than anywhere else. It was the Javanese who developed the canting (pronounced "chanting" and originally spelled *tjanting*) to facilitate and refine the application of wax. It is basically a metal bowl to hold the hot wax, with a spout through which the wax flows out, attached to a wooden handle. The invention of the canting opened up the possibility of producing the wonderfully intricate array of designs seen in Javanese batiks.

The word batik derives from the Javanese word, *tik*, meaning spots or dots. Early batiks were executed by means of tiny dots of wax, which were applied to the fabric to form the design. By the 13th century it had become a highly developed art, a fitting leisure pastime for women of noble birth. They often took months to complete a piece of fabric, just as an aristocratic European lady might have worked at her fine needlework.

Early batik designs were believed to have magical powers which would protect the person who wore them, and individual designs were reserved for particular noble families. The Garuda symbol, which was associated with prosperity and success in life, for example, could be used only by members of the royal courts. Today, this creature, half-man, half-eagle, who carried the god Vishnu, has become the national symbol of Indonesia, just as batik fabric has become the national dress of Java.

The production of batik fabric became the main industry and export of Java, from which it spread throughout the world. It was brought to Europe via Holland after the colonization of

Java by the Dutch in the early 17th century. By the 1830s several factories had been established in Europe, and these used Indonesian techniques, taught by Indonesians, who were brought to Holland specifically for that purpose.

By the 1840s the Javanese were using caps (pronounced "chaps" and originally spelled *tjaps*), a form of block to print the wax on with. These were adapted from an Indian technique, and they made the process faster, an advance that made the imitation batik sarongs produced in Switzerland uneconomic to make.

A group of Eurasian women, called collectively the Indische School of Batik, produced fabric for Dutch colonial officials and their families. Their designs, which were a combination of the traditional forms of Java and the colour and simplicity of Chinese paintings, became fashionable in the early years of the 20th century. Also around the late 1800s the British African print trade began, and more styles were incorporated into batik fabric designs. Africans had produced resist-dyed fabrics for centuries — the Yoruba of west Africa used cassava paste as a resist, while the

people of Senegal used rice paste. In India, where cotton rather than silk was used, the batik industry reached its zenith in the 17th and 18th centuries.

Western production of batik on a large scale collapsed with the general economic decline after World War I and it reverted to being the domain of the individual craftsman in Indonesia. In Europe artists and craftsmen continued to work in batik, developing and experimenting with its possibilities. In the 1920s modern dyestuffs started to replace traditional vegetable dyes, changing the appearance of batik fabric by bringing deeper, darker and more varied shades to the range of possible colours.

Batik is undergoing a revival in appreciation and interest in the West. In addition to the traditional uses of batik fabric for clothes and soft furnishings, the medium's potential is being explored and applied as a fine art, with artists seeking expression through dye instead of paint. However, it is still to Indonesia, especially to Java, that the batik enthusiast goes to learn about the process and the art at first-hand.

BELOW Traditional batiked material from Indonesia.

EQUIPMENT AND MATERIALS

—◇—

In the projects described in this book you will gradually gain the knowledge you need to accomplish a wide variety of batik pieces. The basic methods, equipment and materials you will need are discussed in the projects and I have introduced new techniques in this gradual way so that newcomers to the craft are not overwhelmed and discouraged before they have even begun. You do not need to be able to draw in the first few projects, and motifs are printed for your use where necessary until you gain confidence to find or make up your own. All of the projects do, however, use a number of basic pieces of equipment and materials, and I have listed these below, together with the quantities you will need. The only exception is the first project, the greetings cards, for which you need only the first 11 items.

You will need

◊ Plastic sheet to protect your work surface. Large bin liners, cut open, can be used. Choose white rather than black so that you can see any dye.

◊ Cotton wool.

◊ Sponge, 1in (2.5cm) thick by 12in (30cm) square.

◊ Rubber gloves — the thin ones like hairdressers' gloves are best.

◊ Iron — preferably use an old one in case you get some wax on it.

◊ Newspaper.

◊ Measuring spoons. You will need to be able to measure 1 tablespoon, 1 teaspoon, ½ teaspoon and ¼ teaspoon.

◊ Dyes — 1oz (25gm) pots of MX 4G (brilliant yellow), MX G (turquoise), MX G (peacock blue), MX 5B (cerise) and Kenactive Black 2647. Apart from the black, these are Procion fibre-reactive dyes; there is not a ready-made Procion black.

◊ 2 pt (1 litre) measuring jug.

◊ 1lb (500gm) sodium carbonate (washing soda) or soda ash.

◊ 1lb (500gm) sodium bicarbonate (baking soda).

◊ 1lb (500gm) urea — this is obtainable from specialist shops.

◊ 2lb (1kg) batik wax — this quantity should be sufficient for all of the projects, although you could start off with a 1lb (500gm) packet. This is available from specialist shops.

◊ Wax pot — some cheaper alternatives are discussed on page 288, but if you are going to do a lot of batik, you should buy a wax pot from a specialist shop. I have used a wax pot set on mark 5 for all the projects in this book.

◊ Natural bristle brushes, small and medium sizes and both flat and round for making different marks.

◊ Cantings — small, medium and large spouts should be sufficient, with perhaps one novelty multi-spout. Indonesian cantings are the best if you can get them.

◊ Soft, absorbent cloths (rags will do).

◊ Scouring kit — a large saucepan, detergent and wooden tongs (see page 290).

◊ Fabric — 6yd (5.5m) of 36in (90cm) wide fine cotton should be ample for all the projects in the book and allow for some mistakes too. It must be 100 per cent cotton, not polycotton. You will also need 1yd (1m) silk, although 18in (46cm) would be sufficient. All fabric has to be prepared — that is, scoured and ironed — before you start a piece of work. If you buy 6yd (5.5m) cotton and want to scour it all at once you can put it into the boil wash of your machine with half your normal amount of ordinary washing liquid, although this will vary according to the softness of your water. Do **not** boil silk.

LEFT A wax pot, caps, cantings and wax brushes.

BELOW The five basic dye colours you will need.

Chemicals, dyes, hot wax should all be treated with respect. Follow the safety tips throughout the book and you will have fun and peace of mind.

SAFETY FIRST

● Do not inhale the fine dye powder, and if it comes in contact with your eyes rinse them immediately in plenty of clean water.

GREETINGS CARDS

The simplest kind of batik you can do is on paper using ordinary white household candles to apply the wax resist. You can use almost any kind of paper as long as it is not coated with a shiny finish and it is not too flimsy — photocopying paper, which is usually about 80gsm, is suitable. Making these greetings cards introduces you to working with the soda solutions, mixing and applying dyes, ironing out and the "halo" that results from wax seeping when you iron your work.

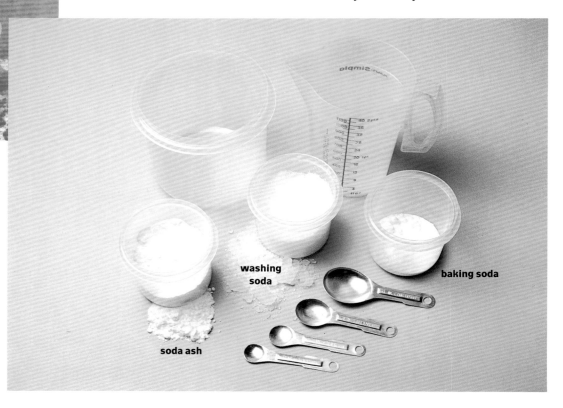

washing soda

baking soda

soda ash

You will need
◊ Basic equipment, first 11 items
◊ Sheets of white paper, 11½ × 8¼in (A4, 297 × 210mm)
◊ Hair dryer (optional)
◊ Two or three white household candles
◊ Card to make a viewing window (use an empty cereal packet)
◊ Ready-made, cut-out window cards to mount your finished work
◊ Stick glue or spray adhesive for fixing

1 So that the dye penetrates the paper properly you should prepare it with a solution of 1 teaspoon baking soda and 1 teaspoon washing soda dissolved in 1½pt (900ml) warm water. You can use soda ash instead of washing soda, but it is twice as strong so you need add only ½ teaspoon to the water. If it is kept in an airtight container this solution remains usable for 10—14 days.

2 Lay a sheet of paper on a flat, non-absorbent surface, such as formica or glass. Use cotton wool to apply the soda solution evenly over the paper. Soak the paper thoroughly but do not rub it so hard that you begin to roughen the surface. Leave the paper to dry completely; wax will not penetrate where there is water. If you want to speed up the drying time use a hair dryer, or iron the paper between sheets of newspaper with the iron set to low. Ironing may cause the paper to crinkle, but this often adds more interesting effects. You could try both ways — smooth and wrinkled.

3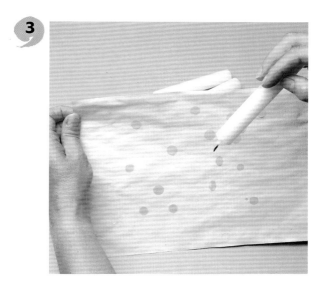

4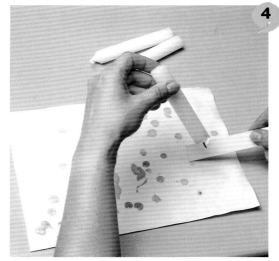

5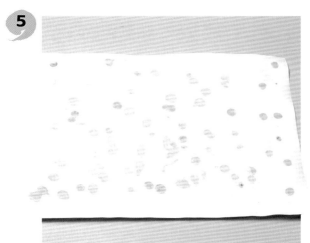

6

7

8

3 Place your prepared sheet of paper on the work surface. Light a candle and, as the wax melts, let it drip onto the paper. Experiment, holding it 3in (7.5cm) above the paper, then 12in (30cm) above the paper. Tip the paper at an angle, and move the candle quickly across the sheet.

4 Use a piece of cardboard to push the molten wax around the paper.

5 Notice the changes in the tone and degree of transparency of the paper as the hot wax cools.

6 Cover your work surface with plastic sheeting to protect it from the dye. Mix ¼ teaspoon yellow dye powder to a paste with a few drops of the soda solution. Add 2 tablespoons (30ml) soda solution to this paste. The dye is ready to use. If you want a paler colour dilute the dye powder still further.

7 Use a large brush or a piece of cut sponge to colour two stripes of yellow on your waxed paper. Wear rubber gloves when you do this or your fingers will go yellow, too.

8 Mix blue or turquoise dye powder in the same way and paint or sponge on two blue stripes. Leave it to dry completely. You can speed this up with a hair-drier, but don't hold it so close that you melt the wax.

SAFETY FIRST

- Good ventilation is important at all times but especially when you are ironing off wax. Work with your iron to one side so that your face is not directly above it. You may even wish to wear a mask as protection against the wax fumes released by the heat of the iron.

9 The wax is removed by ironing out between sheets of newspaper. Always make sure that there is a thick layer of newspaper under your batik to protect the surface below. Place two sheets of newspaper on top and use the iron on cotton heat. You will see the wax melting and being absorbed into the newspaper. Continue to iron, putting fresh sheets of newspaper above and below your work, until no more wax comes out.

10 When the wax is ironed out it also spreads into the paper around the original waxed areas, creating a "halo" effect. These "halo" areas will now also resist the dye, leaving abstract, unwaxed shapes, which can be dyed a third colour if you wish.

11 When the dye has dried completely use a viewing window to select areas, and you will have three or four "alien landscape" cards to send to your friends.

GIFT WRAPPING

How about making some exclusive wrapping paper for a special present or a waterproof jacket for a precious book? You can melt some ordinary candles or use bought batik wax, which comes in the form of granules and which is a mixture of paraffin (candle) wax and beeswax. Paraffin wax is brittle, cracks easily and sometimes flakes off. Beeswax is soft and pliable when it is cool and adheres well to fabrics. The combination of the two balances out their properties so that the wax will crack to give the traditional batik effect when it is folded but not so much that it flakes away. The ratio is about 70 per cent paraffin to 30 per cent beeswax. This project involves using a soft bed, mixing colours and applying extra wax to remove "halos". It also introduces you to using caps.

You will need
◊ Basic equipment, plus
◊ Sheets of soda-treated paper,
   16½in × 11½in (A3, 420 × 297mm)
◊ Small blanket or towel

Cap-making kit
◊ Masking tape
◊ Scissors/craft knife
◊ Empty cereal packets
◊ Boxes
◊ Corrugated card
◊ Kitchen rolls
◊ Corks

1

2

SAFETY FIRST

● If you ever get hot wax on your skin, plunge it immediately into cold water. This will quickly solidify and cool the wax, which is then easy to peel off.

1 Whichever kind of wax you decide to use you will need a way of melting it and keeping it hot. The safest, most reliable equipment is one of the thermostatically controlled, electric wax pots that are available from specialist suppliers. Here, the batik wax granules are beginning to melt.

2 To apply the wax make some home-made versions of Indonesian caps, the copper printing blocks developed by the Javanese to print repeat patterns on lengths of fabric and so speed up the process of batik. Your caps can be made from cardboard rolls or from cut and folded card, held with masking tape if necessary. Cutting with pinking shears gives an interesting tool, and corrugated card is a good material to use because the loops serve as a reservoir for the wax. You could also use corks or wooden cotton reels, but do not use any form of plastic, which will melt in the hot wax.

3

4

5
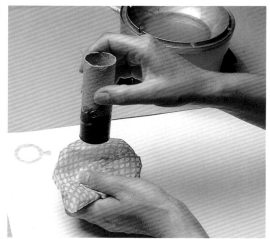

6
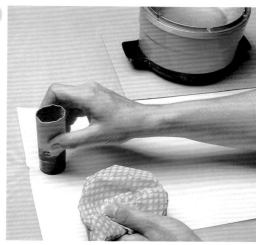

7

8
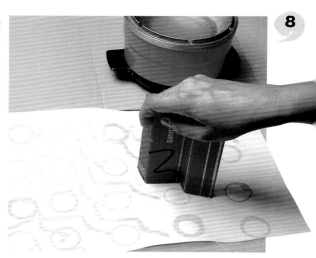

HINTS AND TIPS

WAX POTS

Cheaper alternatives to a purpose-made wax pot include:
- A double-boiler saucepan (bain-marie) in which boiling water in the bottom container melts the wax contained above. The water must be constantly checked to avoid boiling dry.
- An old saucepan on a thermostatically controlled hot plate. You must clean spilt wax on the hot plate regularly.
- A second-hand electric frying-pan with a temperature control.

3 To get the best print from your caps there should be a soft surface under your paper to press into. Lay a folded blanket or towel under the plastic sheeting on your work surface to give a soft bed.

4 Lay a sheet of paper on top of your printing bed. Heat the wax until it has melted, and put your cap into the wax. Cardboard sometimes fizzes the first time you put it in, so don't worry. Count to 10 to allow the wax to penetrate and warm the card.

5 As you lift it from the wax gently shake off the excess wax once or twice. Hold a pad of material underneath it to catch any further drips as you take it to the paper.

6 Print the wax onto the paper by pressing the cap down firmly. If the wax stays white and opaque it is not hot enough. The paper should go darker and become more translucent when it comes into contact with the wax.

7 You can do more than one print before going back to the wax pot, but each successive print will leave a finer deposit as the wax is used up and cools. Three or four impressions are usually the maximum.

8 Combine different cap prints to build up a pattern.

9

10

11

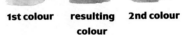

1st colour resulting colour 2nd colour

The colours and patterns you achieve will be as varied as your imagination.

9 Mix the dye using ¼ teaspoon of dye powder and 2 tablespoons (30ml) soda solution for each colour (see page 284). Red, yellow and blue have been used here. You can apply the dye in stripes or paint different colours inside the various wax-surrounded shapes.

10 When the dye is dry, iron out the wax. If you do not want the "halo" shapes, cover the unwaxed areas with wax while they are still warm from ironing, which makes it quick and economical on wax, and then iron out again. All the "halos" will disappear.

11 Try mixing your dyes to see what other colours you can get.

SUN CALENDAR

◇

Working on fabric is slightly more complicated than producing batik paper, but it is not difficult and the process can still be kept simple while giving effective results. The fabric must be 100 per cent natural fibre — cotton, linen, silk, for example — or viscose rayon. Any man-made fibres in the fabric, as in cotton polyester, may appear to take up the dye only for it to wash out at a later rinse stage, giving disappointing results. When the dyes are mixed with an alkali (the solution of sodas), a chemical reaction takes place that allows a permanent bonding of dye and fibre — hence the name, fibre-reactive dyes. Once the chemical reaction between dye and alkali has begun it continues for 2—4 hours, after which the dyestuff will no longer be fibre-reactive. As with synthetics it may appear to take up, only to wash away later, although it can be used up on paper batiks if you can't bear to throw it away. The dye powder, however, can be stored indefinitely if it is kept in closed containers, in a cool atmosphere and away from the light.

You will need
◊ Basic equipment, plus
◊ 2 squares in prepared fabric, 8 × 8in (20 × 20cm) and 3 × 3in (7.5 × 7.5cm)
◊ Small blanket or towel

Cap-making kit
◊ Masking tape
◊ Scissors/craft knife
◊ Empty cereal packets
◊ Boxes
◊ Corrugated card
◊ Kitchen roll

1 Burning a small sample of a fabric is a good way of testing the fibre content, and the kitchen sink is a safe place to do this. Hold a lighted match to a piece of the fabric. Synthetic threads will burn quickly and leave a hard plastic residue; natural fibres burn slowly, leaving a soft ash.

2 You will need a piece of prepared cotton about 8in (20cm) square. Any oils or dressings in the fabric may prevent the dye from penetrating, and they must be removed by scouring. This is achieved by boiling the fabric for 5 minutes in a solution made to the proportions of 2 teaspoons detergent to 2pt (1 litre) water. You can use 2 teaspoons washing soda crystals instead, but this may affect the surface of your boiling saucepan. Rinse the fabric in clear water, allow it to dry and iron to a smooth finish. The fabric is now prepared and is also pre-shrunk.

3

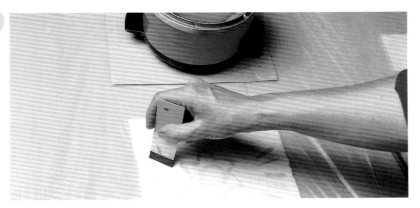

4

6

5

3 Lay the prepared fabric on a soft bed and
heat the wax to approximately 270°F (132°C).
Have your home-made caps ready, and wax
the areas you wish to remain white. If the wax
is at the right temperature you will see the
change in tone of the fabric just as you did
with the paper. If the wax is white and opaque
the fibres are not being penetrated by the wax
and will not resist the dye.

4 Mix ¼ teaspoon yellow dye with 2
tablespoons (30ml) soda solution (see
page 284).

5 Apply the dye with a piece of cut sponge.
Remember to wear rubber gloves.

6 Dye the test piece for experimenting with
overdyeing later. Leave it to dry naturally; this
will depend on the temperature of your room.
You can speed up the drying time with some
warm air, placing the fabric in an airing
cupboard, for example, or hair-drier, but if you
use a hair-drier take care not to melt the wax.
Apply wax to the dried fabric in the areas you
want to keep yellow. The facial detail can be
added with a small brush.

7

8

9

7 Mix red dye as yellow above. Try it out on your test piece of fabric. Add more dye powder if the colour is too weak or more soda solution if the colour is too strong. Apply to your square and allow to dry.

8 Use a brush and cap to wax the areas you want to stay orange.

9 Mix blue dye and test it on your sample piece before applying it. When the dye has dried completely remove the fabric from the plastic sheeting and iron out the wax between sheets of newspaper.

You can mount your finished piece and perhaps attach a calendar below it. You can buy ready-made window mounts, or you could get the piece mounted at your local art shop.

DOLLY BAGS

◇

When you apply the colours all over the fabric each time the range of colours you can achieve is limited to the shades resulting from overdyeing. Painting on the dye in "pools" of fabric surrounded by wax, in the technique known as pool dyeing, gives tremendous possibilities for colour combinations to exist side by side, and the opportunities are limited only by your dye-mixing abilities. Using the dye in this way requires the addition of urea, which is a by-product of natural gas. In this process small amounts of dye are painted onto the fabric, rather than the fabric being immersed completely in a dye bath as in traditional batik, and urea is used to delay the drying process. This is important because fibres and dye react while the fabric is wet, and the longer this process takes the better the fixation of the dye will be – so, no speeding up of the drying from now on. Urea also helps to dissolve the dye more easily and thoroughly, maximizing the colour intensity. This project also involves the use of a sponge "brush", saving colours with wax and boiling out wax.

You will need
◊ Basic equipment, plus
◊ Prepared cotton, 21¾ × 16½in (52 × 39cm); the bag made to imperial measurements will be slightly larger than the metric dimensions in order to keep the figures simple
◊ Lining material, 21¾ × 16½in (52 × 39cm)
◊ Blanket or towel
◊ 2 wooden sticks, 6in (15cm) long – old brush handles, straight twigs, for example
◊ Small paint brush (optional)
◊ Soft pencil, 4B
◊ Ruler

Cap-making kit
◊ Masking tape
◊ Cardboard tubes
◊ Corrugated paper/cereal box card
◊ Scissors/craft knife

Making up the bags
◊ Scissors
◊ Pins
◊ Thread
◊ Sewing machine or needles if you prefer to sew by hand
◊ 1yd (1m) lacing to make the drawstring handles

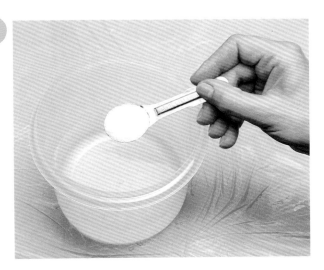

1 To make up a urea solution dissolve 1 teaspoon of urea with 1pt (600ml) warm water. If you are going to use it straight away do not use water warmer than 122°F (50°C) because fibre-reactives are cold dyes and must not be heated above this temperature. This, like the soda solution, is usable for 10–14 days if it is kept in an airtight container.

2 Using the selective dyeing process you can make three bags with different colour schemes. The bags have a base with a diameter of 5in (12cm) and the sides are 5 × 15¾in (12 × 38cm) (all seams are included in the specifications). Mark the three strips and bases on the prepared cotton with a soft pencil and lay it on a soft bed.

3

4

5

urea solution

soda solution

6

3 Make a sponge "brush". Push one of the wooden sticks into a piece of sponge and strap it firmly in place with masking tape. Trim it to a point, and it is ready for use. The sponge will hold more wax than a normal brush, enabling you to work for longer before having to recharge it with wax. These home-made tools are also excellent for applying dye. Heat the wax and use your sponge "brush" to apply a continuous line of wax, following your pencil lines, to separate the three strips. If you do not do this dye will spread to areas it is not wanted.

4 Make your cap prints in each section, making sure that each shape has a continuous wax boundary. If the wax sticks to the plastic beneath the fabric you know it has penetrated! It will also keep your work in place while you are dyeing, preventing the unwanted transfer of colour.

5 Colour fastness is obtained by combining the urea solution with the soda solution in the ratio of 1 part urea to 2 parts soda. For this project add a few drops of urea solution to ¼ teaspoon of dye powder to form a paste, then add 2 teaspoons urea solution and 4 teaspoons soda solution. This will be about full strength; if you want paler colours reduce the dye powder.

6 When all waxing and dyeing is completed and dried remove the fabric from the plastic sheet and iron out the wax. You will probably have noticed that the fabric becomes soft while it is warm from ironing but stiffens again as the residue of wax in the fibres cools. You may wish to retain this quality, because the residue makes the fabric water-repellent. However, if you want the fabric less stiff, more wax can be removed by boiling the fabric in water in an old saucepan for 5 minutes, then

plunging it into cold water, using wooden tongs to transfer it from saucepan to bowl. The wax solidifies on the surface of the cloth and can be rubbed or scraped off. This process can be repeated to remove more wax. Finally, boil in soapy water to remove all surplus dye. Allow the dye to set in the fabric for 24 hours before using this method.

Leave the saucepan of water in which you have boiled the fabric to cool, and the wax will form a skin on the surface, which can be removed, dried and used again. You must dry wax thoroughly before reusing it, otherwise it will spit in the wax pot, like hot fat in a frying-pan.

7

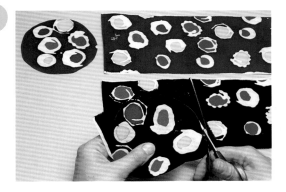

8

9

DYEING TIPS

- If you want to mix all your colours before you start to dye, mix them just with 2 teaspoons urea solution. They will remain usable for 24 hours, and you can add the soda solution to each colour just before use to give fresh, potent dyes.
- Do not saturate the fabric until puddles of dye form underneath, because these may run over the surface of your wax boundaries to the neighbouring areas. Water has only so much surface tension before it breaks down and spreads.
- If you paint on the lightest colours first you can cover any mistakes by a darker colour afterwards.
- If your wax boundaries allow dye to seep, let the dye dry, wax the colour you want to keep, then overdye with a darker colour.

7 Once the wax has been removed to your satisfaction, cut out the fabric ready to make up your bags. Allowing ¼in (5mm) seams, sew the sides together. On each side make a buttonhole ½in (1cm) long and running from ¾in (2cm) to 1¼in (3cm) from the top edge.

8 With right sides together, sew the base to the bottom edge. Turn right side out. Cut and sew the lining material in the same way but omit the buttonholes. Leave unturned.

9 Put the lining inside the bag, turn in ¼in (5mm) seams on both and sew together. Sew two lines of stitching around the top of the bag, one at the top edge of the buttonholes the other at the bottom edge to provide a channel for the drawstring. Thread through the drawstrings, one entering and one exiting from each buttonhole.

If you want to make a larger bag, multiply the radius of the base, by 6.284 (approx 6¼) to give you the appropriate length side.

HINTS AND TIPS

REMOVING DYE

An easier and more effective way of removing wax is to put your work through a dry-cleaning machine. The chemicals dissolve all the wax but the brightness of the colour is not lost, as does happen to some extent with boiling out. Your waxy batik will have no effect on other items in the dry-cleaning machine, and the dyes will not run.

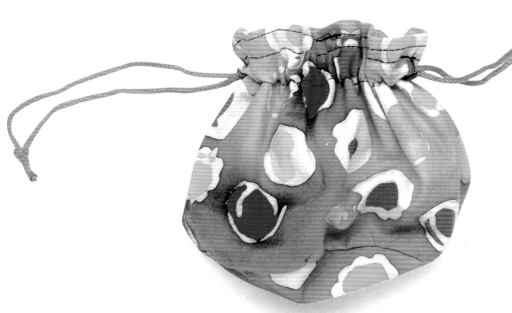

GARMENT FABRIC

◇

Large pieces of fabric can be quite easily batiked. The waxing is done in stages on a soft bed, and the fabric is then immersed in dye to ensure full penetration and evenness of colour.

You will need
◊ Basic equipment, plus
◊ Blanket
◊ Plastic bucket with a minimum capacity of 1 gallon (4.5 litres)
◊ Bowl with a minimum capacity of 1 gallon (4.5 litres)
◊ Paper and fabric for experimenting with caps and dyes
◊ 2yd (2m) prepared fine cotton

Cap-making kit
◊ Masking tape
◊ Scissors/craft knife
◊ Empty cereal packets
◊ Corrugated card
◊ Kitchen roll
◊ Empty card from wide roll of adhesive tape

1

2

3

HINTS AND TIPS

FIXING COLOURS

● **Fixing is improved in a humid atmosphere. Short bursts of steam from an electric kettle, introduced intermittently over the 2–3 hour drying period, can provide the necessary humidity.**
● **The evenness of colour can be enhanced by adding the salt in three stages in the first 15 minutes of the dyeing process. However, the fabric must be removed each time more salt is added, which makes the procedure a bit too complicated for a beginner. For this reason I have suggested that all the salt be added at the same time.**

---

1 Make some cardboard caps and experiment on paper with them until you have a design you are happy with.

2 Try the caps on fabric to see how many prints you can get from each dip in the wax and how they change as the wax cools and runs out.

3 Make as large a soft bed as your blanket and work surface will allow. Lay down the first section of your fabric, and arrange a chair at either side to hold it off the floor while you are waxing. Lift the fabric at intervals as you work to prevent it from being stuck to the plastic when you want to move on to the next section.

CALCULATING THE DYE BATH INGREDIENTS

Multiply the dry weight of fabric before waxing by 20 — e.g., 6oz (150gm) × 20 = 120fl oz (6pt)/ 3000ml (3 litres). For each 2pt (1 litre) of dye bath you need:

- ½–2 teaspoons dye powder
- 2 tablespoons (50gm) salt
- 2 teaspoons (5gm) soda ash or 4 teaspoons (10gm) soda crystals

4 When the first waxing is complete prepare the dye bath. These ingredients are enough for about 6oz (150gm) dry weight of fabric, which is about what 2yd (2m) cotton should weigh. Dissolve 6 tablespoons (150gm) salt in 3fl oz (100ml) warm water and set aside. Dissolve 6 teaspoons (15gm) soda ash (or 12 teaspoons/ 30gm soda crystals) in 3fl oz (100ml) warm water and set aside.

5 Make a paste of 1½–6 teaspoons yellow dye powder in warm water. Do not use water warmer than 122°F (50°C). Add some more water so that it will pour easily.

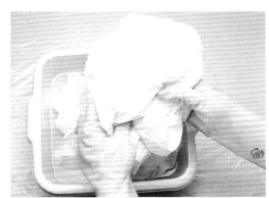

6 Add 6pt (3 litres) water to the dye and stir. Add the dissolved salt and stir. Salt is added to this dye recipe to facilitate penetration, to promote an even quality of dyeing and to get the best colour from the dye powder.

7 Immerse the waxed fabric and test piece in clean, cold water and shake off the excess.

8 Transfer the fabric to the dye bath. Immerse it completely, agitating it to ensure good penetration of the dye.

9 Remove it after 15 minutes and put it in a bowl.

10 Add the dissolved soda to the dye bath, then return and immerse the fabric for a further 45 minutes, stirring occasionally. Remove the fabric, rinse in cold water until the water runs clear, then hang to drip dry. This is part of the fixing process.

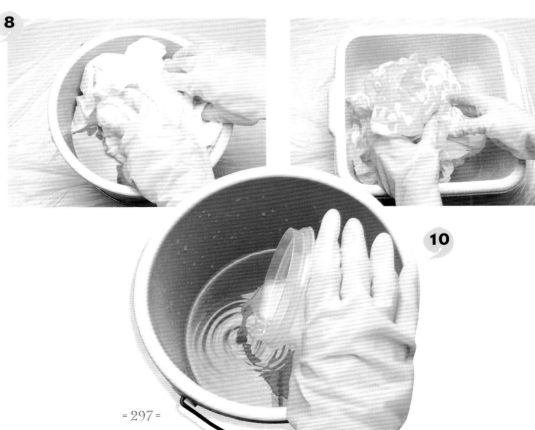

11 When the fabric is completely dry return it to the soft bed and do the second waxing. This time wax everything you want to stay yellow.

12 Follow the same recipe and procedure as before, but using blue dye powder instead of yellow. Test the colour on your sample piece first.

13 As the fabric moves around in the dye bath some of the wax will be bent and crack, and dye will be able to penetrate the fibres. This is what gives batik its traditional crackle effect. Wax cracks more readily and cleanly when it is cold, and this is why the fabric is soaked in cold water before it is immersed in the dye bath. The cracking is further controlled by crushing the fabric to a greater or lesser extent before and while it is being dyed.

It is easier to boil out the bulk of the wax from a large piece of fabric rather than ironing it. Dry clean it to restore the original softness, and then it will be ready to make up into the article of your choice. If you machine-wash the article at home afterwards do so on a cool wash – 104°F (40°C) – and wash separately for the first few washes, especially if you have used intense colours.

CUSHION COVER

As we have seen, it was the Javanese who invented the canting. Although it is not easy to use, once you have mastered the techniques you will find that the canting will provide a continuous flow of hot wax that will enable you to fine line or dot work that would not otherwise be possible. There are many different shapes of these metal wax reservoirs available, but they all have one or more spouts through which the wax flows. The diameter of the spouts is one of the factors dictating the width of a line or the size of a dot of the wax applied to the fabric; speed, heat and angle of use are others.

Wax can be most easily applied to fine cottons and silks because the wax can penetrate more quickly than on thicker or more coarsely woven fabrics like linen. You will draw a more confident, freer and finer line if the tool can move smoothly and easily across the surface. If you go more slowly to allow wax to penetrate a thicker fabric you will be more likely to produce wobbly, more uneven and thicker lines. The heat of the wax also affects the speed with which it flows through the spout and how much it spreads in the fabric, and this is particularly evident when you are working on fine fabrics, such as silk. Remember that the same spout will produce lines of different widths on different fabrics and with the wax at different temperatures.

You will need
◊ Basic equipment, plus
◊ Soft pencil, 4B
◊ Wooden frame
◊ Drawing pins
◊ Prepared cotton, 17 × 17in
  (43 × 43cm)

1 An abstract design, which will give you maximum freedom to experiment with the cantings, is suggested for a cushion cover. Lay the prepared piece of cotton on your work surface and use a soft pencil to mark the diagonal and horizontal crosses lightly as a guide to keep the design symmetrical.

2 At first you will find that canting work is easiest on stretched fabric. You can use an old picture frame, if it is firmly jointed and not warped. Pin the centre of each side and then the corners. The fabric needs to be taut, but take care that you do not pull the weave out of alignment, or the image will be distorted when you take the fabric from the frame.

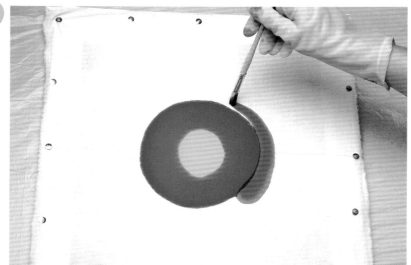

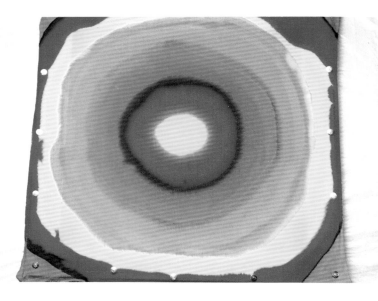

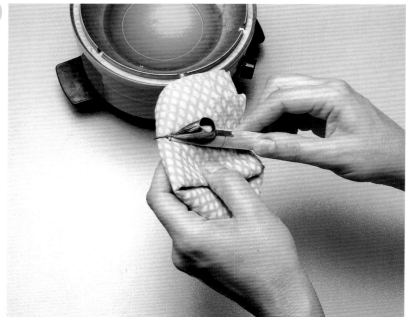

3 Before you begin waxing, mix the dyes – 6 tablespoons (90ml) of each should be plenty. I have used red, yellow and turquoise. Apply the dyes to the fabric, allowing them to mingle with each other at the edges to create a colourful, softly diffused effect.

4 Keep the colours light and bright. Allow the fabric to dry completely.

5 Heat the wax and put the canting in it for at least 30 seconds so that the metal bowl can warm up and help to keep the wax hot. Fill the reservoir about half full so that wax does not flow over the top while you are working. Use a piece of soft, absorbent cloth to remove excess wax and to catch any drips as you carry the canting from the wax pot to the fabric.

6

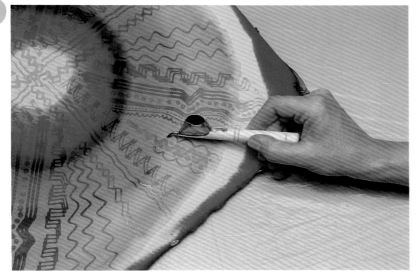

7

6 Rest your frame at an angle and also hold the canting at an angle as you work. The angle affects the flow of wax from the spout, and you will have to experiment to get the flow you want, but do not hold it at such a sharp angle that wax flows out of the back onto your fingers!

7 When waxing is complete, mix up 3fl oz (90ml) of black dyestuff using ½ teaspoon dye powder and apply it over the fabric with a sponge. Remember to have the sheet of plastic underneath to catch any drips and to wear rubber gloves to protect your fingers. Fibre-reactive dyes increase in intensity when they are overdyed, and this is particularly true with black, which looks darker and richer when it is applied twice, as was done here to cover the underlying bright dyes. When the fabric is completely dry, iron out and dry clean before making up into a cushion cover.

FISH ON SILK

◇

Silk is a much more delicate fabric than cotton, and it requires a different treatment and a different technique. It has to be prepared for the same reasons as cotton, but it should never be boiled. A rinse in warm water containing detergent is sufficient. The wax can be cooler because the weave is so fine, and you can use a canting with a smaller spout because the wax will penetrate the fabric easily. The dyes will look less intense than on cotton and linen, and they will also react differently.

You will need
◊ Basic equipment, plus
◊ Prepared silk, 6 × 6in (15 × 15cm)
◊ Sheet of acetate, 11½ × 8¼in (A4, 297 × 210mm)
◊ Cardboard frame with an image area 5¼ × 5¼in (13.5 × 13.5cm)
◊ Masking tape
◊ Mixing palette
◊ Small, soft dyebrush – watercolour brush size no. 4

1
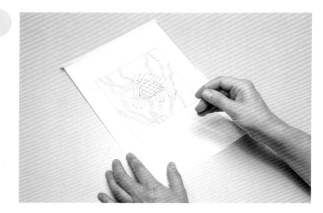

1 Keep to quite a simple image to begin with. You can use the fish shown here or draw an image of your own. Because silk is so fine you will be able to see through it and use it as you do tracing paper to do your waxing. Put a layer of acetate between the image and your silk to prevent the wax picking up any ink, which might transfer to the silk when you are ironing out the wax.

2

3

4

5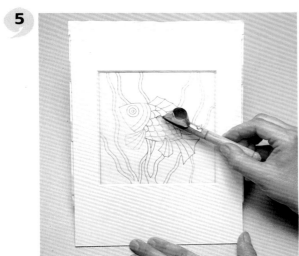

6

7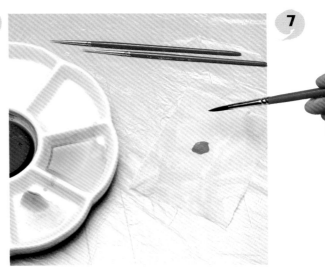

2 You can use a cardboard frame on which to stretch the silk. Although you can use corrugated box card, the best kind is heavy mounting board or the card used for shop displays. If you use the fish the cut-out window needs to be 5¼ × 5¼in (13.5 × 13.5cm). Tape the prepared fabric to the frame so that it is taut but not distorted. Position the stretched fabric over the image.

3 Tape it securely at the top, but just catch the sides and bottom with small pieces of tape so that you can separate the layers to check your progress.

4 Working with the fabric and canting at an angle, draw a line of wax around the perimeter of the image area, using the edge of the frame to guide the canting. This line will prevent the dye from spreading into your cardboard frame.

5 Following the lines of the image underneath, wax around the different "pools" of colour that you want. Make sure there are no gaps in the lines themselves or at the points they join to prevent dye from spreading to unwanted areas.

6 You will need very small amounts of dye for the fish. Mix a solution of 1 teaspoon urea solution and 2 teaspoons of soda solution and use them to mix the colours you want. Use a palette and treat the dye powder as if it were powder paint, mixing it with the chemical solutions as if they were water.

7 Test the colours on a sample.

8 Remove your stretched fabric from the acetate-covered image and paint on the dyes.

9 When the dye is completely dry, which happens much more quickly on silk than on cotton, wax the whole area before ironing out to prevent "halos" from forming.

10 Be very careful when you iron out silk. Creases that form at this stage are very difficult to remove. It is better to use unused newsprint, and do not pick up your ironed piece until it has cooled completely, otherwise it will be distorted when the wax cools. Ironing flat again can sometimes be difficult.

You could sandwich your finished batik between two layers of perspex and hang it against a window or mount it on a white backing sheet and frame it. Spray adhesive is an efficient and easy way of mounting silk on paper.

WINDOW BLIND

◇

When cotton batik is held against the light the effect is similar to that of stained glass windows. The dyes are seen at their very best, the light giving extra vibrancy to all the colours. A window blind is, therefore, a good way of displaying your batik expertise. Choose a small window for your first attempt. This project will cover an area 26in (66cm) wide and 44in (112cm) long.

The materials allow ½in (12mm) at the side edges for turning and 4in (10cm) at the top and bottom for fixing to the blind kit. The fabric may shrink when it is boiled, so cut the material at least 1in (2.5cm) larger all round than the measurements given for the prepared fabric.

You will need
◇ Basic equipment, plus
◇ Prepared fabric, 27 × 52in (69 × 132cm)
◇ Wooden frame, 27 × 27in (69 × 69cm)
◇ Drawing pins
◇ Tape measure
◇ Long ruler or straight edge
◇ Masking tape
◇ Soft pencil, 4B

Plan of window blind

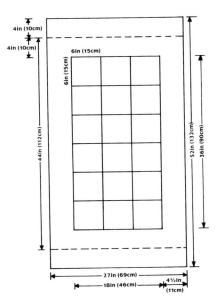

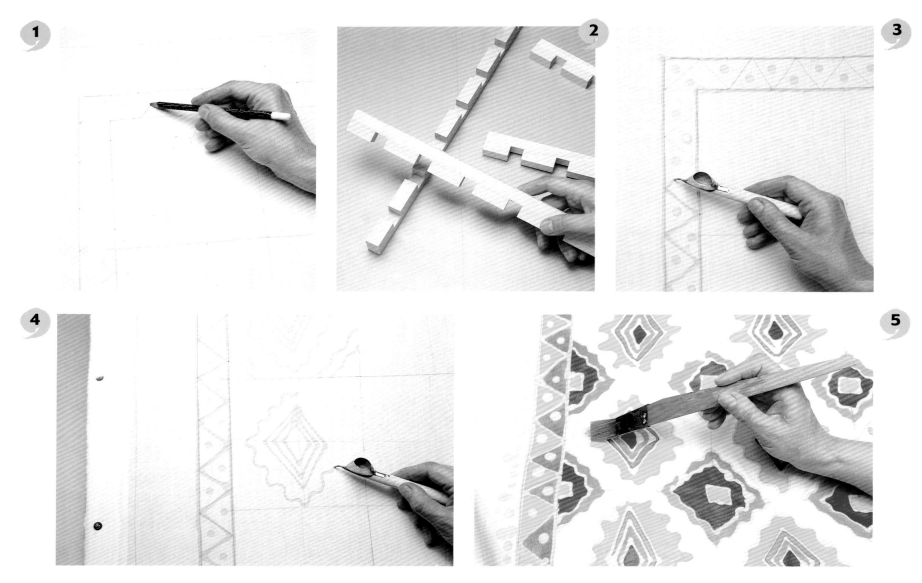

1 Lay the fabric on a firm surface and use a soft pencil to mark off 4in (10cm) at top and bottom. Draw a margin inside these lines of a further 4in (10cm) and on each side a margin of 4½in (11cm). The inside area is 18in (46cm) by 36in (90cm), so the repeat motif has been made 6in (15cm) square to fit three times across and six times down. Mark these squares. The border pattern needs only a ruler's width line marked in to keep the width of the snake line constant, with the points 1in (2.5cm) along the edges.

2 A frame about 27in (68cm) square would be ideal for stretching your fabric so that it can be worked in two manageable sections. These adjustable frames, which slot together, are available from most craft shops in a range of sizes; although you could use an old picture frame.

3 Wax in the border pattern. When the first section is complete move the fabric up the frame and position the second half. Move it carefully so that you do not crack the wax lines; otherwise the colours will seep where you do not intend them to.

4 The only extra guides you might need are the vertical and horizontal crosses so that you can place the points of the diamond shapes in each square. Let your canting run freely and enjoy applying the undulating lines. They will all look sufficiently similar to work well visually but different enough to add interest.

5 It is easier to apply dye if the fabric is in a complete length. If it is laid on a plastic sheet the dye may collect and cross over the wax lines. Laying it on an absorbent surface, such as newspaper, can make this less likely, but tends to suck the dye away from the fabric. If

6

7

8

you can suspend the material in some way there will be fewer colour accidents and the finished design will look more the way you intended. You can suspend the fabric from a shelf or door lintel, which is how I applied the smaller areas of colour here. Remember to work from light to dark with your dyes and wax them as they dry to prevent any accidents with darker colours later.

6 The final background was applied with a sponge while the fabric was suspended between two lengths of 2in (5cm) square wood resting on the work surface.

7 It is better to work horizontally when larger areas are being dyed because the fabric will hold the dye, which will not drain away to the base, as happens when hanging vertically, resulting in some colour loss at the top.

8 When all the dye is completely dried, wax all over to avoid "halos", remembering to lift the fabric between applications of wax. Iron out and either leave the fabric stiff and waterproof, or get it dry cleaned after ironing and spray it with fabric protector and water repellant so that the blind can be wiped down. Your batik fabric is ready to turn into a roller blind and bring the beauty of stained glass to your window.

PORTRAITS

◆

The techniques you used to make the Sun Calendar — successive waxing and dyeing to build up the image — can be used to reproduce photographs. This time, instead of using caps on cotton, you will wax with a canting onto silk. Silk is used because of its transparency, which allows you to see the image easily through the fabric. Choose an image with quite a lot of contrast — it could be your partner, child, pet or even the car! It doesn't matter if it is in black and white or colour.

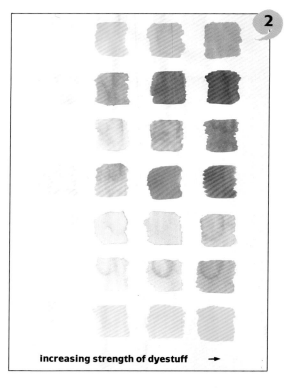

increasing strength of dyestuff ➡

You will need
◊ Basic equipment, plus
◊ Image — photograph or picture from a magazine, for example
◊ Enlarged photostat of the chosen image
◊ Acetate
◊ Prepared silk, 11in (2.5cm) wider all around than projected finished image
◊ Cardboard frame with inside dimensions of projected finished image
◊ Unprinted newsprint

1 Enlarge the image on a photostat machine. As a guide, increase the face to measure at least 6in (15cm) from crown to chin. Cover the image with acetate.

2 Plan to have three tones in addition to white. These do not have to be greys — you might like to work in tones of one colour by mixing different strengths of dyestuff.

3 Prepare and attach your silk to the cardboard frame (see page 303). Tape the image in position behind the stretched silk and draw the line of wax around the image area (see page 303). Wax in the areas to be kept white using a brush or sponge for large areas and soften the edges by applying the wax as dots with the canting.

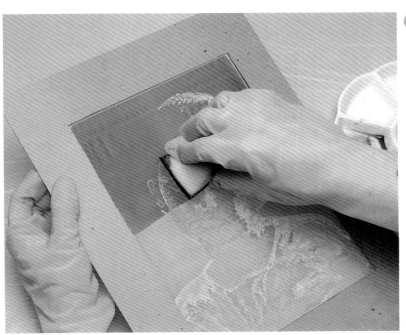

4 Remove the silk from the image ready to dye the first tone. Mix the lightest dye (tone 1) and apply it with a piece of sponge. Do not overload the sponge with liquid or the wax outline to your image will be unable to contain the dye. Remember to wear rubber gloves.

5 Use the dotting technique to wax the areas to be saved as tone 1.

6 Mix the next dye, tone 2 and test on the reverse side of the picture.

7 Apply the tone with a soft sponge.

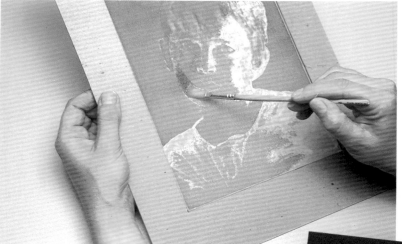

8 Apply wax to save the areas of tone 2.

9 Mix the last and darkest dye, tone 3, and apply as before. When it is completely dry, wax the remaining areas to avoid "halos" forming after ironing out.

Iron out the wax, leaving the silk to lie flat until it is cool. Mount for display.

Owl Picture

In all the other projects in this book you have used wax as a resist so that you could selectively dye areas of paper or fabric. Another use for this resist is to "undye" areas of an image. By using ordinary household bleach on fabric that is already dyed a strong colour, you can "discharge" the dye — that is, remove the dye already in the fabric.

Varying the dilution strength of the bleach and/or the length of time it is in contact with the fabric allows you to create an image in varying tones of the original colour. The strength of the bleach solutions and contact times given here are only approximate, and you will have to experiment on the particular fabric you are using because dyes react in different ways.

You will need
◊ Basic equipment, plus
◊ Prepared, pre-dyed cotton 11 × 11in (28 × 28cm)
◊ Household bleach
◊ Wooden frame
◊ Drawing pins
◊ Plastic tray larger than the fabric
◊ Sodium metabisulphite
◊ Masking tape
◊ Soft pencil, 4B

SAFETY FIRST

● **If any bleach gets onto your skin or into your eyes, rinse immediately in lots of cold, clean water.**

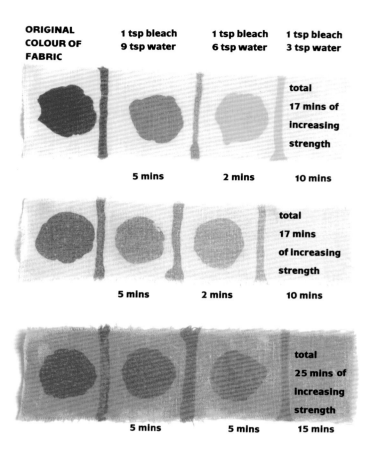

ORIGINAL COLOUR OF FABRIC	1 tsp bleach 9 tsp water	1 tsp bleach 6 tsp water	1 tsp bleach 3 tsp water
			total 17 mins of increasing strength
	5 mins	2 mins	10 mins
			total 17 mins of increasing strength
	5 mins	2 mins	10 mins
			total 25 mins of increasing strength
	5 mins	5 mins	15 mins

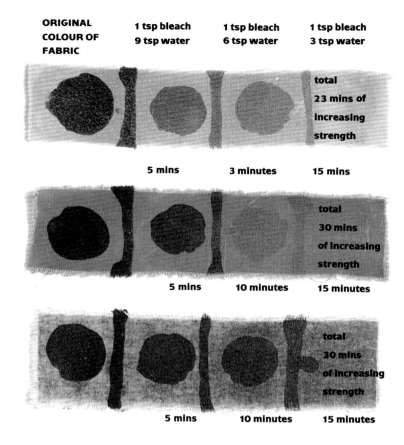

ORIGINAL COLOUR OF FABRIC	1 tsp bleach 9 tsp water	1 tsp bleach 6 tsp water	1 tsp bleach 3 tsp water
			total 23 mins of increasing strength
	5 mins	3 minutes	15 mins
			total 30 mins of increasing strength
	5 mins	10 minutes	15 minutes
			total 30 mins of increasing strength
	5 mins	10 minutes	15 minutes

1 Some dyes discharge more readily than others, so always do a test on a small piece of your fabric before you start your main work. Never use neat bleach — it will rot the fibres — and never use bleach on silk — it will rot the fabric completely. The strongest solution you should use is 1 part bleach to 3 parts water. It is better to extend the time than to increase the strength of the bleach.

2 Black dyes discharge to very different colours according to the bias of colour in the make-up of the dye.

3 Transfer your image to the fabric using a light box or using masking tape to keep everything in place against a window. Until you are confident enough to draw freehand, it might be sensible to avoid black fabric,

because it is harder to see through. If pencil does not show up on your fabric use white chalk or pastel.

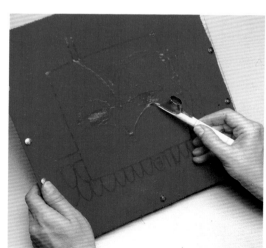

4 Pin your prepared fabric to the frame and use cantings or brushes to wax the areas or lines that are to be the darkest tone.

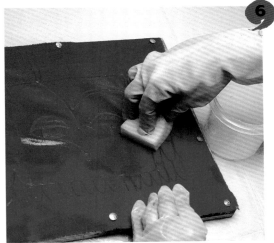

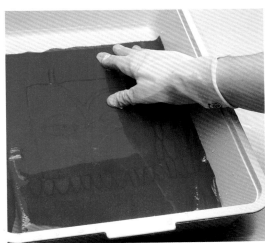

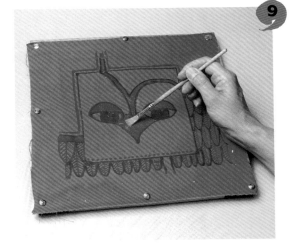

5 Prepare the neutralizing solution in readiness for step 8 later. Dissolve ½ teaspoon of sodium metabisulphite to 2pt (1 litre) water, which should be at a temperature of 105°F (40°C). You will find sodium metabisulphite on the home-brew counter, where it is sold for sterilizing equipment.

6 Mix a weak bleach solution of 1 teaspoon bleach to 3 tablespoons (45ml) water and apply it with a sponge or cotton wool. Protect your hands with rubber gloves.

7 When enough dye has discharged, which should take 5–10 minutes, rinse the fabric in cold water.

8 Transfer the fabric to the sodium metabisulphite solution and leave for 15 minutes. This will neutralize the bleach and prevent it from damaging the fibres. Rinse again in cold water.

9 Remount the fabric on the frame and when it is completely dry, wax the areas you want to stay the tone achieved by the first bleaching/discharging.

10 Mix a stronger bleach solution of 1 teaspoon bleach to 2 tablespoons (30ml) water, and apply as before. After 5–10 minutes rinse in cold water, then transfer to a fresh solution of sodium metabisulphite, which must be renewed each time it is used. Wax to save the last tone before the final bleaching.

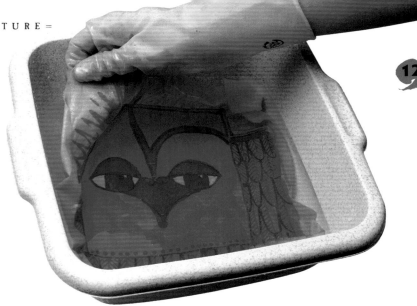

11 This time mix a strong bleach solution of 1 teaspoon bleach to 1 tablespoon (15ml) water.

12 When all the dye has been removed, rinse and neutralize as before.

13 When it is completely dry, iron out the wax.

Mount and frame.

WALL HANGING

—◆—

Bleach can also be used to increase the possible range of colours when you are working on images that you do not want to be outlined by a white wax line. When you do successive immersions in dye some colours are lost — for example, if the first colour is yellow, subsequent dyeing with blue will create green; if the first colour is red, subsequent dyeing with blue will create purple, and in neither case will any of the fabric be blue. In this project, which uses red and blue dye, the discharge process is used to regain the blue.

You will need
◊ Basic equipment, plus
◊ Prepared cotton, 24 × 36in (60 × 90cm)
◊ Soft pencil, 4B
◊ Blanket
◊ Plastic bucket with a minimum capacity of 1 gallon (4.5 litres)
◊ Bowl with a minimum capacity of 1 gallon (4.5 litres)
◊ Cork
◊ Kitchen roll (cardboard)
◊ Plastic tray
◊ Bleach
◊ Sodium metabisulphite
◊ 2 pieces of ½in (14mm) dowel, each 2ft (60cm) long

To make up
◊ Scissors
◊ Pins
◊ Thread
◊ Sewing machine or needles

1 On the prepared fabric use a soft pencil to mark margins of 2½in (6.5cm) at the top and bottom to form the channels for the rods to fit in, and a 1in (2.5cm) margin on either side for a hem. These lines will act as guidelines for waxing. Lay the fabric on a soft bed and wax the white border pattern with cork and kitchen roll caps.

2 Draw an oval in the centre. It does not have to be perfect, and an uneven shape will be more interesting.

3 Position the eyes about halfway up the "face". Support this area over a frame so that you can hold the fabric at an angle to wax in the white part of the eyes.

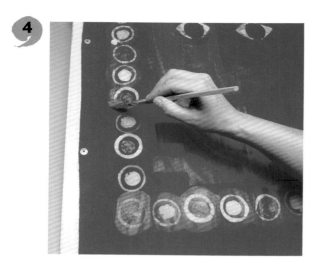

4

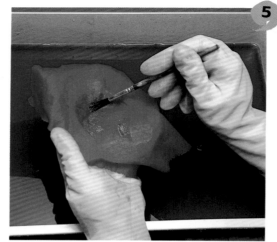

5

6

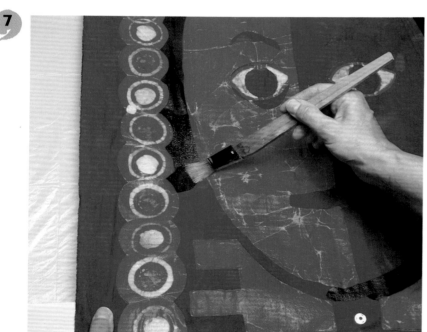

7

8

4 Prepare a red dye bath (see page 297). Remember to dye a test piece to try out overdyeing colours and discharge strengths and times. Complete the border, using a brush to wax areas to stay red. Use a sponge "brush" to wax in the side of the mask face that is to stay red. This will allow you to apply the wax quickly, making it easier to draw the lines.

5 Prepare a blue dye bath and test the colour on your sample. Adjust as necessary.

6 If you want to avoid too much crackle on the face, use a tray to hold the dye because it will be easier to keep the fabric flat.

7 When the fabric is rinsed and completely dry, return it to the work top and wax the areas that are going to stay purple. To avoid wax sticking to the plastic sheeting, lift the material as you wax. You may find it easier to mount the fabric on a frame.

8 Mix a medium strength solution of bleach, preparing enough to cover the unwaxed areas and using proportions of 1 tablespoon bleach to 6 tablespoons water. Test on your sample piece to check the timing. You will find that the red dye discharges completely before the blue, so as soon as all the red is gone you can rinse out the bleach solution. Neutralize and rinse (see page 313).

9

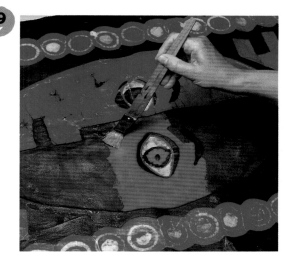

10

9 If you want to intensify the blue dye, apply it as in pool batik. When it is completely dry, wax over to avoid "halos" forming after ironing out.

10 If you want to iron out so that the fabric retains a residue of wax for waterproofing do so on a surface that is large enough to accommodate the whole piece so that it will cool flat. Otherwise, such a large piece may distort like silk.

Turn in and sew the sides. Turn over wide hems at the top and bottom to take the wooden dowel by which the finished piece will hang. The bottom rod will weight the work, making it hang better. If you prefer a softer finish have the work dry cleaned then spray it with a fabric protector.

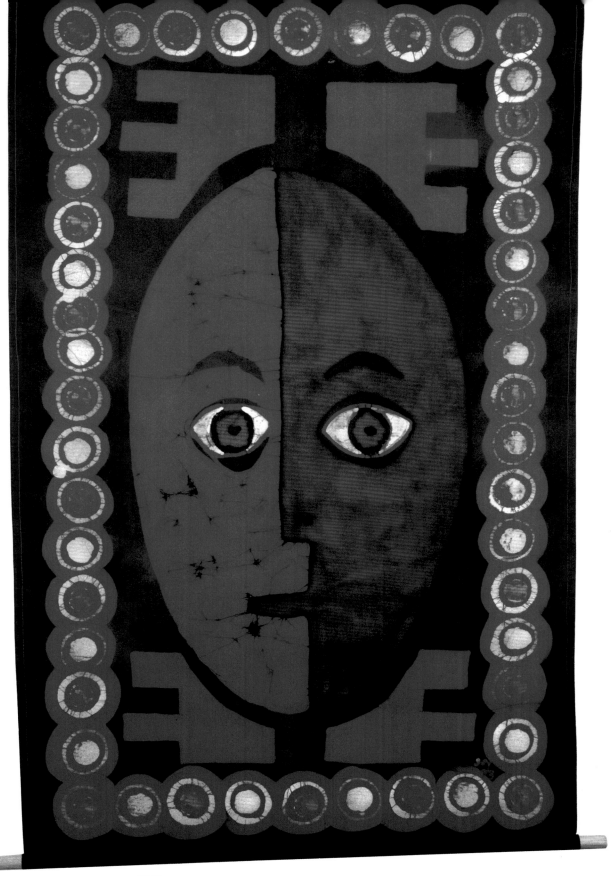

GALLERY

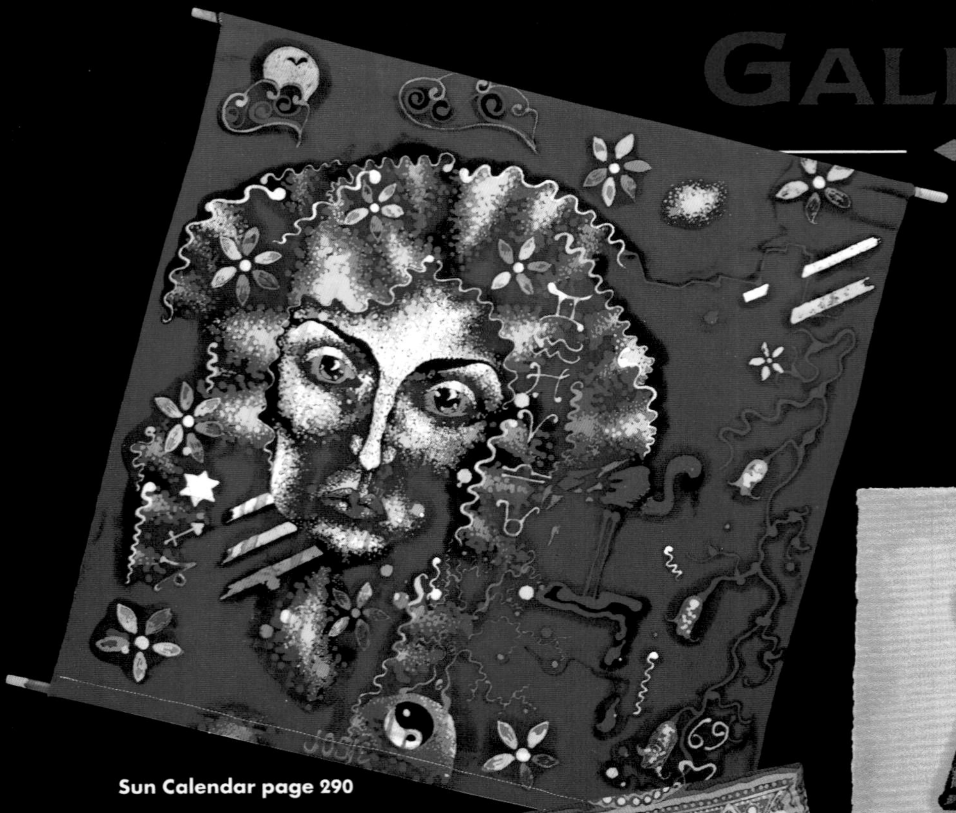

Sun Calendar page 290

Cushion Cover page 299

Owl Picture page 311

Portraits page 308

Wall Hanging page 315

Here are some inspirational ideas to take you further with your newly acquired skills. Each piece refers you back to the project that uses similar techniques.

Fabric Painting

Master a whole range of techniques such as sponging, stencilling and printing to create sensational effects

Introduction

Painting on fabric offers you the opportunity to create sensational effects on ordinary household items. Liven up a dull T-shirt or an old pair of jeans; design table linen to match your china, cushions to match your wallpaper and loads of other exciting things.

You don't have to be a great artist to master the art of fabric painting as many simple and effective designs can be done freehand. As your skills develop you can attempt more ambitious designs which require a steady hand, such as copying a motif from a book or magazine, or even making up your own design and transferring it onto fabric.

There are numerous ways of applying the paint to the fabric. Stencilling is an excellent way of covering a large area or creating a repeat pattern, for example on a tablecloth. Printing with sliced vegetables, fruit and flowers is a novel way of creating abstract patterns onto fabric – and it's dead easy: simply apply paint to the surface or edge of

the object with which you are painting and print it directly onto the fabric. Throughout the book there are projects that incorporate masking, sponging, printing and painting on dark fabric so you become familiar with a whole range of fabric painting techniques.

Fabric paints come in many forms so you can create many different effects with puff, glitter and pearly paint. Colours can be easily mixed and applied to both natural and synthetic material. Furthermore, by ironing the newly-painted fabric on the wrong side, the article becomes colour-fast which means that it can be machine-washed time and time again. For best results new fabrics should be washed and ironed before paint is applied so

that any dressing is removed which would prevent the paint from being absorbed. Remember to always place a piece of paper underneath the fabric onto which you are painting.

This book is specially designed for beginners: no expensive equipment is needed nor any special skills. Although suggestions have been given for colours and designs in all the projects there is no reason why you shouldn't try different combinations of colours and patterns. In many of the projects there are illustrations of alternative ways of painting the items to encourage you to use your imagination and, more importantly, to have fun with the paints.

Basic equipment you will need for painting on fabric.

Butterfly T-Shirt

Plain T-shirts in a wide range of colours and sizes are available all over the place, and if you buy them from a market they cost very little. Alternatively, you could give a new lease of life to an old T-shirt. I have drawn a butterfly design, but there is no limit to the patterns and motifs that you can try. This is an ideal project for experimenting with some of the specialized fabric paints, such as glitter paints, and puff paints, which change when they are exposed to the warmth of a hair-drier.

You will need
◊ Tracing paper
◊ Pencil
◊ Scissors
◊ Plain T-shirt
◊ Newspaper
◊ Pins
◊ Tailor's chalk or coloured pencil
◊ Fabric paints (including puff and glitter paints)
◊ Mixing palette
◊ Paintbrushes (various sizes)
◊ Hair-drier

1 Trace the butterfly template from the outline on page 349 and cut it out. Cut out the holes in the wings.

2 Put newspaper inside the T-shirt to stop paint seeping through to the back. Pin the template to the front of the T-shirt and draw around the shape with a coloured pencil or tailor's chalk. Use a coloured pencil to add other details — the antennae, for example — freehand.

3 Paint in the wings using whatever colours you wish. Use a no. 6 paintbrush for the small dots and a ¼in/5mm brush for the larger ones.

4 Add other colours. Allow the paint to dry for about 20 minutes before painting another colour next to it.

5 Add lines of puff paint around the patterns on the wings.

6 Add some spots of glitter paint around the neckline.

7 Outline the wing shapes in a different colour puff paint. Puff up the paint using a hair-drier.

Abstract Patterns

This is an ideal way of decorating lengths of plain fabric so that you can make them up into curtains, table linen, cushion covers or even clothes. Look around your home and you are sure to find countless bits and pieces — sponges, combs, jar lids, pen tops, pegs — that can be used to make interesting patterns. You could also experiment with food — pasta or potatoes, for example — to create some unusual designs.

You will need
◊ Items for printing — combs, cotton reels, pen tops, etc.
◊ Newspaper
◊ Fabric
◊ Masking tape
◊ Fabric paint
◊ Mixing palette
◊ Paintbrush (medium size)
◊ Iron
◊ Cloth

1 Assemble the items you think would make interesting shapes. You might find it helpful to make a rough sketch of your overall design before you begin.

2 Cover your work surface with newspaper and lay out the fabric, if necessary, using masking tape to keep it in position.

3 Mix the colours you want to use in a palette.

4 Apply paint to the object — I used a comb — taking care not to use too much paint or the outline will not look crisp and neat.

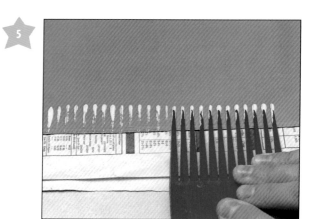

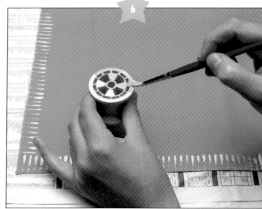

7 Incorporate the shape into your design. Leave to dry.

8 Use a different colour with your next object. I used a small piece of sponge, which gives an interesting and uneven texture.

9 Leave the third colour to dry before you apply the next series of coloured shapes. When you are satisfied with the pattern, iron under a cloth to fix the paints.

5 Use the comb to transfer the paint to the fabric. Continue all around the edge of the fabric, then leave to dry for about 20 minutes.

6 Take your next object — I used a wooden cotton reel — and paint the surface with a different colour.

Printing with Flowers

This simple project uses flowers and leaves to decorate fabric, which could be used for cushion covers, table or bed linen or even curtains. Some kinds of plant material work better than others — flowers and leaves with sturdy, unfussy outlines give more successful prints than more delicate shapes. Try buddleia, ivy and conifer leaves and flowers such as daisies. The backs of leaves with prominent veins work especially well.

You will need
◊ Rough paper
◊ Coloured pencils
◊ Newspaper
◊ Fabric of your choice
◊ Masking tape
◊ A selection of flowers and leaves
◊ Fabric paints
◊ Mixing palette
◊ Paintbrush (medium size)
◊ Iron
◊ Cloth

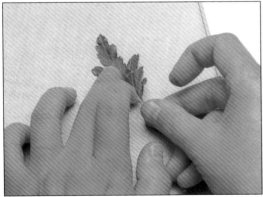

1 Position the flowers and leaves in a pleasing design. Make a rough sketch of the design and colour in the shapes so that you have a reference when you start to print.

2 Cover your work surface with newspaper and spread out your fabric, taping it in position if necessary. Mix your paints and paint some of the leaves.

3 Using your sketch as reference, place a leaf on the fabric, pressing it firmly but gently. Hold it down for 10 seconds, then raise an edge to see if the impression has printed. If you are happy with the result, carefully lift the leaf to avoid smudging the paint. Continue building up the design with other leaves.

4 Now paint a flower, placing it as indicated on your rough sketch. Fill in any gaps in the design and don't worry if some of the flowers look rather abstract. Leave to dry before ironing under a cloth to fix the paints.

Folk Art Picture

This charming image is achieved by applying a series of stencils, one after the other, and painting each in a different colour. You could frame the completed image, as I have done, or you could paint two and make up a pair of cushion covers.

You will need
◊ Tracing paper
◊ Pencil
◊ Stencil card
◊ Masking tape
◊ Craft knife or scalpel
◊ Piece of canvas or calico, approximately 13 × 11in/33 × 28cm
◊ Scissors
◊ Newspaper
◊ Stencil brush (¼in/5mm or ½in/12mm)
◊ Fabric paint
◊ Mixing palette
◊ Iron
◊ Cloth
◊ 4 buttons

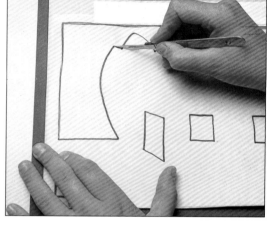

3 Cut out a piece of canvas or calico and place it on some sheets of newspaper. Tape the first stencil – the background to the picture – securely in position over the canvas and paint it – I used blue. Carefully remove the stencil so that you do not smudge the edges. Leave to dry for a few minutes.

4 Tape the second stencil – the house front and chimney piece – accurately in position and apply dark blue paint. Use a paintbrush to paint around the window areas.

1 Trace the stencil designs on pages 350 to 352, drawing each of the outlines onto equal-sized sheets of paper so that they will all fit together accurately.

2 Tape each traced stencil onto a separate piece of stencil card, taking care to position each outline in the same position on each piece of card. Cut out the holes in each stencil.

5 Leave the paint to dry before you use the next stencil.

6 Tape the next stencil – the front door and roof – in place. This time use brown paint. Again, leave to dry.

7 Tape the next stencil in place and then paint the side of the house purple. Leave to dry before using the last stencil, the foreground and trees, which are painted green.

8 Iron under a cloth to fix the paint and sew a button in each corner.

Child's Wall-hanging

This charming parade of stencilled animals would look great on a child's bedroom wall. The project uses simple, colourful hand-stitching and stencilling, which combine to give an old-fashioned, slightly folksy effect. You could make a similar piece using numbers or letters instead of animals.

You will need

◊ Tracing paper
◊ Pencils
◊ Stencil card
◊ Masking tape
◊ Craft knife or scalpel
◊ 8 pieces of cream-coloured fabric, each measuring approximately 5 × 5 in/12.5 × 12.5 cm
◊ Fabric paints
◊ Mixing palette
◊ Stencil brushes ¼ in/5mm and ½ in/12 mm
◊ Sponge (natural sponge is best)
◊ Iron
◊ Cloth
◊ 2 pieces of coloured fabric, each measuring approximately 50 × 8 in/128 × 20 cm (I used blue)
◊ Pins
◊ Scissors
◊ Needle
◊ Coloured embroidery silks
◊ 2 buttons
◊ Bias binding, tape or ribbon, approximately 4 in/10 cm

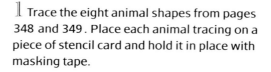

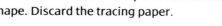

1 Trace the eight animal shapes from pages 348 and 349 . Place each animal tracing on a piece of stencil card and hold it in place with masking tape.

2 Use a craft knife or scalpel to cut out each shape. Discard the tracing paper.

3 Cut out eight squares of cream-coloured fabric.

4 Use masking tape to hold each cut-out animal in position on a square of fabric.

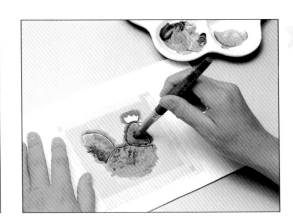

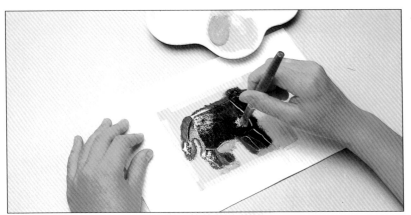

5 Prepare your paints, then colour the pig's body using a stencil brush.

6 Colour the pig's feet brown and add a band of brown across its body.

7 The cockerel has a blue-green body and a bright red comb.

8 Add some yellow and orange to the feathers in the cockerel's tail.

9 Colour the cow's body black and its hooves and udder pink. Make some spots by sponging on some white paint.

10 Paint the rest of the animals, using the photograph of the finished wall hanging as a guide. Turn under the edges of each square and iron under a cloth to fix the colours and press down the turned-back edges.

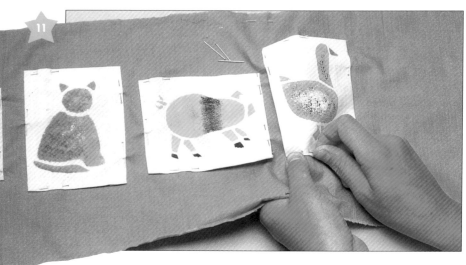

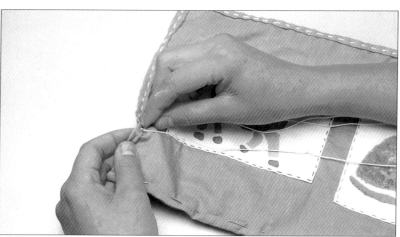

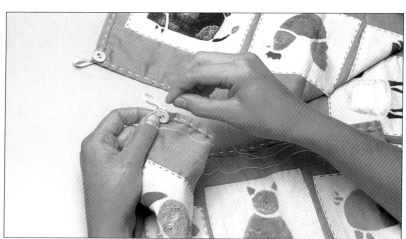

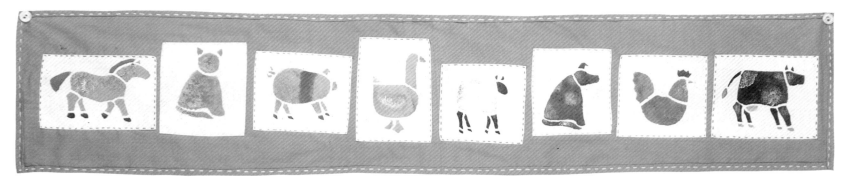

11 Place the two rectangles of fabric together and pin. Space the eight animal pictures evenly along one of the long rectangles of fabric, pinning them in position.

12 Use coloured embroidery silk and straight stitch to sew each square in place.

13 Turn the edge of the large rectangle into a neat hem on the front and hand sew with yellow embroidery silk.

14 Sew a button in each of the top corners and add loops of tape, bias binding or ribbon from which to hang it.

Shopping Bag

The combination of the attractive fruit design and the durable nature of this simple canvas drawstring bag makes it the perfect way to carry heavy fruit and vegetables home from the market. Although I have supplied simple templates for the motifs, you could decorate it with an alternative pattern so that the bag could be used to carry school things or your sports kit.

1 Trace the fruit motifs from the templates on page 347 and cut out.

2 Cut two pieces of canvas. Place the templates on the canvas, pin them in position and use a pencil to draw around the outlines.

3 Use your traced outlines as a guide to fill in the details of the fruit.

4 Use a ruler to add the check tablecloth pattern.

5 Mix your paints. You will need yellow for the bananas, purple for the grapes (you can add some white, yellow and orange for a lighter shade of purple) and green for the apples.

You will need
◊ Tracing paper
◊ Pencil
◊ Scissors
◊ 2 pieces of canvas, each 18 × 16in/45.5 × 40.5cm
◊ Pins
◊ Ruler
◊ Fabric paint
◊ Mixing palette

◊ Paintbrushes (3 sizes)
◊ Fabric paint pen (blue)
◊ Iron
◊ Cloth
◊ Sewing machine
◊ Sewing thread
◊ ¼in/5mm cord, 30in/76.5cm long
◊ Safety pin

6 Use short strokes to apply the first colour. Aim to create a three-dimensional effect.

7 Paint the apples and bananas.

8 Colour the stalks and leaves of the apples.

9 Add the detail to the grapes, using dark green for the tendrils and brown for the stalks.

10 Add detail in brown to the bananas to make them look as natural as possible. Leave

the paint to dry for about 20 minutes, then iron under a cloth.

11 Paint in the white squares of the tablecloth border pattern and outline the squares with a blue fabric painting pen.

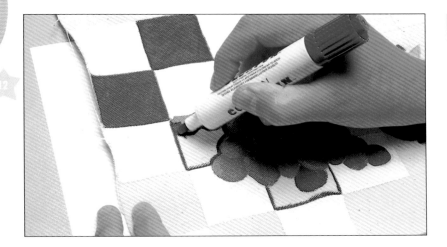

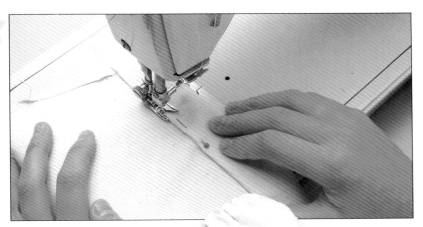

12 Colour in alternate squares and leave to dry for about 20 minutes. Iron under a cloth. Decorate the second piece of canvas in the same way if you wish.

13 With right sides together, sew one side of the bag with a sewing machine.

14 Open the bag so that the middle, inside seam faces you. On each side at the top, turn 2in/5cm of the raw edge inwards at an angle. Machine stitch into place. Fold back the bag with right sides together and machine stitch along the bottom and side. Turn right side out.

15 Use a safety pin to thread through the cord as a drawstring. Bind the ends of the cord to stop it from unravelling.

Animal Cushions

Scatter these lively animal cushions on a child's bed or arrange them in a group on a chair. Watered-down fabric paints have been used to achieve the background colours, while thicker paints are used for the detailed markings. Simple embroidery stitches in brightly coloured threads have been added to enhance the details of feathers, whiskers and so on.

You will need
◊ Tracing paper
◊ Pencil
◊ Scissors
◊ Pins
◊ White cotton fabric, approximately 20 × 10in/51 × 25cm for each cushion
◊ Newspaper
◊ Fabric paints
◊ Mixing palette
◊ Paintbrushes (small and medium)
◊ Coloured embroidery silks
◊ Needle
◊ Sewing thread
◊ Sewing machine
◊ Kapok or other toy stuffing
◊ Buttons for eyes
◊ String for pig's tail

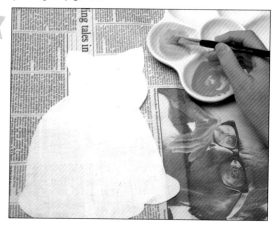

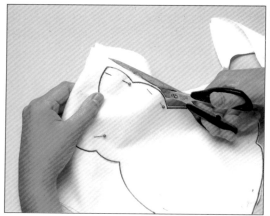

1 Trace the animal templates on pages 344 to 346 and cut out.

2 Pin each template to a double layer of fabric and cut around it.

3 Place each animal shape on some newspaper and prepare your paints.

4 Water down the paints that you are going to use for the background — for example, use orange for the cat — but do not make the colour flat; it will look more natural if it is quite streaky.

5 Add spots on the back and head and a nose and tail, using the photograph on page 337 as a guide.

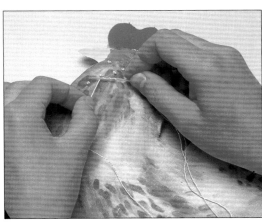

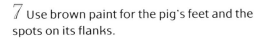

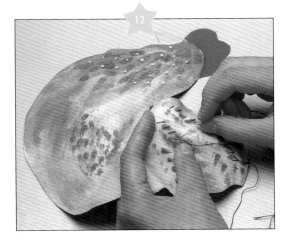

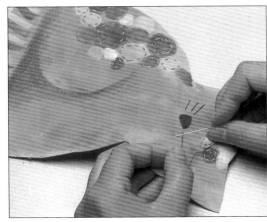

6 Make the pig in the same way and remember to include two ears.

7 Use brown paint for the pig's feet and the spots on its flanks.

8 The cockerel is more difficult. The background is a combination of green, purple, pink and yellow. Apply each colour separately but try to achieve a soft, feathery effect with no harsh edges to the colours.

9 Add a yellow beak and bright red comb.

10 Iron both sides of each of the animals under a cloth when you have finished them to seal the paints.

11 Use embroidery silks to stitch details on the cockerel's neck feathers.

12 Stitch some additional feather detailing to the cockerel's back.

13 Stitch around the spots on the cat and embroider the whiskers. Remember to stitch the cat's paws.

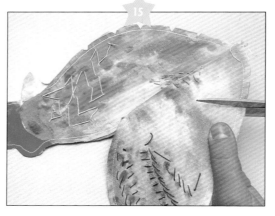

14 Pin the two pieces of the cushion together and use a sewing machine to stitch around the edge, leaving about 2in/5cm open along the bottom edge.

15 Carefully snip the curved edges up the stitching line so that the seams lie flat.

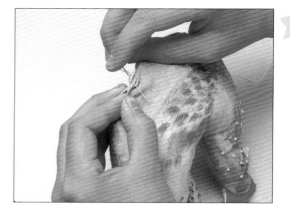

16 Turn the cushion to the right side, using the wrong end of a paintbrush to push out the seams, especially around the cockerel's beak and comb. Fill the cushion with Kapok or any soft toy stuffing material, pushing it into the head and tail with a piece of wooden dowel or the wrong end of a knitting needle.

17 Sew up the open seam. Repeat steps 14–17 for the pig and cat.

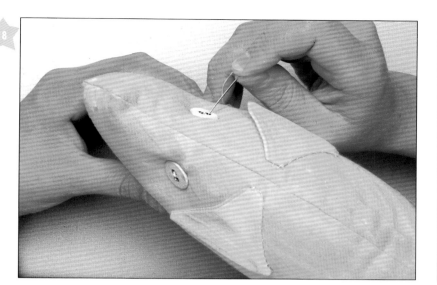

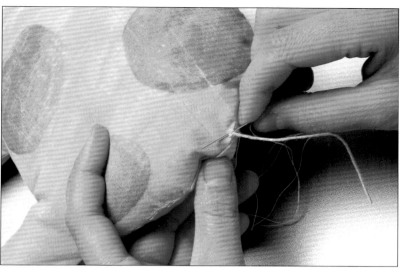

18 Stitch on buttons for eyes and remember to add the pig's ears.

19 Make a tail for the pig by painting some string pink and sewing it onto the pig's back.

Pillowcases

Simple stencilling techniques allow you to decorate plain cotton pillowcases with
a fresh floral design, and once you have mastered the techniques there is no
need to stop at pillowcases: you can decorate a duvet cover and sheet to match.
I have supplied templates for the flowers, but you may prefer to design
your own motifs.

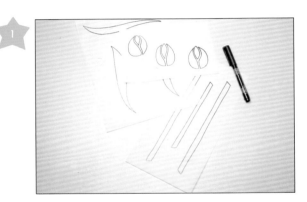

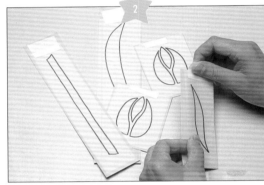

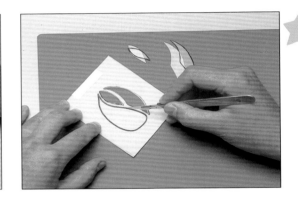

You will need
◊ Marker pen
◊ Tracing paper
◊ Masking tape
◊ Stencil card
◊ Craft knife or scalpel
◊ 2 plain cotton pillowcases
◊ Newspaper
◊ Fabric paint
◊ Mixing palette
◊ Stencil brush
◊ Iron
◊ Cloth

1 Use a marker pen to trace the stencil patterns from the outlines on page 342.

2 Use masking tape to hold the traced shapes securely in position on the stencil card.

3 Cut around the shapes with a craft knife or scalpel, working on a cutting mat or a piece of thick cardboard. Discard the tracing paper.

4 Put some pieces of newspaper inside the pillowcase to protect the other side from any paint that seeps through.

5 Position the stem templates on the pillowcase, securing them with masking tape.

6 Mix the paint colours. Paint in the stems with a small (¼in/5mm) stencil brush and use different shades of green.

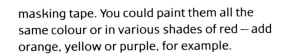

masking tape. You could paint them all the same colour or in various shades of red — add orange, yellow or purple, for example.

11 Allow the paint to dry, then iron with a piece of cloth over the paint to fix the colours.

7 Dab rather than use brush strokes for a "sponging" effect and take care not to splash the paint onto the rest of the pillowcase.

8 Repeat until there are stems across the pillowcase — about eight in all. Remove the stencils.

9 Position the leaf stencils and secure them with masking tape. Colour the leaves as you

did the stems, holding the stencil firmly down with your fingers so that paint does not bleed under the cut edge.

10 Position the flower stencils and hold them in place with

Doll

This simple doll makes a delightful gift for a child older than five or six years of age. You could design a different outfit if you preferred, or you could base the doll's appearance on someone you know. If you wish you could add extra details such as a hair ribbon, a hat or a piece of jewellery.

You will need
◊ Sketch pad
◊ Coloured pencils
◊ Tracing paper
◊ Pencil
◊ Piece of white fabric, 13 × 10in/33 × 25cm
◊ Pins
◊ Scissors
◊ Newspapers
◊ Kapok or other toy stuffing
◊ Sewing machine
◊ Sewing thread
◊ Fabric paints
◊ Mixing palette
◊ Paintbrushes (various sizes)
◊ Iron
◊ Cloth
◊ Needle
◊ Buttons

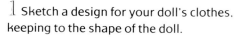

1 Sketch a design for your doll's clothes, keeping to the shape of the doll.

2 Trace the doll's template from page 343 and cut out. Fold the white fabric in half (so that it measures 13 × 5in/33 × 12.5cm) and pin the template to it, making sure that the pins go through both layers. Cut out the outline, adding a seam allowance of ⅛in/3mm all round.

3 Using your sketch as a reference, pencil guidelines on the cut-out doll – hairline, top, trousers, shoes and so on. Add the details to front and back.

4 Cover your work surface with newspaper and paint the front of the doll. Begin with the background colour of the blouse – I used blue.

5 Next paint in the shoes and trousers and then the mouth, cheeks and hair.

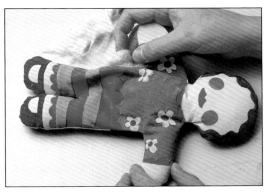

6 Allow the paint to dry, then add details such as the flower pattern to the top and the frills around the neck and trousers.

7 Paint the face pale pink and leave to dry. Paint the back of the doll to match. Iron.

8 Place the two pieces, right sides together, and machine stitch all the way around the doll, leaving a gap of about 2in/5cm under one arm. Carefully snip into the curves, up to the sewing line, at the neck, between the legs and at the ends of the arms and legs so that the seams lie smoothly.

9 Turn the doll the right way out. You may find it helpful to use the wrong end of a paintbrush to push the arms and legs through. Fill the doll with Kapok or any other soft toy stuffing, adding little pinches at a time and using a piece of wooden dowel or the wrong end of a knitting needle to push the filler down into the arms and legs. Stitch up the underarm seam opening.

10 Sew on buttons for the eyes.

11 Paint on the eyebrows.

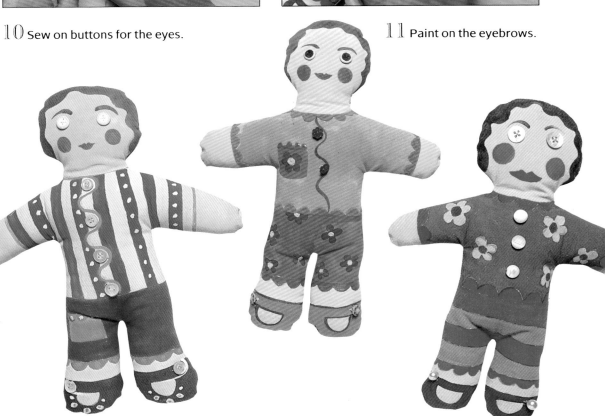

Templates

PILLOWCASES

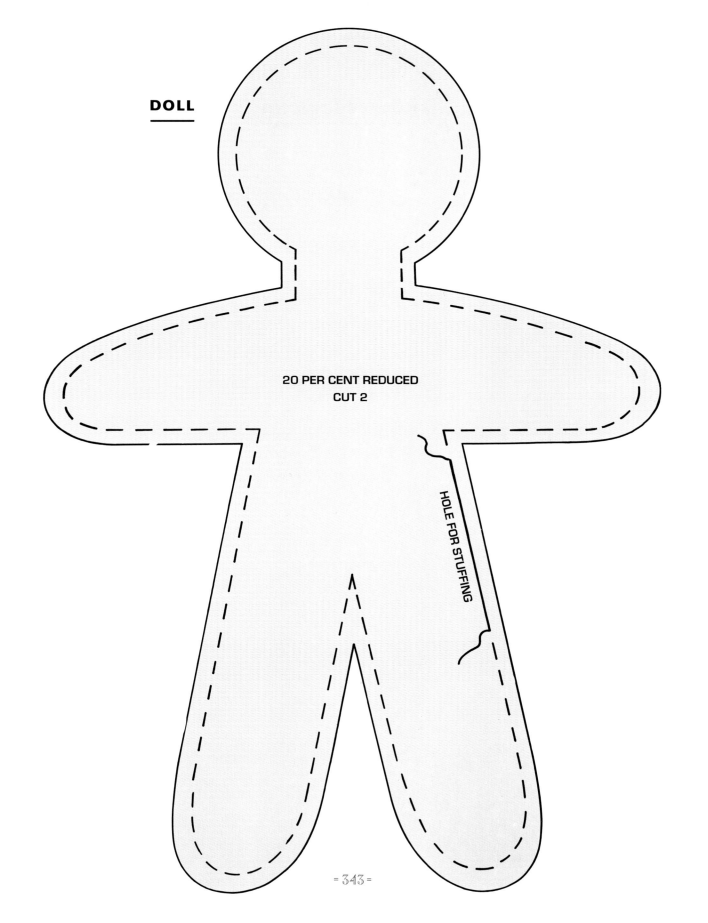

DOLL

20 PER CENT REDUCED

CUT 2

HOLE FOR STUFFING

ANIMAL CUSHIONS

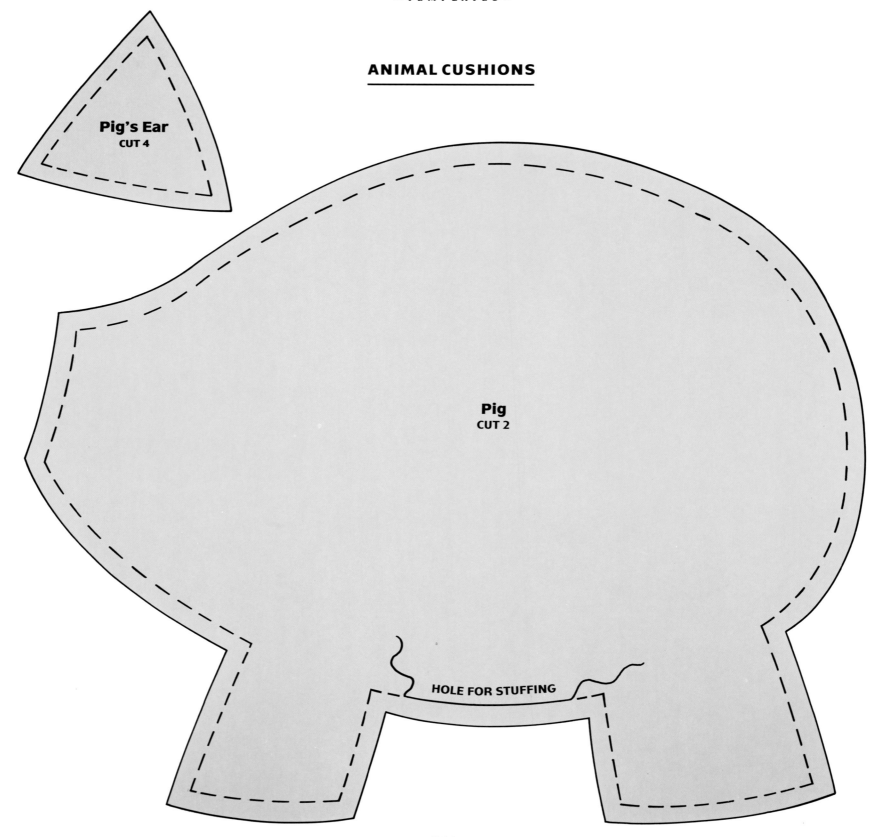

Pig's Ear
CUT 4

Pig
CUT 2

HOLE FOR STUFFING

ANIMAL CUSHIONS

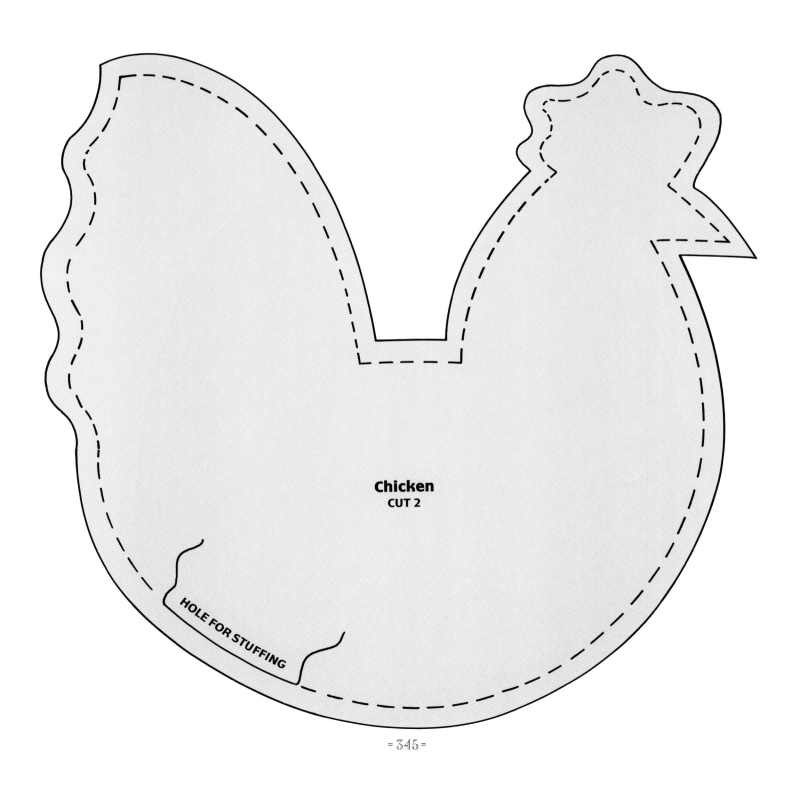

Chicken
CUT 2

HOLE FOR STUFFING

ANIMAL CUSHIONS

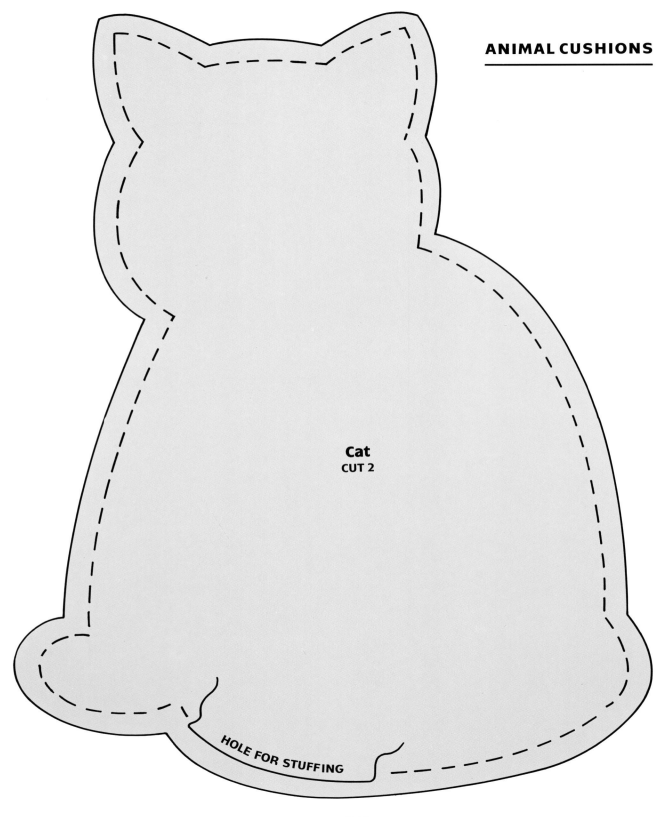

Cat
CUT 2

HOLE FOR STUFFING

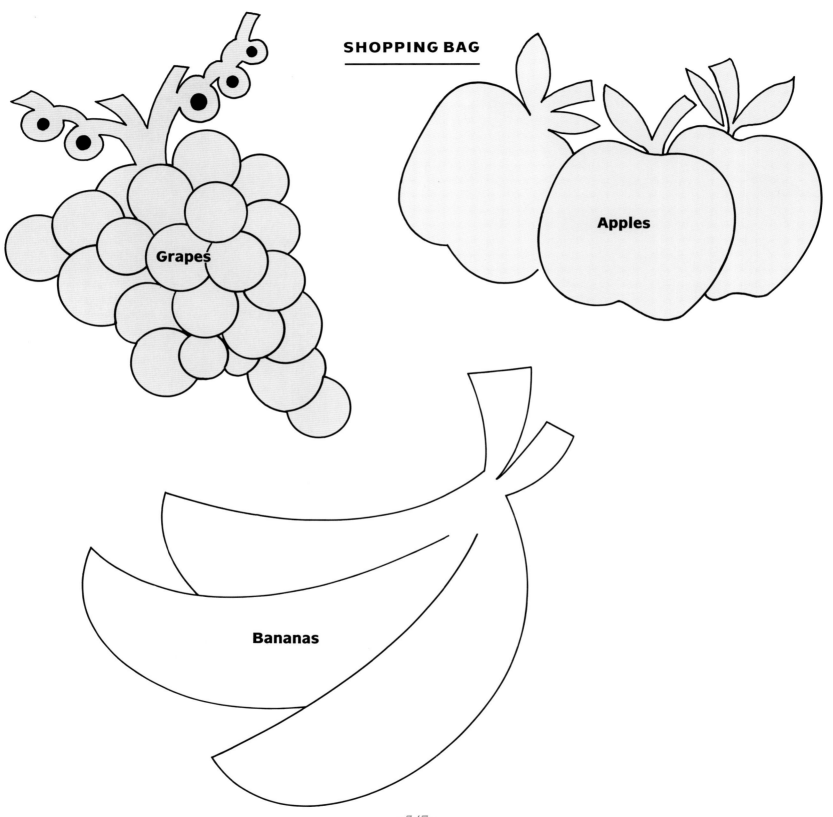

SHOPPING BAG

Grapes

Apples

Bananas

ANIMAL WALL HANGING

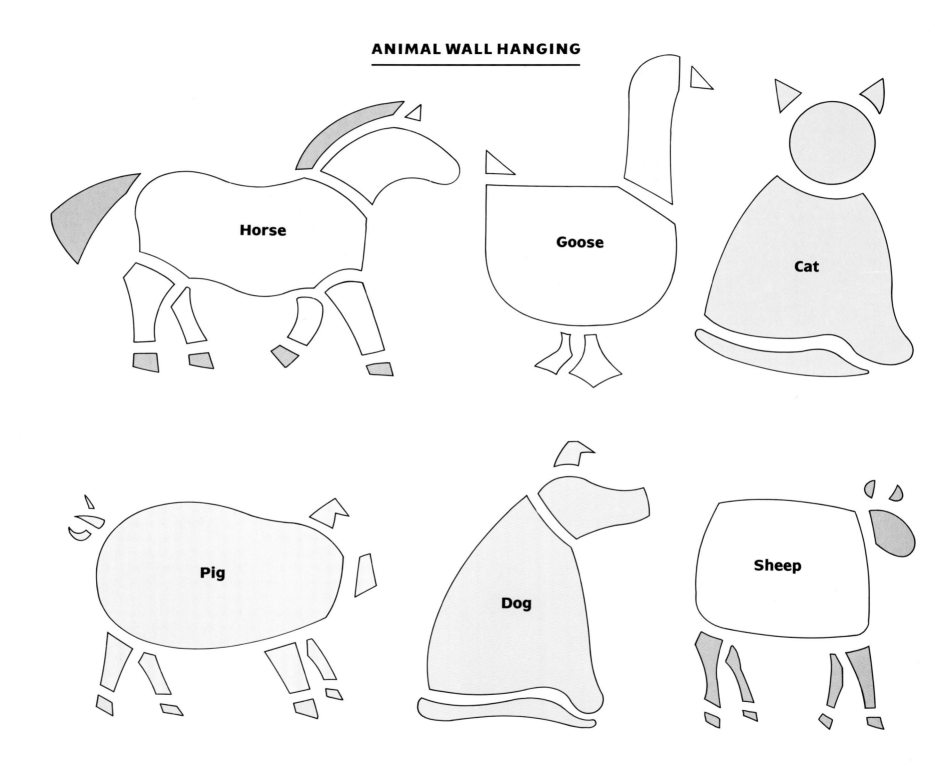

Horse

Goose

Cat

Pig

Dog

Sheep

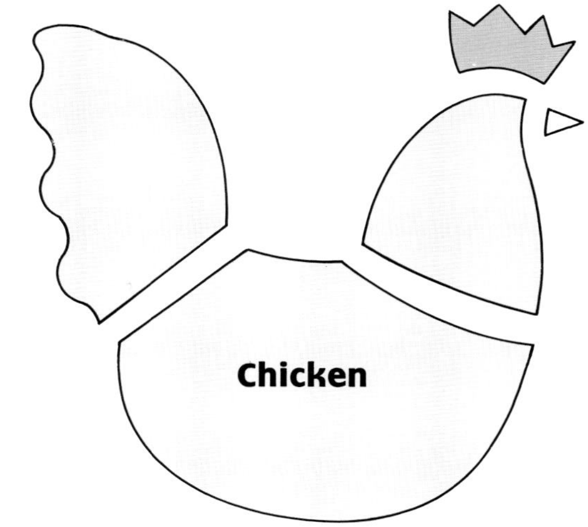

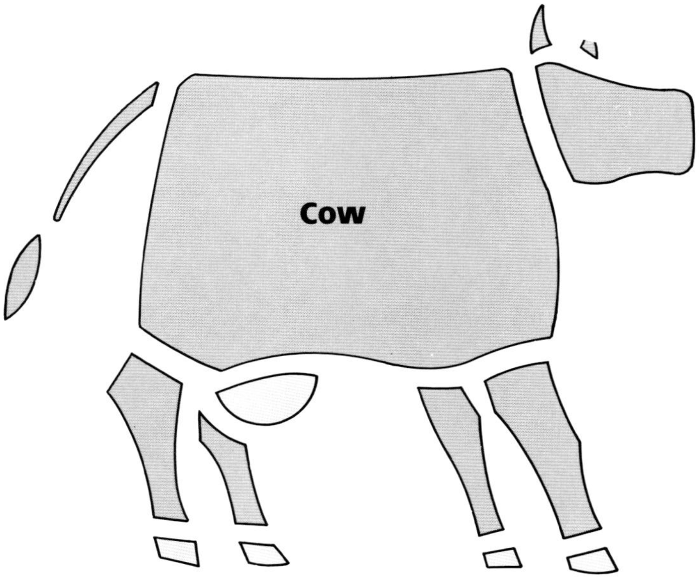

BUTTERFLY T-SHIRT

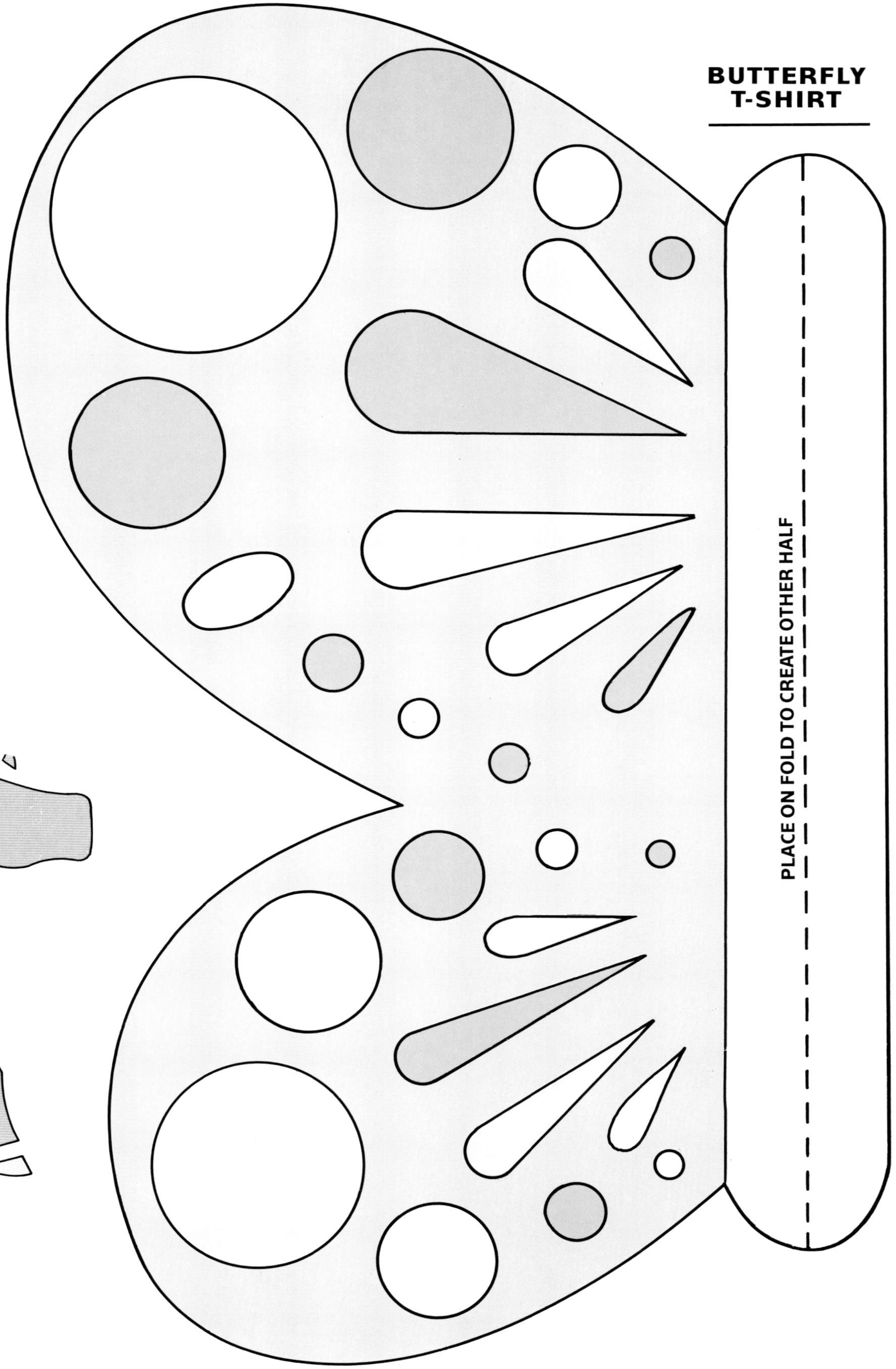

Chicken

Cow

PLACE ON FOLD TO CREATE OTHER HALF

FOLK ART PICTURE

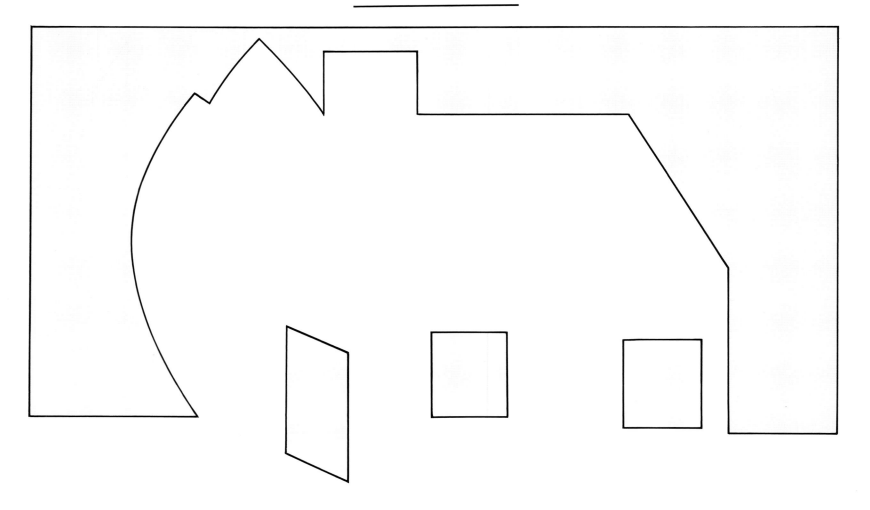

FOLK ART PICTURE

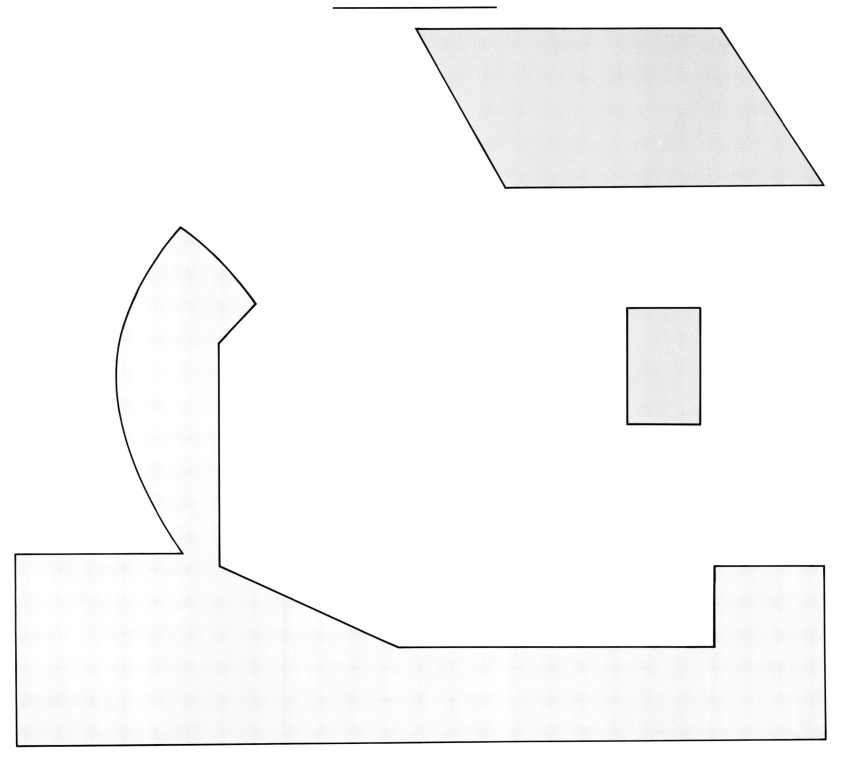

FOLK ART PICTURE

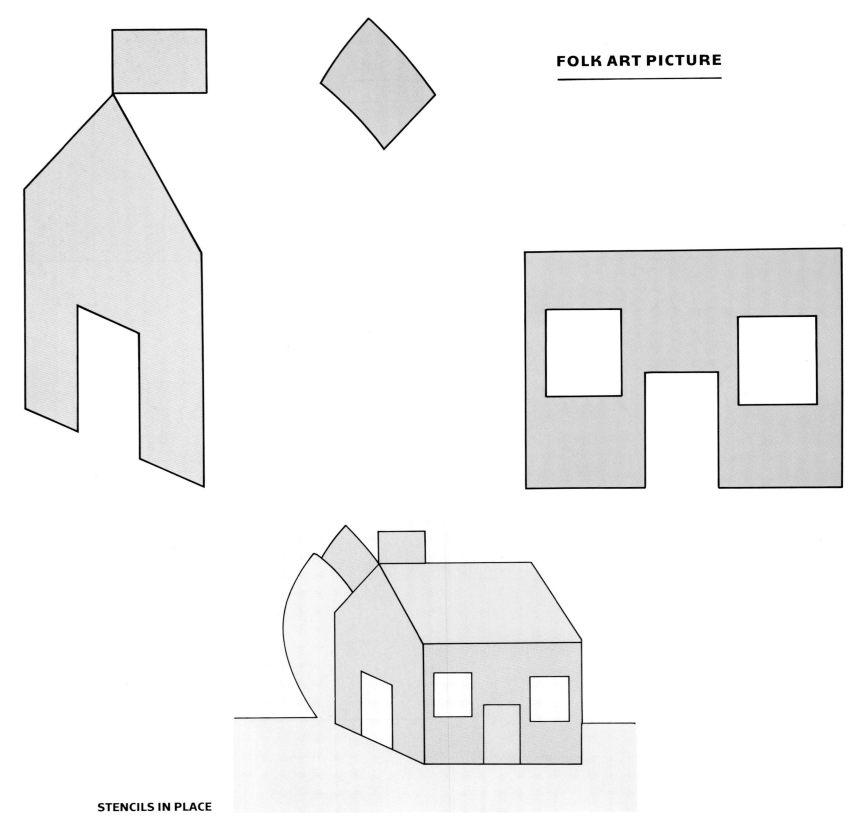

STENCILS IN PLACE